Praise for *The Gen Z Effect*
and
Tom Koulopoulos and Dan Keldsen

"For years, I have experienced enterprises losing the wisdom of generations because of generational divides. This book offers hope and prescription for stemming that loss. It comes at a critical time in the evolution of organizations."
—Jim Champy, author of *Reengineering the Corporation*

"Working with some of the world's largest retailers I see first hand how critical it is to understand and integrate *The Gen Z Effect* into an organization's strategy for growth. Tom and Dan provide a clear view of the disruptive force that Gen Z is already having on our businesses and our world, as well as the sort of future we can all look forward to."
—Stephanie Fischer, president & CEO of the Global Retail Marketing Association

"A superb book that exemplifies a critical skill for the present and future: bridging the generational chasms across knowledge workers. The stories of leadership role models are inspirational, and reinforce the idea that success is based on unique ways of thinking and being not just age."
—Bruce Rosenstein, managing editor, *Leader to Leader*; author of *Create Your Future the Peter Drucker Way*

"*The Gen Z Effect* is an inspirational showcase of ideas where learning, gaming, technology, and age collide."
—Nicholas Bonardi, lead audio designer for Rocksmith and Rocksmith 2014 at Ubisoft

"Dan and Tom provide a timely, pragmatic alternative to the polarized perspectives that promote division and deny progress at a critical time in world history. *The Gen Z Effect* offers a mindset that will immediately appeal to those who prefer the roles of playwright or actor, to that of the critic."
—Robb Webb, chief human resources officer, Hyatt Hotels Corporation

"*Who's influencing who?* That's the needling question of *The Gen Z Effect*, a must-read for built-to-last Boomers and build-it-again Gen Z alike. The insight of Koulopoulos and Keldsen—that influence will trump affluence—makes it clear that privilege and power are no longer the levers that move minds, mouths, and markets."

—Alan Kelly, founder & executive director, Playmaker Systems, LLC; author of *The Elements of Influence*

"Koulopoulos and Keldsen have the pulse on a critically important sea change in how we think about ourselves, society, and the forces of change interacting and impacting us all. Read this and slingshot yourself forward to be influential in a multigenerational, hyperconnected, global society."

—Blackford Middleton, MD, MPH, MSc, chief informatics officer and professor at Vanderbilt University Medical Center

"This ground-breaking work provides a much-needed framework for corporate strategists and marketing executives to capitalize on the most valuable demographic trend that has ever existed: the Gen Z Effect."

—Luke Hohmann, CEO of Conteneo; author of *Innovation Games: Creating Breakthrough Products Through Collaborative Play*

"In *The Gen Z Effect*, authors Dan Keldsen and Tom Koulopoulos show us a new model of working, of engaging our customers, of continuous learning—and of living. Gen Z is blurring the lines between all of us. It's about time."

—Jill Dyché, author of *The New IT: How Technology Leaders are Enabling Business Strategy in the Digital Age*

"Generational differences impact our values, beliefs and actions. Why? Because that is how we historically defined ourselves. Technology is changing this. *The Gen Z Effect* provides thought-provoking insights about the impact of technology and how simplified accessibility and collaboration beyond traditional boundaries can lead to a civilization that works together to co-create a better world."

—Heather Ishikawa, co-author of *Now You're Thinking!*; national director at Pearson TalentLens

"*The Gen Z Effect*'s six forces are all about democratization—of technology, information access, learning, power, and even *identity*. This raises the possibility of collective insight into science and humanity, and collective action to improve them. This book not only illuminates how these forces work, but how we, as educators and business leaders, can bring out the best collective action."

—Kate Pugh, academic director, Columbia University Information and Knowledge Strategy; author of *Smarter Innovation* and *Sharing Hidden Know-How*

"This book shows how the 'generational' perspective of human behavior and attitude is dissolving. The generations are increasingly using technology and new perspectives to work together to solve today's biggest challenges. Here's my advice: read *The Gen Z Effect*, understand the six forces that are creating this shift and establishing the 'last generation,' and use them to bring your influence into the future."

—Chris Goward, author of *You Should Test That!*; founder of WiderFunnel Marketing Optimization

"Koulopoulos and Keldsen reveal the compelling forces behind Gen Z and their impact on managing, learning, and innovating in the new knowledge economy. Their in-depth investigation into *The Gen Z Effect* sheds new light on how to design strategies to leverage the best of hyperconnected, hyper-dynamic and agile organizations."

—Eric Tsui, professor at The Hong Kong Polytechnic University

THE
GEN Z
EFFECT

THE
GEN Z
EFFECT

THE SIX FORCES SHAPING THE FUTURE OF BUSINESS

Thomas Koulopoulos
and Dan Keldsen

First published by Bibliomotion, Inc.
39 Harvard Street
Brookline, MA 02445
Tel: 617-934-2427
www.bibliomotion.com

Printed in the United States of America

Library of Congress Cataloging-in-Publication Data

Koulopoulos, Thomas M.
  The Gen Z effect : the 6 forces shaping the future of business / Thomas Koulopoulos and Dan Keldsen.
      pages cm
  Includes bibliographical references and index.
  ISBN 978-1-62956-031-1 (hardcover : alk. paper) — ISBN 978-1-62956-032-8 (ebook) — ISBN 978-1-62956-033-5 (enhanced ebook)
  1. Internet and children 2. Technology and children. 3. Business enterprises. 4. Organizational change. 5. Intergenerational relations. I. Keldsen, Dan. II. Title.
  HQ784.I58K68 2014
  004.67'8083—dc23
                    2014031543

To Mia and Anastasios,
Your love and your brilliance keep me young
by teaching me how much I have yet to learn. ~ tk

To Sandra, Julia and Logan,
For allowing me to disappear into the writer's cave
and for pulling me out of it to be with the great family we have. ~ dk

CONTENTS

ACKNOWLEDGMENTS

Writing is an act of learning.

No matter how well versed you are in a topic when you start to write, by the time you are done you've discovered how much more there was to know. Learning is a process guided by countless teachers, mentors, advocates, and supporters; it is an intellectual journey of discovery; and perhaps the greatest of these discoveries is how much you have to learn from others about that which you thought you knew so well.

At a time when the Internet provides us with all we need to know, books still have gravity. We're convinced that much of that is because of how many minds meld to form a book. Which is why this book must begin by thanking the many brilliant and supportive people who helped us with their insights, anecdotes, and encouragement.

First, our thanks to the people who make up so much of the narrative of this book. They are the Gen Z prototypes after which we will all model ourselves and our organizations. These include: Robb Webb, who serves as a living model for leading-edge Human Resources, both as a professional and by what Hyatt is accomplishing worldwide; Bill Gribbons, who has built an amazing user experience lab at Bentley University; Carlos Dominguez at Cisco, a self- labeled tech "nowist" whose ability to stay young in mind is exceeded only by his passion for sharing what he knows; Nicholas Bonardi at Ubisoft, whose passion for tying the best of gaming, learning, and music should serve as an example for anyone involved in modern education; Craig Kielburger, co-founder with his brother Mark, of Free the Children, perhaps the most inspiring and impactful non-profit shaping Gen Z; Daniel Debow, who is redefining the notion of performance reviews; George Achillias, whose insights about Gen Z created a constant stream of "aha" moments; Kevin Davis, whose reputation as "The Dataman" demonstrates exactly why we all have so much to learn about Big Data and behavior—it yields RESULTS; long-time friend, colleague, and visionary, Jeetu Patel, who is leading one of the hottest companies in Silicon Valley and whose youthful energy never seems to ebb; Justin Levy, whose efforts at Citrix are changing how we all look at the possibility and value of remote work and what it means to our lives; Stephanie Fischer, who has created what has to be one of the most influential groups of marketing professionals on the globe with the GRMA; Suman Mulumudi, the 16-year-old who caused us to reconsider the enormous potential that Gen Z will bring to the future; as well as; Patti Anklam, Vivek Bhaskaran, Tim Brewer, Lee Bryant, Professor Sandra Deacon Carr, Laura Carstensen, Randy Corke, Dr. Ellen Domb, Damien Duchamp, Leslie Fine, Arjan Haring, Dr. Joseph Keebler, Wayne Kurtzman, Rick Ladd, Robert Lavigne, Joe Miller, Michael Mueller PhD, Rajat Paharia, Robert Rasmussen, Rebecca Rienzo, Marc Smith, Professor Eric Tsui, Kevin Werbach, and Ty White.

Second, we are incredibly fortunate to have one of the most professional teams in the publishing industry behind us. Although big ideas can flood your mind, it is the relentless attention to the details of translating those ideas into a meaningful and comprehensible structure that prevents you from drowning in your own euphoria.

Our agent John Willig is a powerhouse of experience with the decisiveness of a drill sergeant (and a haircut to match) that only comes from decades in the industry. His quick ability to sum up ideas, point out the obvious, and provide direction was often the factor that added clarity and tipped the scales on many difficult decisions.

Our publishing team at Bibliomotion, lead by Jill and Erika, is creating the next great success story in an industry sorely in need of disruption. Erika's uncanny ability to tune in to a topic was especially important in bringing the big idea of Gen Z down to earth. Along with Audra, Jill S., and Shevaun, we always knew the Bibliomotion team had our backs.

There is a saying among authors that towards the end of the writing

Acknowledgments

process you become "one with the book" as you read every page and paragraph over and over. But you also experience the equivalent of becoming snow–blind to your own writing. We are very grateful to our editor, Susan Lauzau, who brought an eagle eye and uncompromising attention to detail, which allowed us to see our writing with microscopic vision.

Third, there was a large a cast of friends and colleagues who helped us throughout; a list so long that we hesitate to include anyone for fear of whom we will inevitably leave out. Erin and Sunil who helped to stress test and refine our ideas; Lynn for her encouragement and faith in Gen Z; Aleise and Sharon for keeping the rest of TK's plates spinning; Kim for inspiring with her always positive outlook; and many other friends who helped keep us sane and centered.

Finally, we are grateful beyond measure to our families for their ongoing inspiration and support. For Sandy, this was the first time through the process of living with an author, which is not an easy task, but one that she was especially supportive of through her constant encouragement and enthusiasm.

And, of course, there are our own Gen Z'ers, Mia, Adam, Logan, and Julia who are the reverse mentors to whom we turn to understand the human side of the changes that we talk about. Through their eyes and experiences they teach us every day how much we have to learn, how narrow our view can become, and how much more amazing, than anything contained in these pages, Gen Z will become. Most of all, they give us hope for tomorrow, and provide the purpose we need to leave a legacy on which they can build a future deserving of their talents, ambition, and optimism.

Tom and Dan
Boston 2014

INTRODUCTION

The Gen Z Effect

We always put ourselves at the end of history. It's what humanity does best, repeatedly. Each generation sees itself as the pinnacle of civilization. Their model of the world, their science, their society is always the best there can be. Which is why we believe we have more pressing matters to deal with in solving today's problems than in worrying about the hypothetical problems of tomorrow. After all, we reason, if we don't get through the mess we're in today there will be no tomorrow. Yet somehow tomorrow does arrive, and with it even greater challenges and opportunities.

So why focus specifically on the topic of generations, and why Gen Z? What about those bigger problems? What about, for example, the escalating threat of terrorism; the uncertainty of climate change; the tension of income disparity; the despondence among youth caused by global unemployment; looming financial crises in the world's economies, with global debt at $223 trillion, or 313 percent of global GDP;[1] the burden of climbing energy costs and an imperative to move toward renewable sources of energy; and the stark contrast of a world awash in billionaires while nearly 1 billion humans lack access to clean water and 2.5 billion lack basic sanitation.

Here is the reason to focus on Gen Z: in working with hundreds of organizations—from small businesses and global corporations to nonprofits and government—we have found that the greatest impediments to the collaboration and cooperation needed to solve these problems are the generational chasms we have been taught to expect and accept. These divides are so ingrained in our way of thinking that we do not question them. To the contrary, we dig in our generational heels, build ideological fortresses around our worldview, and plow the trenches between us even deeper. Nowhere is that tendency more counterproductive than in the setting of an enterprise, which, by definition, works best when its members are aligned around a central strategy and vision.

This is why we are so impassioned by the call of Gen Z to bridge the generational divides that have stood in our way for so long, undermining our ability to innovate in what is quickly becoming a post-generational world. **Post-generational thinking requires that we not only change our individual perceptions of the boundaries between generations, but also build organizations that can do the same.**

The foundation of the Gen Z Effect—the big shift we are all part of, including every previous generation—is a new set of behaviors that finally allows us to work across generations, and which is driven by technologies that are increasingly shared across all ages, promoting an awareness of the world and a collective engagement in economic and social institutions. It's a world in which:

- Grandmothers are on iPads Skyping children who have not yet learned to walk.
- A child in Kenya whose parents make less than $5 a day is attending an open online course at MIT.
- An unemployed Baby Boomer is crowdfunding her latest innovation on Kickstarter.
- A middle-schooler is building revolutionary new medical devices using a 3D printer.

These are all examples of the Gen Z Effect at work, and what these people have in common is the desire to change and the ability to simply and affordably connect to each other and to humanity's accumulated knowledge. Many small steps for billions of beings, one giant leap forward for humanity.

Yet, generational boundaries have been a standard part of the way we operate a business; they've shape our organizations, described our markets, and defined our assumptions about one another. We rarely question the logic behind using these arbitrary delineations to identify groups of people, and to a large degree, we take pride in the group to which we belong. It is a piece of our identity we didn't choose—like our ancestry, the color of our hair, or the shape of our eyes—but nonetheless we take credit for it, and in doing so we create canyons of misunderstanding.

From Matures to Millennials, the force of accelerating change has been compressing the time between each generation into smaller and smaller intervals.

Consider that, while it was typical to see two distinct generations in the workforce simultaneously during the first half of the twentieth century, in the past fifty years we have seen a progression to three and four generations working simultaneously—and each of these is far less delineated in terms of the specific age boundaries between the generations.

With work-life expectancy increasing,[2] by 2020 we will easily have five generations working shoulder to shoulder.

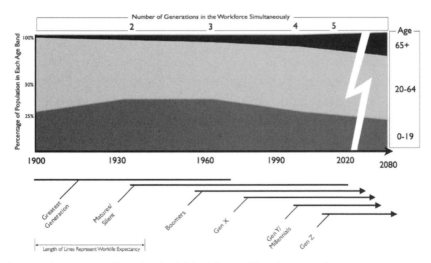

Figure I-1: Generations in the Workforce Simultaneously

Between 1900 and 2080 there will be seven distinct generational groupings. Each horizontal line below the chart indicates the work-life span of each of these generations. The shaded horizontal bands in the chart represent (from top to bottom) the percentage of the population (vertical axis) in the following age groups: sixty-five and over, twenty to sixty-four, and birth to nineteen. As the percentage of people sixty-five and over increases, the percentage of the population in the birth to nineteen band decreases. In addition, the number of generations in the workforce at the same time increases (top horizontal axis) from two in the early 1900s to five by 2020.

But even five generations working together is barely the beginning of the generational mash-up we foresee. By 2080, increasing life expectancy and work-life expectancy, together with shrinking intervals of technology turnover and innovation, will create an unprecedented fifteen generational bands in the workplace, based on each age band being about four years in span and expecting people to work from age twenty to age eighty. It challenges us to imagine what this sort of organization and world might look like, with so many distinct behaviors and attitudes about everything from the way we communicate and collaborate to how we perceive business risk and social value. But an organization could not function that way; there would be no hope of aligning interests and values; no chance of constructive collaboration. That is exactly why the unifying power of the Gen Z Effect is so important to the future of every organization. Still, trying to envision exactly what this future will look like is a challenge.

THE GRAVITY OF THE FUTURE

So, what can we say for certain about the future and Gen Z? Only that both will be stranger than anything we can dream of. Here's why.

As a child I had the hardest time grasping the concept of the rate at which objects fall to Earth. For those who may have had similar difficulty, or simply do not recall, a quick recap: all objects fall at the rate of 9.8 meters per second per second. It's that "per second per second" part that gave me trouble. It's easy to envision an object falling at a given speed, say 100 meters per second. The math here is anything but impressive. You can travel 100 meters in one second or 200 meters in two seconds. But that's not the way gravity works. If you drop an object from twice as high it does not take twice as long to reach the ground. It only takes 1.4 times as long.[3] The reason is that the higher the object the more time it has to accelerate. The simplest analogy is to think of pulling onto a highway. When you accelerate from 0 to 105 kph in ten seconds you are actually covering more ground with each passing second.

What does this have to do with the future and the Gen Z Effect? **Well, the future has its own form of gravity that pulls us toward it faster and faster: it's called technology.** And when it comes to technology, we simply cannot project change at the same rate going forward as it has occurred in the past.

Imagine that the last hundred years have been the first few seconds of that acceleration as we enter the highway. During that time, our ability to connect, expand, and accelerate the pace of every aspect of our world—from politics and economics to business and leisure—has changed in ways that would have been unimaginable to people living in the early twentieth century (something we'll talk more about in the chapter on hyperconnectivity).

However, an even greater rate of accelerating change awaits us over the next one hundred years. Today's connected enterprises are barely a prelude to the hyperconnected world we are quickly evolving toward. The change that happened in a hundred years will now happen in less than half that time—much less.

If we stay on the exponential trajectory we've been on for the past sixty years, by the year 2100 we will have more interconnected computing devices than there are grains of sand on all of the world's beaches—in fact, we'll have one hundred times as many! Imagine computers in everything from the food we eat to the clothes we wear to the cars we drive (or that drive us) to the implants that are part of us. The fabric of technology that will be woven into every aspect of our lives is driving the Gen Z Effect.

Most importantly, the Gen Z Effect will change the nature of business not only by making technology innovation move faster but by allowing value creation and exchange to permeate every corner of the globe. Billions of people who are today outside the economic mainstream will be suddenly thrust into a maelstrom of interconnected commerce, ten billion human beings all entwined in one great, interconnected, global value chain.

Trying to fathom the specific changes this will bring to the way we do business stretches our imagination well beyond its limits and nearly to the realm of science fiction. And because it seems so unimaginable, we discount the possibility of that change as though it were part of some distant dystopian view that is too far off to require action today.

MOVING BEYOND GENERATIONAL FICTION

For businesses, the Gen Z Effect and the opportunities it offers to move beyond generational fiction are striking. We came to the premise of a post-generational world with a healthy skepticism, but the research we did and the many cases detailed in these pages reinforced our belief that Gen Z is coming at us faster than we ever anticipated. It's time to start eliminating the generational rifts.

- IBM has put in place a Results-Oriented Work Environment (ROWE) that resulted in 50 percent higher productivity as well as a $700 million savings.
- Hyatt is using design thinking to break down generational barriers, in the process becoming one of the most admired companies to work for.
- Cisco revolutionized the way it shares behaviors across generations through its use of reverse mentoring; yet, only 15 percent of companies are doing the same.
- Dove crossed the boundary from twentieth-century paid media to twenty-first-century social media, creating a global movement that removes generational stigmas associated with beauty.
- The Gen Z-focused nonprofit Free the Children has become the largest Facebook cause in the world without spending a single penny on advertising.
- Lowe's is using behavioral data to cut across age demographics and identify underlying patterns in how and why customers buy.
- Prestigious universities such as Stanford, Harvard, and MIT are giving away their courses for free, disrupting the very foundation of higher education—a foundation that they built.
- As many as four million new businesses each year suddenly have access to capital they couldn't have dreamed of.
- Seventy-four percent of professionals believe that the patent system needs to be significantly overhauled, while 20 percent believe it serves no useful purpose.

THE SIX FORCES

Rarely is it possible to narrow down the forces that are shaping organizations into a few neat categories. Rarer still is the assurance that a prescription can be written to help organizations navigate uncertainty and change—especially at a time when both seem to be testing the limits of our endurance. Yet that is the purpose of *The Gen Z Effect:* to define the forces shaping the future of post-generational organizations, to understand them, and to identify specific ways we can leverage them to build more successful enterprises.

Six forces are driving the Gen Z Effect, and we will examine these individually in each of the following chapters. These six forces are the main characters of this book, and they've been carefully chosen not only for their overall impact on business but also for their ability to disrupt current notions of *how* we do business. The Gen Z Effect is propelled by:

> **Breaking Generations**: facing the imminent and immensely disruptive population redistribution that equalizes the number of humans globally in each of the thirteen five-year age groups from birth to sixty-four.[4] (i.e., ages 0–4, 5–9, 10–14, ... 60–64)

> **Hyperconnecting**: moving toward exponential hyperconnectivity among people, computers, machines, and objects.

> **Slingshotting**: exploiting disruptive advances in user experience and affordability that turn what was the cutting edge of technology into the norm, allowing large segments of the population to catch up, seemingly overnight, with technology pioneers.

> **Shifting from Affluence to Influence**: leveraging the ever increasing ability to influence world events through communities that cut across age and other demographic boundaries, without the benefit of access to large pools of capital.

> **Adopting the World As My Classroom**: pushing toward global availability and affordability of education through all levels of schooling and for any age.

> **Lifehacking**: breaking through barriers, taking shortcuts, and otherwise outsmarting the system so that we can focus on outcomes rather than processes, making meaning and purpose the center of our personal and professional experience.

The six forces driving the Gen Z Effect are not subtle generational shifts. Instead, they challenge some of the most basic beliefs about the way we operate across all generations.

ONE LAST THING

In the spirit of Gen Z, we've written this book in a way that makes sharing its content and collaborating using its ideas easy. In addition to the supplemental material on the website GenZEffect.com and the rich e-book version, you will see in this printed edition short segments of text in boldface—inline with the narrative—that capture the essence of the ideas we talk about. Like this one: **Generational thinking is like the Tower of Babel: it only serves to divide us. Why not focus on the behaviors that can unite us?**

We've limited the length of many of these nuggets to postable and, where possible, tweetable lengths, so that you can easily use them in social media. In the e-book version of *The Gen Z Effect* you can even post and tweet directly from the e-book. We've also included a "Put It Into Action" section at the end of each chapter, featuring key questions that help you assess how prepared you and your organization are for the coming of Gen Z. There's also a list of Gen Z leaders—both people and organizations—who are setting the pace.

Share these sound bites and bring to life your own conversation about Gen Z. Some of our ideas you may agree with, while others may stir skepticism. In either case, they are the seeds of a conversation that we hope you will take to the next level by breaking down the generational Tower of Babel and building in its place a future rich with new ideas and perspectives.

At TheGenZEffect.com, you'll find a detailed assessment that allows you to measure your own Gen Z ranking against those of thousands of your peers. This appraisal will guide you toward a better understanding of the behaviors and attitudes that may lead you into or away from Gen Z. You'll also find ongoing examples, commentary, conversation, and even debate around the many nuances of the Gen Z Effect.

To borrow a phrase popularized by the early-twentieth-century economist Joseph Schumpeter, "creative destruction" of the past and present is always the first act in building the future.

The good news is that this future of business has a playbook, and you're holding it.

1

Meet Gen Z—The Über Generation

Every generation wants to be the last.

—CHUCK PALAHNIUK, *LULLABY*

In this first chapter we will define Gen Z and the Gen Z Effect, describe the basic drivers of the shift to a post-generational world, and look at why we believe Gen Z is the last generation of the twenty-first century and the beginning of a new era of innovation and creativity.

Consider for a moment that much of what we've learned about how the world works has been built on what we've viewed as an immutable truth: that generations represent distinct and separate groups of people with a common set of beliefs, experiences, and values about the way the world works. As each cohort passes through life they become further entrenched in their generational beliefs, stifling innovation and disruption and protecting the wealth of ideas, power, and influence they have built through their efforts.

What if the notion of distinct generations has become a convenient fiction? What if—because of dramatically changing global demographics, the accelerating pace and simplification of technology, hyperconnectivity, universal education, and new ways of getting around impediments to innovation—we are being thrust into a post-generational world?

That's the big idea behind this book: the Gen Z Effect compresses and eliminates many of the generational boundaries that have separated us for

so long. Suddenly, we find ourselves with the ability to bypass difficult-to-use computer technology. Older generations who found technology impossible to master are rapidly overcoming their fear and loathing of computers by leap-frogging directly into a post-PC world where mobile, touch, voice-enabled, and wearable devices no longer need users' manuals or training. Grandparents are as likely to use Facebook as their grandchildren.[1] Technology, which once divided us, is now uniting us.

At the same time, the ability to constantly reeducate ourselves, well after and outside of K-12 and university classrooms, build vast personal networks, and amplify the influence of these networks through social media and online communities is no longer restricted to the affluent and powerful but available across ages and demographics. However, this book is not just about the next generation, and it is definitely not intended to leave the generations of the twentieth century behind; it's about a set of six unifying forces that will become pervasive and profound in the way they shape every aspect of life, no matter your age.

WHO IS GEN Z?

We need to be clear from the outset on one important point: while we believe passionately in the evidence that the Gen Z Effect allows us to cross chasms and unify generations, at its inception Gen Z starts with a new set of behaviors, which are foreign, even awkward, to those of us who arrived on the Earth last century. These behaviors are most vividly portrayed in children born in the past decade. For purposes of drawing a line of when Gen Z begins, we'll start with a band of ten years on either side of the year 2005. Keep in mind, as we discussed in the introduction, that generational boundaries have become increasingly blurred over the past century. So, as the topic of Gen Z is popularized, you are likely to see start dates for Gen Z in many sources that will span from 1995 to 2015. Putting a hard starting point on Gen Z is not something we are obsessed with since one of our key themes throughout the book is that Gen Z is not just a birthright but rather a set of shared behaviors that can be adopted through conscious choices.

Although much of what we talk about in this book has its roots in changes that started long before 2005, it is the specific attitudes and behaviors of children born near or after that point that are most influencing the way we look at the future. These kids are not just digital natives, they are hyperconnected junkies whose expectations will radically change business forever. In fact, we view Millennials as beta testers for the true digital natives of Gen Z.

For Gen Z, technology is invisible; it's just part of the way the world behaves toward and interacts with them. They are blind to the distinction between technology and the natural behavior of certain objects. For them, technology is just another thread in the fabric of their lives. As a hatchling is imprinted with the vision of whatever it first sees as its mother, those born into Gen Z are imprinted with technology.

In the same way that you expect a bee to sting, a dog to play, a bird to fly when approached, a child born into Gen Z expects objects to have behaviors, even personalities. Although the idea of attaching behavior and personality to objects is not entirely new, after all; every child who has ever owned a stuffed animal has attached a personality to it. However, what is new is the way in which these behaviors and personalities are now manifest in what these objects actually do, rather than what we imagine they do. The result is a two-way interaction with "smart" objects being the new norm and the deus ex machina all around us, rather than the "dumb" objects, whose "personality" was imposed and one-way from the owner to the object. The phenomenon amazes those of us old enough to remember when that was not the case, but it is nothing exceptional for a five-year-old. In short, technology is only technology for those of us who haven't grown up with it.

A good friend of ours, Lynn, recently shared a story about her two-year-old daughter, Julia, which demonstrates this better than we ever could. Julia, as is the case with 38 percent of all toddlers in American households, has regular use of a tablet.[2] In her case it's an iPad. She calls it her "paaad"—she cries for it in the same way infants cry for a pacifier, and it is just as frustrating for her when she can't have it. Julia is a bright child, and one of her favorite games on the iPad is the matching game Concentration, in which she has to flip cards on the touch screen by tapping them to reveal matching pictures. When Julia gets a match she screeches with excitement at her genius. It's her favorite game and she plays it endlessly. Nothing unusual there. You've surely seen some form of this game played by your kids, grandkids, nieces, and nephews—you've likely even played it yourself.

Recently, however, Julia's mom decided to dig up the deck of real Concentration cards that she had used with her ten-year-old son when he was Julia's age. Lynn was thrilled at the idea of sharing the "old world" experience with Julia and watching her discover the wonder of playing the game with the physical cards. As Lynn laid out the cards, Julia's excitement mounted. She clapped gleefully, knowing what was about to come. If only Lynn had known what was going on in Julia's mind.

With the cards laid out in neat rows and columns, Julia reached out and quickly tapped one. Nothing. Julia had a puzzled look on her face. She tapped again, this time harder, then harder, and harder still, until she finally burst into a rage, tossing all of the cards about by swiping her hand back and forth across the well-laid-out grid. In Julia's mind *this* paaaad was clearly broken.

Before you dismiss Julia's meltdown as just another cute example of how detached children have become from reality due to technology, consider that this *is* her reality. To Julia, objects should exhibit certain behaviors, perhaps the most important of which is an intelligent ability to interact with us. Those objects that do not follow these rules are simply broken.

We doubt that you would have a problem including Julia in Gen Z. In the same breath you'd likely be quick to describe all the ways in which Julia's behavior somehow robs her of the wonder and amazement of living in the real world. It's tempting to carve out the generational chasm. But wait: Julia is going to be your customer, your employee, your next great entrepreneur, your senator, perhaps, or, someday, your boss. You get the picture, right? We can't take away Julia's expectations for how the world should operate any more than I can take away your expectation that an apple falls from its branch to the ground. But to live in Julia's world you also have to believe that in some cases apples talk back to us and tell us when they are ready to be eaten.

This is why we need to look at Gen Z not as just a generation, but as a new set of behaviors and attitudes about how the world will work and how we will need to respond in order to stay current, competitive, and relevant. Increasingly, it doesn't matter when you were born, being part of Gen Z is a matter of adopting these behaviors—or, at the very least, understanding them and the value they bring. **Simply put, Gen Z is not just a birthright; it's a conscious choice to adopt new behaviors.**

In the nineteenth century, French historian Alexis de Tocqueville wrote, "Among democratic nations, each generation is a new people." However, what de Tocqueville, as well as those of us born in the last century, could not have foreseen was the closing gap between generations and the emergence of micro-generations, separated by just a few years but having grown up with entirely different technology experiences.

The reality is that all of the parameters that traditionally defined generations are changing, compressed into ridiculously small intervals. A two-year-old and a six-year-old could well be considered of different generations based on the type of tablet technology they use. In which case, we might as well define generational boundaries to correspond to Samsung's product release schedule!

This micro-generational experience is uncharted territory for all of us. It's not the way we are used to thinking about generations.[3] Consider how, in just a few decades, electronic communications have progressed from fax to e-mail to instant messaging to texting to Twitter; in successive bands of four to five years, each of these methods has overtaken the previous one as the preferred means of communication among each newly minted group of digital natives.

As each new medium of communication has emerged, something completely nonintuitive has occurred: technology behavior has percolated up through older users, not just down from them.

Because of the emergence of micro-generations, it is useless to consider what comes after Gen Z. There is no post-Gen Z, no Gen 2.0, no Gen AA, no Gen Alpha. Gen Z is the last generation worth labeling. That's good news because, unlike past generations, Gen Z's behaviors and attitudes are not confined to a demographic defined by a band of years; instead, they are a conscious choice, and the benefit of making that choice is the essence of this book.

In embracing the Gen Z Effect you become part of Gen Z. The barriers and the artificial perimeters of generational boundaries no longer limit your ability to be part of the future—only you can do that!

Although it may seem daunting to absorb all of the changes we will talk about, the Gen Z Effect will have a positive impact; it will radically reshape our institutions, expectations, and behaviors and offer a means to solve the greatest problems facing our organizations and our world.

So, what does this mean for *you*? Understanding and embracing Gen Z means that you will be able to:

- Manage and work with the broadest possible range of ages
- Benefit from intense collaboration in your work
- Build professional relationships that leverage the energy of youth and the wisdom of maturity
- Embark on a journey of lifelong learning, unlearning, and relearning
- Enjoy interacting with your kids and grandkids, nieces and nephews, without a technology divide
- Embrace the value of disruption and uncertainty
- Thrive in a world of accelerating change

We know that's a tall order to fill, but we're not trying to convince you to do something you wouldn't have to do anyway. We're just giving you fair warning so you can prepare for the changes that are coming. The Gen Z Effect will bring as radical a shift in attitudes and behaviors as humankind has yet experienced. Those of us who choose to be part of Gen Z will play a pivotal role as the last distinguishable generation of the information age and the first generation of the age of hyperconnectivity.

Don't underestimate the tremendous power inherent in embracing this shift. If you're part of Gen Z then you are the bridge between the behaviors that got us to where we are today and those that will bring us into the future. Like it or not, you are the torch bearer for all that's good and bad in the world: progress and prosperity, community and connectivity, but also wealth inequity, terrorism and political unrest, climate change, and economic volatility—all of these happened on your watch. However, you are also, if you choose to be, part of a real hope of solving these enormous challenges.

The promise of the Gen Z Effect is that it allows us to choose behaviors that point the way forward rather than anchor us to the past. Gen Z will lead the world into a new era of possibility, but we will also have to endure enormous disruption as we swap out behaviors so entrenched that they might as well be encoded in our DNA. Yet, even DNA mutates over time. The same can be said of Gen Z, which has been steadily taking shape—during a two-hundred-year prelude—as a society informed by changing demographics and rapidly evolving technology.

Look around today, and you will notice examples—hints, really—of how once fundamental structures, such as those shown in table I-I, are giving way to something entirely different, and how attitudes are shifting right along with them.

Table I-I: Attitudes Before and After Gen Z

	Before Gen Z	Transition to Gen Z
Internet access	A privilege	A human right
Influence	Purchased	Earned
IP/Patents	Value creators	Barriers
Failure	Avoided	Embraced
Gaming	Non-value-add play	Foundation for engagement
Uncertainty	Prepared for	Predicted
Retirement	A destination	A journey
Connectivity	A luxury	A necessity

So, how do two authors, one born as a Baby Boomer and one as a Gen Xer, get into the heads of Gen Z? The same way that we hope you will, by first opening up our own minds to the possibilities that exist beyond our experiences, and then allowing ourselves to be amazed by the value in the attitudes and behaviors of Gen Z.

As you read through this book you may experience a temptation to discount both of these—attitudes and behaviors. It's easy to do; we still live in the shadow of a generational world. However, try to view Gen Z in the way that one of the people we interviewed, Suman Mulumudi—profiled later in the book—put it to us: "It is not experience itself that hurts, but the fact that people treat experience like a crutch. They forget that where they can really see new technologies is where they haven't had experience. I truly believe if you have not failed, then you have not succeeded, because if you have not failed, you have not tried anything uncertain, you have not thought outside of the box."

Suman Mulumudi, by the way, is fifteen years old. We agree with him and would amplify his analogy. **Experience is sometimes more of an exoskeleton than a crutch; it gives us the ability to do amazing things but it lacks flexibility and eventually it defines what is possible in ways that we are simply unable or unwilling to question.**

One more thing worth pointing out is that we are not saying that *every* new behavior is one we should blindly accept as part of Gen Z. As with all change, a healthy dose of skepticism doesn't hurt in separating valuable behaviors from destructive ones. The danger is in discounting what's new just because it does not fit our experience. Simply put, don't allow the constraints of the past to define the limits of the future. So much of what we will talk about—the cases and examples we will use and the suggestions we will make—can only be fully understood through their application. Trying to decide if a new behavior makes sense is like trying to decide if a new product, one we've never experienced, makes sense. Only experience can make that determination.

In 1984 John Dvorak, the technology writer for the *San Francisco Examiner,* said, "The Macintosh uses an experimental pointing device call a 'mouse.' There is no evidence that people want to use these things." [4] Well, of course there was no evidence, because the first commercially available mouse did not exist until 1983! In fairness to Dvorak, his point of view was no less valid than most projections of how disruptive new technologies will perform in the market. Looking backward, there is one path to the present; looking forward, there are infinite paths to the future. It's always easier to pick the right path looking backward.

An academic discussion about the future is one thing; it's another thing altogether to live it. Only through experience can we decide which of the many paths to the future is the one worth taking. So, we offer a warning: Gen Z requires a mind that is open, willing to evolve, and tolerant of the discomfort of change.

THE BEGINNING OF THE END OF GENERATIONAL BOUNDARIES

We can't go much further without defining Gen Z and the Gen Z Effect. We will use the terms throughout the book, and it might be easy to confuse one with the other, but there is a difference. Gen Z is a set of behaviors and attitudes about the way the world works. You can be born into it or you can choose to be part of it. **The Gen Z Effect is what happens when the simplicity and affordability of technology unites generations more than it divides them.**

Welcome to Gen Z if:

- You are a Boomer in the process of starting your next career rather than heading off into retirement.
- You were born around or after the year 2005.
- You're just starting your career but expect to never end your education.
- You believe that innovation comes from crossing the boundaries that separate us rather than staying within them.
- You're a leader who wants to stay young in the way you think and you encourage others to do the same.
- You believe in challenging conventional wisdom—even if it's your own.
- You are an educator who does not want (or no longer wants) to teach a curriculum that puts you on a pedestal of unassailable experience.
- You believe that 2.7 billion people with Internet access is still 4.3 billion people short.
- You are unwilling to accept that affluence is the only path to influence.

This doesn't mean that we will all wake up one morning and make the decision to be Gen Zers. The current demographics of the world just don't support that sort of sudden shift. Broad generational differences live on today in the people who were born into the last five generations, because those at the beginning and those at the end of the spectrum were born into very different worlds, and different people react differently to change.

What is happening—and it's accelerating—is a steady closing of gaps between earlier generations and the near elimination of the gaps for future generations. There are two ways in which the Gen Z Effect does this.

Making Technology Simple Is Complicated Stuff

The first way in which the Gen Z Effect closes generational gaps is through the simplicity and availability of new technology—such as mobile devices and tablets—that make it much likelier that people across all ages will adopt it.

9

But the simplification of technology is the result of a long and complicated journey. The simplest technologies mask enormous complexity that the user neither sees nor cares about.

Take as an example e-books, which today you are as likely to find in the hands of a preschooler as in those of an eighty-year-old retiree. E-books actually have a long history, with the first ones introduced through the pre-Internet (ARPANET) Project Gutenberg in 1971. Project Gutenberg was intended to build a digital online library of books that were no longer protected by copyright. Forty years later Gutenberg still exists, and includes more than forty thousand books. You can access it at Gutenberg.org. However, we doubt that most of you have since it is a far cry from the many advances in e-books that have come—and gone—since. Nineteen years later, in 1990, Sony made an attempt to enter the market with its Data Discman, which read books— mostly reference books—on CD-ROM and resembled a laptop more than an e-reader of today. It was a classic case of force-fitting the future into the packaging of the past. CDs were Sony's offspring from the mid 1970s. The Data Discman was more of a novelty and ended up going head to head with laptops, which had substantially greater screen real estate for reading.

It was another eight years before the first true handheld e-reader, the Rocket, released in 1998 by NuvoMedia, evolved to the point that it was a somewhat independent and portable device. We say "somewhat" because the Rocket required you to download your e-books from your PC using a serial cable (a predecessor to USB).

Yet, e-book readers were still barely a speck of dust lying on the monitor of consumers' radar. Fast-forward to Amazon's introduction of the Kindle in 2007. Within two years of the Kindle's introduction, e-book reader sales had increased to about three million units per year. From that they jumped to about twenty million units in 2012.

However, something curious happened just after that peak was reached. E-book reader sales started to drop—and continue to fall today. But, wait, isn't e-book popularity increasing? Yes, but the e-book is not the same as the e-book reader. What's happened here is a classic case of simplification slingshotting technology into a larger orbit of users; it's an example of how technology providers so often get technology right and behavior wrong.

This is why we get it wrong: one of the most common models used to explain the expansion of technology is that of exponential curves. These are growth patterns that show and project how a given technology spreads over time based on an exponential increase in some aspect of its use, power, or capacity. One example is the often-touted Moore's law, which predicts the doubling of the number of transistors on an integrated circuit every two years.

But there is a flaw in the way we apply exponential growth patterns to technology; namely, we believe that any single technology or device will follow the exponential curve in perpetuity. This has never been the case. Instead, what happens is that multiple technologies follow what are called sigmoid curves, or, as we will refer to them, power curves. These are curves that eventually plateau—think of an S curve rather than a J curve, as shown in figure I-I. Power curves don't go on forever; they take off slowly, ramp up quickly, and eventually taper off and often, drop.

Individual computer and information technologies follow a sigmoid, or power, curve function. While each power curve eventually reaches a point

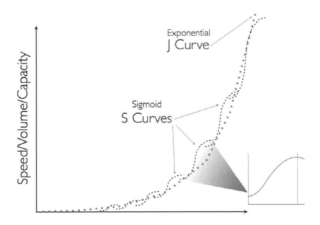

Figure 1-1: Power (Sigmoid) Curves versus J Curves

While individual technologies, as in the case of the many generations of e-books, may each follow their own "S" curve, eventually tapering off and disappearing, the overall behavioral curve represents a cumulative exponential growth in the use of, and in the impact of technology. The problem is that technology providers and markets continuously lose sight of the behavioral curve and instead become obsessed with a specific technology.

of deceleration and ultimately stalls, the effect is that each also progressively builds on the last following a cumulative exponential rate of growth. We call this cumulative effect the behavioral curve. By projecting the behavioral curve we can gain visibility into the future, although the specific technologies that will continue the increase in speed, volume, or capacity of computing devices may not yet exist.

The failure of any one technology to grow exponentially doesn't stop exponential change in the overall impact of multiple technologies on our behaviors.

Consider the music industry, where vinyl records gave way to audiocassette tapes, which were replaced by CDs in the early 1990s and then overtaken by the digital MP3 format in the early 2000s. The number of songs that you could carry with you continued to grow exponentially, but the devices you used changed as each medium eventually reached the end of its power curve. We've shown in figure 1-1 that the results are separate individual power curves for each technology, the cumulative effect of which is to follow an exponential curve in the overall growth and impact of technology. We call this sustained ability to grow across multiple technologies a "behavioral curve." Later, in chapter 3, we'll look at how this phenomenon has played out over the last seventy years, causing us to perpetually live on the elbow, or inflection point, of the behavioral curve.

To capitalize on the Gen Z Effect, you need to understand the behavioral curve so that you can effectively jump from one technology power curve to the next at just the right time. The Kindle Fire HDX is a great example of a company stepping off of the power curve just in time to get back onto the next technology defining the behavioral curve. The HDX is still able to download an increasingly larger number of books, but it is no longer just an e-book reader, it is also a tablet—and at the time of this writing one of the most cost-effective tablets on the market.

By jumping the prior e-reader power curve, Amazon has kept the Kindle experience current with the trend toward e-book consumption as part of an integrated set of mobile behaviors rather than a separate stand-alone e-book experience. Amazon went further than other tablets to enhance the experience and support the behavioral expectations with its Mayday button. Mayday provides users with the ability to access support for the device directly, not just by talking to Kindle customer support but by viewing live video of the support agent on their Kindles. Live assistance that functions like a full-time technology nanny makes using a Kindle as easy as switching on a light and amazingly age agnostic. Most importantly, it makes Amazon a leader in defining the next power curve of user experience.

Now contrast that with the path that Sony has followed. Although Sony introduced its first e-reader two years before Amazon launched the Kindle, that head start did not provide a long-term advantage. As Amazon jumped the power curve, Sony began its exit from the e-book market by closing its e-book store and transitioning all of its users to Kobo, another leader in e-book content and devices. (We should point out that while Sony is not in the e-book market, at the time this book is being written, it is still actively playing in the tablet marketplace.)

This sort of not-so-graceful exit has been typical of Sony in other markets, including digital music, which it abandoned when Apple stepped in and stole the pole position from Sony with the iPod. Sony followed the same fateful path when it lost out to Panasonic's VHS videotape format over its own Betamax format and players. These abrupt exits are certainly better than following the power curve's descent into obsolescence, but they invariably create negative sentiment among customers who have invested heavily by hitching their cart to the promise of the brand.

In a post on goodereader.com one loyal Sony customer, who identified himself as Jeff P., shared the following comment in response to an open letter from Sony stating that customers always come first.

HORRID! HORRID! HORRID! I've [been a member] since November 2007. The only readers or tablets I've ever [used] were Sony so that I could use the reader software. I once told a sales clerk that I didn't need the extended warranty because I was buying a Sony. Almost every piece of electronic equipment I have is Sony. I won't buy another Sony ANYTHING. Yes, you say customers are first, well, I'm the first customer to tell you that you've made a HORRID mistake and I'm never going to buy another Sony product EVER.[5]

Although both Amazon and Sony have made the transition to the next power curve—tablets—Amazon is doing so in a way that reinforces the meaning behind its brand, while Sony, clearly, is feeling the repercussions of failing to do so.

Staying on the power curve for too long with a single technology creates rifts between generations as the distance between successive technologies widens.

Companies that try to ride the tail end of the power curve as it descends conjure up images of the final scene in *Dr. Strangelove*, which features Major Kong riding a nuclear bomb out of the B-52 bay doors to certain annihilation. The difference is that Kong had a firm objective in mind. These companies are simply falling into an empty abyss. Staying on the long-term behavioral curve while shifting seamlessly from one power curve to the next is a hallmark of companies that leverage the Gen Z Effect. Companies like Amazon are able to develop the type of relationship with the Gen Z marketplace that ultimately brings the technology to increasingly larger audiences. By consistently simplifying devices and processes, they ease the transition from one technology to the next, thereby allowing the entire marketplace—undivided by generations of technology—to collaborate and share in the experience.

It's Only Technology If You Don't Grow Up With It

The second way in which the Gen Z Effect unites generations is by creating a new set of behaviors that pretty much mandates the use of certain technologies for anyone who wants to remain an active part of society. In other words, rejecting the technology creates significant impediments in being able to interact with others. This is in large part why texting has seen incredible growth as a communication medium. Estimates of texts sent daily, which include instant messaging as well as SMS, point to about twenty-two billion messages.[6] According to data from the Pew Research Center, "18–24 year olds send or receive an average of 109.5 texts a day, more than double the comparable figure for 25–34 year olds, and twenty-three times the figure for text messaging users who are 65 or older."

Each age band is increasing its use of text messaging at roughly the rate of

30 percent each year, in large part because if you don't text you will end up isolating yourself from many of your coworkers, family, and friends. But this behavior will change in ways that are going to take many people, and companies, by surprise (via the phenomenon of slingshotting, which we cover in chapter 4). As Alvin Toffler asserted in *Future Shock*, we are in for "[a] sense of shock felt by those who were not paying attention."

It's also important to note that the Gen Z Effect is not an entirely new phenomenon, nor is it limited to the sixty-eight years since the advent of digital computers. In fact, it has been present in some form for the last two centuries of technology innovation.

When automobiles were first introduced, drivers needed a level of competency and daring that terrified most people. Estimates for the number of automobiles it would take to saturate the market were made based on the number of chauffeurs that were projected to be available. That may sound absurd today, but in 1920 the death rate from automobile accidents was twenty times higher than it is today. Driving was risky business.

Unlike modern automobiles, which don't require much knowledge to start and drive, early automobiles were complex machines. Even Henry Ford's Model T had no fewer than seven different controls that you had to master—not an easy task, but one that millions of people quickly learned in order to not be left behind. The same holds true for many of the technologies that we take for granted today; we learn and relearn because it's the only way to stay in the game.

There are many more generations of technology in the century between you and your grandparents than there were in the two thousand years between Plato and Gutenberg.

The ability of youth to influence a society is not new either. This was as true in the nineteenth century, when Ivan Turgenev wrote his novel *Fathers and Sons*—which described the tension between generations as youth started to move away from traditional Russian values toward Western values—as it was in the twentieth century—when hippies shaped sentiment by protesting the Vietnam War and distrusting everyone over the age of thirty.

What has changed dramatically since these examples, and what provides the foundation for so much of the Gen Z Effect, is the way in which behaviors, attitudes, and opinions are amplified by media and the Internet.

Any activists before this century needed to attract the likes of CBS or the *New York Times* to get their message out. Not so for Gen Z. A well-crafted—or sometimes not-so-well-crafted—Twitter campaign can create a firestorm of popular opinion, from the political commentary on Florida Senator Marco Rubio's sip of water as he delivered the Republican response to President Obama's State of the Union Address[7] to the unintentional comedy of a woman attempting to take a selfie at the Sochi 2014 Olympics.[8]

So what is going to drive all of this change? In research we've done over the past five years on more than six hundred individuals spanning the ages of eighteen to eighty-five, and in working with hundreds of organizations that are facing the very real struggle of a multi-generational workforce with a new set of behaviors and attitudes, we've identified six forces that are driving the Gen Z Effect. These six forces—breaking generations, hyperconnecting, slingshotting, shifting from affluence to influence, adopting the world as my classroom, and lifehacking—form the bedrock for Gen Z's behaviors and are our first step in understanding the future of business. It is these influential forces that we'll explore one by one in the following six chapters.

GEN Z IS A CHOICE NOT A BIRTHRIGHT

We're still talking about generations, and that's missing the big idea behind the Gen Z Effect and this book—that generations are the wrong way to group people. We refer to Gen Z as *the* last generation because our six forces—population distribution, shifting influence, universal education, hyperconnectivity, slingshotting, and lifehacking—are blurring and contorting shared experience and the lines between generations so dramatically that it will soon be impossible to differentiate between generations in any useful way. Cohorts will still exist but what they will share is not a common age but rather a common set of behaviors and experiences. If you want to see this today, look at gaming (something we talk much more about in chapter 6). Gamers come in all shapes, sizes, ages, and ethnicities. There is no human demographic that gaming does not traverse. It's the same way with Gen Z, which cuts across all cultural divides.

Mind you, the developmental stages of youth and the cultural experiences we share by age won't be a thing of the past. There's still an experiential difference in stages of life—from needing a pacifier to needing a walker—although we'd claim that the distance between a tablet, the modern-day equivalent of the pacifier, and a computerized walker is far smaller. And, of course, you'll still have particular shared experiences with your classmates from high school or university, or with colleagues from your first job.

We're also not claiming that the growing pains typical from toddlerhood to adolescence will somehow be eliminated by the Gen Z Effect. The hormonal and chemical changes that we, and our parents, went through are the same ones our children will endure. Children will continue to drive their parents crazy because testing limits and challenging authority are inherent parts of discovering and forming an individual identity.

But, as a tool for working together productively, and certainly as a tool for understanding the larger picture of how the world will operate in the twenty-first century, diagnosing and responding to behavioral trends in twenty-year generational bands no longer makes sense. Our claim is that we all have an opportunity—even a responsibility—to adopt the broader zeitgeist of Gen Z. **The bottom line is that the year you were born need no longer be the principle identity of your behaviors and attitudes.**

What our research has shown is the emergence of a set of behaviors and attitudes that crosses generations and defines Gen Z. For example, Gen Zers hold the increasingly prevalent belief that Internet access is a basic human right for everyone rather than a privilege for a few. According to Internet.org, two-thirds of the world's population still does not have access to the Internet, and while penetration of the Internet has reached 2.7 billion people in just a few decades, the annual increase has slowed to just 9 percent globally.

In developed countries where the Internet is widely available and affordable, the impact has been significant in practical economic terms. A McKinsey & Company study found that over the past five years the Internet has contributed to 15 percent of GDP growth in these countries. The study also uncovered that for every job the Internet eliminates due to new efficiencies, 2.6 new jobs are created. **Consider the economic impact to developing countries if we could create affordable Internet access for the world's remaining five billion inhabitants.**

Much of the behavior of Gen Z will grow from this attitude that being connected is foundational to economic growth. For Gen Z this is an obsession that will cross all traditional boundaries, including nationalism, race, and political affiliation. Their gaming and their schooling will happen on a global stage, it will be self-directed, and it will build new forms of global community.

We believe that within the decade we will have an affordable Internet that will allow any human being, without regard to geographic or political location and economic status, to connect with any other human being based on individual interests rather than on the circumstances of his local "tribe." The result will be the beginning of an era of global disruption, innovation, and progress unlike anything humankind has experienced.

With all due respect to the vast body of his work, Thomas Friedman was wrong. The world isn't flat: it's networked and it's both infinitely small, in that anyone can connect with anyone at anytime, and infinitely large, in that the possibilities that arise from hyperconnectivity are endless. This is what we call *distributed convergence,* an ability to be both hyperlocal and hyperglobal at the same time.

Understanding this point is critical to appreciating the power of the Gen Z Effect. In simple terms, we are saying that locality still has meaning, but not in a geographic sense. Locality is defined by your interests rather than your geography or your political borders. Just as adding a third dimension to two dots on a piece of paper allows you to connect the dots by folding the paper rather than traversing a straight line on its surface, hyperconnectivity allows Gen Zers to find whatever and whomever they need to accomplish the task at hand.

While the full impact of the Gen Z Effect may not be felt until 2025 (the latest date by which every last human will have Internet access), we're already behind in understanding and preparing to work shoulder to shoulder with those who embrace this radical new set of behaviors.

So, let's begin our journey through the six forces of the Gen Z Effect that are already shaping our world. The first of these is also the most profound in terms of how it will reshape society. Its unlike any other shift that will alter nearly every aspect of how we think and act as individuals, businesses, and governments: it is the imminent and radical change in population distribution from the pyramid to what we call the skyscraper.

Put It Into Action:
Chapter 1 #ubergeneration #GenZ

Are You Ready for Gen Z?

- How often do you make decisions and judgments about people based on your perceptions of the generation they belong to?
- If you are Gen Z by age, how do you interact with other generations?
- If you are Gen Z by choice, who else around you shares a Gen Z outlook?
- Think of some personal examples of how technology is bridging and unifying generations rather than separating them. How many did you come up with?
- Are you paying attention to new Gen Z behaviors? Do you try to experience them before dismissing them?
- Where do you fall in table 1-1, "Attitudes Before and After Gen Z"?
- How well does your organization follow the behavioral curve as opposed to individual technology power curves?
- How many generations are currently working in your business?
- What are you doing to understand, work, and play with multiple generations?
- How would your business need to change to handle fifteen simultaneous generations by 2080?
- Are you building professional relationships that leverage the energy of youth and the wisdom of maturity, and vice versa?
- Are you limiting your view of the future based on the constraints of the past, or are you constantly testing these limits in order to better react to the future?
- How does your organization reward and engage its employees across age groups?
- Does your organization recognize the personal and professional drivers of your employees outside of work?

Find out whether you're ready for the Gen Z Effect by taking the full assessment at TheGenZEffect.com.

2

Breaking Generations

The best thing about the future is that it comes one day at a time.

—ABRAHAM LINCOLN

In this chapter we lay the foundation for much of the Gen Z Effect, delving into the dramatic changes on the horizon for population demographics by introducing the concept of population pyramids and exploring the way they have been, and will continue, morphing. We'll also introduce influence and affluence pyramids, explain how to avoid the generational traps that we often fall into, and explore the validity of "generation gaps" as well as identify methods that close the gaps by looking beyond generational boundaries.

The year 2080 will be remarkable. Not for its technologies, which will no doubt be light-years ahead of where we are today, but because it will mark the first time in recorded history that every five-year age band, from newborns to sixty-five-year-olds, will account for almost exactly the same percentage of the world's population: 6 percent.

This nearly perfect symmetrical demographic distribution—what we'll call the skyscraper—is without precedent and will exist in stark contrast to the pyramid-shaped global population distribution that has been pervasive for the majority of recorded human history.

Pyramid structures are so deeply embedded in all of our social

21

institutions—from education to economics to politics—that it's no surprise we cannot think outside this intuitive metaphor. **It's as though, over the past five thousand years, the pyramid has become an instinctive framework for thinking about the way the world works.** It's hard to imagine how we would even begin to break free of this entrenched model of society. Yet the underlying shift in global demographics is on a trajectory leading to just that, whether we are prepared for it or not.

THE END OF THE POPULATION PYRAMID

No matter how far back you go, the tendency of every civilization has been toward population distributions that resemble pyramids. With the exception of major natural disasters, famine, pandemics, and wars, population pyramids have remained relatively stable over time, sometimes bulging and at other times contracting, but always regressing towards a pyramid.

Ultimately, two simple factors shape population pyramids. The first is the rate of mortality at each age as we move toward the top. (Statisticians are a bit more blunt, calling it the "death rate" and measuring it as a function of the number of deaths per thousand members of a population at any give age and during any given time period.) In each subsequent age band, moving up the pyramid, individuals are subtracted from the layers. Simply stated, we all enter a population pyramid at its base and we exit as we age and move toward its peak.

However, the role of this first factor—the death rate—has been steadily decreasing in each age band over the past two hundred years because of better health care, improved sanitation, greater access to clean water, and a more stable food supply. Keep in mind that the decrease is due to factors such as reduced infant mortality and better disease control. It's clearly not the elimination of mortality; the overall death rate does not decrease, it's always 100 percent, since even if we reach the top of the population pyramid we are all eventually going to exit. For the time being we'll ignore the temporal aberrations that increase the death rate, which we just mentioned (natural disasters, global pandemics, and so on).

The second factor is the rate of absolute growth in the bottom of the pyramid. (Again, statisticians simply refer to "net growth," which is the number of deaths per 1000 subtracted from the number of births per 1000 in a given period of time.) As birth rates increase so does the population at the base because, for most of human history, the number of births has consistently exceeded the number of deaths. The result is that as the overall population increases you have a larger and usually broader-based pyramid. This is exactly what we saw as the global population more than tripled, from 1 billion in 1804 to 3.5 billion in 1950, and then doubled from that point to the present day. Think about that for a moment. **It took about seven thousand years for world population to grow from several million to 1 billion, 150 years for it to triple, and another sixty for it to double again.**

Over the past sixty years we have seen the formation of a perfect global population storm that includes a dramatic drop in infant mortality, better access to health care, clean water and food, increasing life expectancy, and greater participation in the benefits of a global economy. While all of these started to take root in developed countries, they are increasingly reflected in nearly every major global geography. The result is a global population pyramid that, although still growing in terms of overall population, has been growing more slowly at the base and expanding toward the top in relative terms.

Now do a simple thought experiment and picture what that population pyramid would look like over time as we move toward 2050. What do you see in your mind's eye?

On a global scale the result is astonishingly nonintuitive. During the next eighty years we will see the global population pyramid reshaping itself into a nearly perfect skyscraper.

If you stop to consider the long-term implications of this phenomenon, it's initially cause for concern. For example, how does the well–established notion of social welfare for the top third of the pyramid continue to survive when it's growing faster than the rest of the pyramid, relatively speaking? The flawed but previously unassailable assumption that many social welfare systems have made is that a growing middle class will always support an increasing but radically smaller top third of elderly and retired workers. The very simple economic consequence of that flaw in our generational system of government is ensconced in myriad other social implications of a redistributed global population. To understand just how deep the redistribution of population is, let's look at some of the underlying data supporting the shift from pyramid to skyscraper.

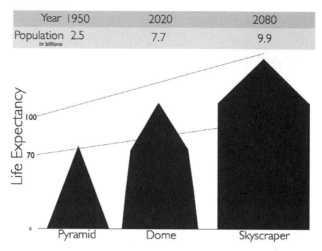

Year	1950	2020	2080
Population in billions	2.5	7.7	9.9

Figure 2-1: The Shift from Pyramid to Skyscraper

The traditional global population pyramid, which existed until 1950, has changed considerably. In its place has evolved a dome with a much broader midsection and subtler tapering as it progresses up through generations. But the dome is only a transitional metaphor as we head into the defining permanent structure of the future: a world with ten billion fully educated and completely connected human beings. How we navigate that transition will likely define society for the next millennium. (The relative size of each shape—pyramid, dome, and skyscraper—represents relative growth in population.)

BUILDING THE SKYSCRAPER

As we've said, by 2080, with global population topping ten billion, the number of people in each five-year age band through age sixty-four will be virtually identical, about 6 percent, or six hundred million each. In the United States that same phenomenon will occur by 2020, when these same age bands will be within 1 percent of one another, from 5.5 percent to 6.5 percent.

Compare the shape of 2080 global population with that of figure 2-3, which shows the global distribution of ages in 1950—about five years into the Baby Boomer generation—when age distribution formed a neat pyramid, with a range from 14 percent of world population at its base to 2 percent at sixty-five years of age, with nearly 50 percent of the population under the age of twenty.

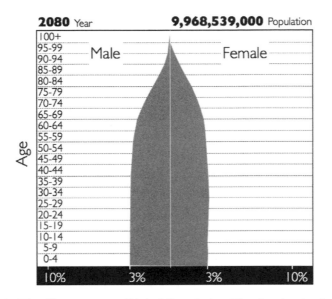

Figure 2-2: The Skyscraper—Global Population Distribution by Age in 2080

The skyscraper represents a nearly equal distribution of population in every age band from birth to age four through age sixty to sixty-four.

This shift is not a globally isolated phenomenon. This same dramatic trend in demographics is mirrored in virtually every developed economy. Even currently lagging and underdeveloped economic regions such as the African continent and the Indian subcontinent will catch up to this distribution within the next fifty years. The long-term impact is undeniable. By 2100, the population distribution across the globe by age will look more like a skyscraper than like a broad-based pyramid.

As age bands at the base of the skyscraper slow in their growth and levels toward the top swell with increasing life and work-life expectancy, we will start to experience distinct changes in many of the defining attributes that have allowed us to draw lines between generational boundaries.

When we talk about the base of the population pyramid some clarification is necessary. How we qualify what constitutes the parts of the pyramid—base, middle, and capstone—is critical if we are to have a meaningful conversation about influence. In our discussion we will look at each of these thirds

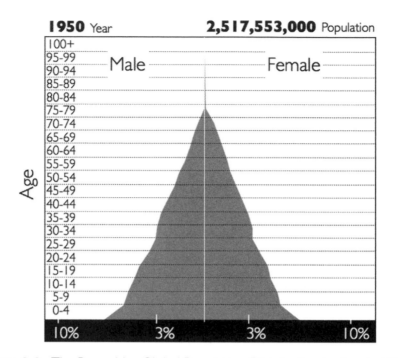

1950 Year   **2,517,553,000** Population

Male   Female

Age

100+
95-99
90-94
85-89
80-84
75-79
70-74
65-69
60-64
55-59
50-54
45-49
40-44
35-39
30-34
25-29
20-24
15-19
10-14
5-9
0-4

10%   3%   3%   10%

Figure 2-3: The Pyramid—Global Population Distribution by Age in 1950

The pyramid represents a classic distribution of population that tapers at a relatively standard rate from birth through eighty years of age.

of the pyramid as representing an arithmetic third of global population—approximately 2.33 billion people at the time this book was written.

Most importantly, this is not just a conversation about wealth. Oxfam has reported that the wealth of the world's eighty-five richest people is equal to that of the world's 3.5 billion poorest people, many of whom, through no fault or choice of their own, have no access to even the most basic human necessities, such as sanitation, clean water, and health care. Based on distribution and density of wealth, that means the wealth in the lower half of our pyramid is equal to the wealth in the top one-millionth of 1 percent (0.0000012142857 percent).

To give that some perspective, look at figure 2-4; if global population were the size of the Great Pyramid of Giza, the world's eighty-five wealthiest individuals would fit in a child's sand pail, about one cubic foot of the pyramid's volume. Their wealth, using the pyramid, would represent 44,000,000 cubic feet. That's an acre of land one hundred stories high.

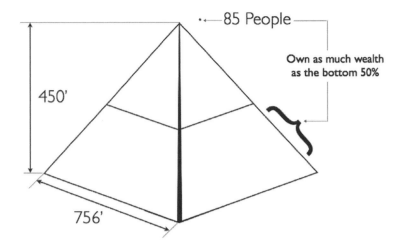

Figure 2-4: Population and Wealth

Picture the world's population represented by the Great Pyramid of Giza: the dot below represents the eighty-five people—less than a sand pail of the pyramid's volume. Yet they own as much wealth as the 3.5 billion poorest people—the 44,000,000 cubic feet that make up the bottom half of the pyramid.

In the context of this discussion about wealth inequality, what is often lost is that the 3.5 billion at the base of that pyramid have, collectively, substantial wealth; it's just that they have little ability to collectively exert influence.

We want to look at population because, ultimately, that is where Gen Z differs significantly in its leveraging of influence. Gen Zers are powerful. They have a built-in media channel to billions in the form of the Internet. And they know how to disrupt. In other words, they know how to mess things up if they don't get what they want. You can look at that as entitlement. You can look at it as being spoiled. Call it what you want; the reality is that when influence is diffused throughout a population rather than concentrated, the effect is a disruption of the balance of power in nearly every existing institution— social, business, and government.

This disruption is not just fueled by the contemporary notion of a digital divide but also by the canyon of economic disparity between those who have access to and are engaged in the world economy and those who do not have access and cannot be engaged. Being disconnected digitally means being disconnected economically. **The last time the world saw anything close to the current level of disparity in global wealth was just before the French Revolution, an uprising that resulted in forty thousand of France's wealthiest men and women losing their heads—literally.**

We are again at a precarious and perilous intersection for the global economy. So, what does this have to do with the Gen Z Effect? A great deal, in our estimation. The difference for Gen Z is that, unlike *any* previous point in history, today the ability to instigate change is not determined solely by affluence but increasingly by influence. This ability to influence, something we'll talk about much more in chapter 5, creates an entirely different social dynamic. It not only makes society more transparent, it also gives a voice to those who would otherwise be silenced and increasingly angered by their lack of influence in shaping society's agenda.

AVOIDING THE GENERATIONAL TRAP

At its core the Gen Z Effect is about rethinking the way age shapes our behaviors and attitudes so that we can avoid falling into the trap of rigid generational categories—these are myths that distract and separate generations by diminishing their behaviors instead of focusing on the benefits of age-based diversity and inclusion.

At the graduate level of education, students have historically been clustered within a fairly narrow age range. They either went directly to grad school from their undergraduate studies or they went back after about five years of work experience. So you had a majority of students in their late twenties, a minority in their early twenties, and an even smaller minority in their early thirties. For the most part they shared the same experiences and social context, so their conversations, case studies, and interests were similar. Sometime in the last ten years that began to change—dramatically. More students started to come in on the back end of longer careers.

For the first time, the professor is not the oldest person in the room. Today there are students from across the age spectrum in graduate school. Many in their fifties and sixties are entering their "Third Act," a time following traditional education (the first act) and a traditional career (the second act). "Third Act" is more than just a catchy term we're slapping on a small number of folks who want or need to work past a certain age. According to our research, 29 percent of the overall population do not expect to *ever* retire. That increases to 37 percent for twenty-two- to thirty-two-year-olds. Don't mistake this for simply a trend born of economic necessity. While many in the workforce have suffered because of the recessions that struck in the early and late 2000s, there is another factor at play, one we've already talked about. We can all work longer because locality and age do not stand in the way of our ability to work.

In fact, we challenge the very nature of "retirement" and feel strongly that this, too, is a term and a concept that has outlived its usefulness. Since 1950 a definitive trend line has emerged, pointing to a narrowing gap between life expectancy and work-life expectancy. Both are increasing, but work-life expectancy is increasing at a slightly faster rate than life expectancy.[1] While that does not mean we will at some point be working after we're dead—at least that's not a claim we're making in this book—it does illustrate how underlying trends are challenging some of the most basic generational beliefs, such as retirement.

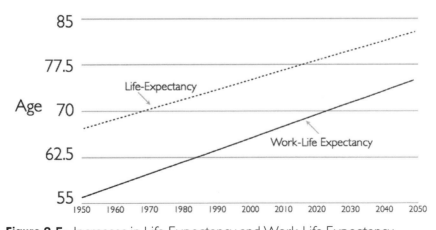

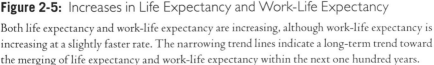

Figure 2-5: Increases in Life Expectancy and Work-Life Expectancy

Both life expectancy and work-life expectancy are increasing, although work-life expectancy is increasing at a slightly faster rate. The narrowing trend lines indicate a long-term trend toward the merging of life expectancy and work-life expectancy within the next one hundred years.

If you're thinking, "But wait, I want to retire! I'm looking forward to it!" don't miss the point. For Gen Z, retirement is not a chronologic watershed that marks the end of work and the beginning of leisure. Gen Z does not expect to, and will not have to, disengage from work that is financially or personally fulfilling. Instead they will simply move into a new stage of life where the balance between, or the purpose behind, work and play may shift. That's why we prefer the term Third Act as a way to describe a period of life when the venue and the rules of how you work may change, allowing you to integrate and balance work as a meaningful part of your life.

THE GENERATION GAP AND OTHER MYTHS

The biggest trap we fall into when trying to think beyond purely generational terms is that of the apparently immutable generation gap. One of the most common misconceptions that comes up in any conversation about the shrinking intervals between generations is the idea that a generation gap must exist, and that it will always be the source of irreconcilable tension and friction between generations. After all, the emergence of a generation gap is just a natural outcome of rebelling against authority and finding our identity as individuals within a group of like-minded peers.

We find it interesting that even the term "generation gap" has become culturally accepted without much scrutiny as to its origins or meaning. The term seems to have originated in the 1960s as a way of describing tensions that arose during a tumultuous period in which Baby Boomers were coming of age and rebelling in a very public and abrasive way against the establishment of the day. At the same time, television began playing an important role in shaping social and political sentiment. The result was a magnification of the difference in values between two generations, one raised in a world of relative anonymity and another propelled to express itself in the public eye.

The term itself was popularized by cultural anthropologist Margaret Mead. However, even Mead had her doubts about its use. In *Margaret Mead: A Biography*, Mary Bowman-Kruhm describes the origins of the term and Mead's ultimate reservations about its use:

Mead may not have coined the term "generation gap," but she popularized its use to refer to the difference in sense of history between those who were born and reared before World War II and those born after it. She later felt the term was a poor one and that "era gap" better represented the conflict that occurs when a culture is in a state of rapid flux, but by that time the catchy term generation gap was embedded in public consciousness.[2]

So before accepting or rejecting the term generation gap, let's think about why it exists and what useful purpose it has served. First, as we've already said, we do not want to diminish the vital role that adolescence and its many changes, from chemical and hormonal to the rewiring of our brains, play in our development.

There is a valuable vigor and perspective to youth that goes beyond attitude and experience. We are not out to change that—not that we could. There are both drawbacks and opportunities presented by a young mind that is more open to—or perhaps more oblivious to—the risks and uncertainties of experimentation and adventure.

However, we do not believe that the difference between a young and old mind is the primary reason we've developed the societal notion of a generation gap. Having a gap means that those on the near side of the gap—the younger generation—can create an identifiable community within which they can find reassurance and empowerment for their ideas. Whether it's a label of hippie, Gen Xer, or Millennial, if you are part of that generation you are now associated with a community of thought, ideals, values, and beliefs. It's not much different from saying that as a member of a political party you subscribe to its platform.

But you probably see the flaw here. Not every conservative believes in the right to bear arms, just as not every liberal believes in taking that right away. Community is convenient but it is flawed as a means of identity when it's painted with too broad a brush.

So, what's the alternative? First, we need to recognize that in the near term we are living and working with five generations and that, over time, the micro-generational phenomenon we talked about will blur the lines between generations entirely. The leaders we talked to who recognize this trend are focused on an empathetic and highly personalized approach to communicating with their employees and the marketplace. Second, we need to work toward engaging 100 percent of our employees and customers. It's a lofty objective, but there are companies that have made it their mission to do just that.

THE HYATT STORY:
LISTENING BEYOND GENERATIONS

Robb Webb, chief human resources officer of the Hyatt Hotels Corporation—which was founded in 1957 and, as of December 2013, had 549 properties globally, including the brands Park Hyatt, Grand Hyatt, Hyatt Place, and Hyatt House—spoke with us about the highly personalized ways Hyatt is dealing with generational issues, and what the company sees as both opportunities and challenges:

> Traditionally, companies used to think of the workforce—such as the ninety thousand employees of Hyatt—as this homogenous group of people that we expect to react exactly the same way, regardless of age. It's interesting that we have all of these management tools that were built for a homogenous workforce—whether it was or wasn't—and we keep using them even if we can see that they may not be as useful as we've come to believe.
>
> For example, Hyatt is a company blessed with very long tenure, great loyalty, and a phenomenal workforce. We celebrate tenure and we celebrate anniversaries, but there's a big part of the workforce that might not think that's such a great thing. We want to keep good workers, but we also want to be empathetic to changing attitudes about work and people's individual, not generational, situations.

Webb found that there is a lot of baggage to unload in the traditional view of generations, and much of it concerns a set of preconceived notions about the behaviors and attitudes that come with a generational label—most of which are popularized stereotypes that we buy into.

The problem seems to be that many people make the same mistake talking about generations that they once did in talking about gender. Well, I don't know about you but I've determined that neither men nor women are all exactly alike. The same holds true for Millennials. We seem to keep saying to them, "This is how we expect you to behave; you're not supposed to want to work anywhere longer than two years; you're supposed to be inwardly focused; you're supposed to feel entitled." With all of these stereotypes we're doing people a disservice because, while there are general traits of generations and the impact of the environment they grew up in, they're still individuals and they react differently.

It's not enough to simply state that treating generations as a one-dimensional stereotype is a problem. You also need to figure out how to go about giving people tools to help them break free of these expectations.

At Hyatt, they've turned to using empathetic interviewing, a technique borrowed from "design thinking"—a toolbox that concentrates on an anthropologically focused approach to observing people in real scenarios in order to understand how to design better products, experiences, and environments. This is in contrast to the typical design approach, which often just wraps a pretty bow around a product that has already been designed by engineers.

Design thinking has its roots in firms such as IDEO and Continuum, but it's being applied outside product design to organizations around the world and in a variety of industries. Hyatt's journey in this area came about from a partnership with Stanford University's d.school, which was formed in 2005 as a creativity-focused business school, intended as the left-brain version of the traditional, quantified, numbers-driven, right-brain-focused business school. According to Webb:

One of the most interesting things we've done is become involved with the d.school. Their design thinking approach—which we've taken to heart as "Hyatt Thinking"—has taught us to practice and teach empathetic interviewing, which is hugely important when you're dealing with guests or people from different backgrounds and generations. Through empathetic listening and interviewing—where you don't guess at what someone wants or likes because they are a certain age—you simply ask and observe. It's one of the few approaches that will give you the opportunity to reach beyond your own experience and preconceptions to learn more about your customers or employees.

"Hyatt Thinking" is a very different way for us to interact with guests and each other, and really empathize with people, put yourself in their shoes, and understand what they're going through. I think it's an especially valuable tool as we're interacting across generations because you're being taught to use this process to go in and ask very open questions and not "lead the witness," if you will. For me, this has been eye opening.

At Hyatt we focus obsessively on the guest experience. By listening more directly to our customers' needs, we have many opportunities to recognize where we and the industry as a whole are failing to provide the best possible experience and meet customers on their own terms—regardless of predefined generational boundaries.

We're moving beyond concerns about Millennials or Boomers. That's not how I want to live my life—in a generational bucket—and that's not what we want at Hyatt.

If you really care for somebody, then you'll find out what's important to them. I think that transcends generations because I can't say that there's a generation that doesn't want to be cared about.

Webb has a passion for transcending generational fiction, refusing to let it stand in the way of working to engage 100 percent of Hyatt's customers and its workforce, regardless of age. Instead, he and the team at Hyatt approach employees in ways that are focused on the employees' needs, not on what may be easy for the company as a one-size-fits-all policy. This attitude is embodied in one of the many stories Webb shared with us about the importance of being empathetic.

Fortune magazine recently named Hyatt one of the 100 best companies to work for.

I was flipping through the *Fortune* issue and I came across the advertisement we ran and, sure enough, there's our bellman Antonio, from the

Park Hyatt in Chicago. I really admire him and wanted to celebrate his appearance in the magazine.

I found out that we had made a big poster-size version of the ad. I grabbed it and the magazine and I called over to the Park Hyatt to make sure Antonio was working. I drove over to the hotel, pulled up, and as Antonio came out to greet me I said, "Hey, check this out," as I unrolled this poster to show him.

He just looked at it in disbelief and said, "Are you kidding me?" Then a husband and wife, who were guests, came out of the hotel, looked at the poster I was holding and then looked at Antonio; they did a double take and said, "Is that you? Oh, congratulations." And both shook his hand. He was a bit embarrassed.

I said, "This poster is for your dad. I've got a magazine for you, but I have another in my office and I want you to autograph it."

Three days went by and I thought, "I really need to go back to have Antonio autograph this magazine."

I didn't think it was a big deal; Antonio had likely forgotten about it, but I wanted to show him that I cared. When I arrived at the Park Hyatt the first thing Antonio said to me was, "Did you bring it?" I snapped back, "I've got it right here."

He reached into his pocket for what I thought was a pen to autograph the magazine, and instead pulled out a piece of neatly folded paper and showed it to me, saying, "I've been practicing what I want to say."

I looked at the paper in disbelief. He had all of this stuff he'd crossed out and then rewritten, over and over—I could tell how much thought went into it. My first thought was, thank God I went back over because asking for the autograph could have been a throwaway comment. My second thought was, "This is why we take Hyatt Thinking so seriously. We all deserve moments like this." Honestly, I'm not sure which one of us was more moved by the experience.

That may seem like a pretty simple act of just caring for somebody else that you work with and trying to put yourself in their shoes, but that's what Hyatt Thinking is about. You're not a generation, an age, a category; you're a person, and we all want to be understood as people, not labels. And you know what? That one act made me feel better than I felt all year.

I have had dozens of those sorts of experiences. My advice, from what I've learned, is give it up, and don't look at people through a predetermined lens; nobody benefits.

That same focus that Hyatt brings to understanding employees seems to be working with customers as well. Since the recession of 2008 to the second quarter of 2014 (when this book was written), Hyatt's market cap doubled, while it was also named recipient of the 2014 Gallup Great Workplace Award for the third consecutive year. Clearly, mastering the ability to engage both customers and employees is rewarding the company handsomely.

CLOSING THE GAP

While a gap of some sort may always exist between age groups with differing experiences, the size of the gap is directly related to how precisely we can define communities. **Define community by your age, and the generation gap will be very wide. Define it through a deep understanding of people's interests and behaviors, and it will be far narrower.**

Although this sort of thinking, based on very specific interests and behaviors, can be interpreted as creating micro-gaps between generations, we prefer to look at it as a way to create communities that are better aligned, more meaningful, and ultimately less likely to define themselves using age-based parameters. This community, rather than generational, focus is what we meant when we talked about Gen Z's tendency toward a hyperlocal view. The result is that, rather than being defined by an age-based generational gap, we are defined by the connections that tie us into a specific community. The same is true of the increasingly prevalent connections that tie us to the way we work.

One of the best examples of this hyperlocal approach is that of remote work, a controversial topic for businesses that cling to the idea that work can only be done in "the office." Being hyperlocal allows us to tie to a community regardless of location. One of the natural outcomes of this for many of us is that work is no longer location-based. However, though remote work is in part about the technology that allows us to be hyperlocal, it's more so about changes in behavior—what businesses expect from their employees, what employees expect from the business, and how employees and managers renegotiate terms of working together successfully. The nature of the physical workplace—whether it is a traditional office or a remote work environment—is also an area where generational boundaries have played a significant role in defining attitudes and behaviors about the type of environment that is conducive to work and collaboration.

While remote work has been possible for decades, it hasn't been until recently that the rise of cable modem Internet access, 4G networks, fiber network home connectivity, and two-billion smartphones and tablets have made remote work a realistic alternative for the vast majority of workers.

If the expectation is that you're available to work at any time, how can a company cling to the notion that work happens only in the workplace? Which fork in the road of work we take—with a formal office down one path and a flexible remote workplace down the other—is influenced by generational thinking and our social norms.

Some unlikely businesses have banned remote work outright, including Yahoo, when CEO Marissa Mayer enacted a ban on working from home full time in early 2013. This announcement came as a "shot heard 'round the world" that had Yahoo employees, Silicon Valley, and recent college graduates, especially, wondering what in the world Mayer was thinking with such a seemingly backward decision. For Yahoo to proclaim itself an innovator and yet set the clock back fifteen to twenty years—especially given its profile as a high-tech, networked company located in Silicon Valley—baffled many people. Some said it was the death knell of remote work, but in our opinion, Yahoo may have veered from the trend of remote work but only for its singular purposes. The move has done nothing to alter the overall trajectory, and the trend toward remote working continues unabated. In fact, a report by The Future Laboratory even went so far as to say that, "In the near future the term 'office' will be obsolete and the drab surroundings we associate with the executive life will be erased as a new model for work emerges. This emerging vision of the workplace will facilitate flexible working patterns in a society in which nine-to-five working is increasingly the exception rather than the rule."[3]

Still, although remote work has become standard practice for many knowledge workers, it is far from the norm. We spoke with Justin Levy, head of global social media for Citrix, about the challenges and opportunities of what he calls "work-shifting." He discussed how Citrix manages its own eight thousand–plus employees and the issues he sees with other companies trying to find the right on-ramp to make remote work within their own organizations.

> Remote working is not without its difficulties, and when I talk to people who remote work in different companies, from solopreneurs to people at large companies like Citrix and even bigger, that is one of the areas that doesn't get talked about enough and that people don't acknowledge. If you have spent most of your career having to be in an office, a day outside the office sounds golden. To be that person with the headphones at a Starbucks or to sit on your couch and that's good once in a while to do that, as an entré to full-time remote work, or simply as a change of pace from daily work. Enabling and trusting employees to be able to make their own decisions about where and how they work is a challenge that is still foreign to many managers, or even among employees with different ideas about what it means to be 'at work'."

As we point out in chapter 5, "Shifting from Affluence to Influence," there's a certain "dues paying" mentality that may be at work here. If managers and executives had to work their entire careers in the office, why shouldn't new hires, young or old? Changing this outlook is at the heart of what we mean by Gen Z being not necessarily a group you're born into but an attitude that you choose. For example, if you lead a big company, does that mean you have to run it as big companies have run in the past? Levy explained:

> At Citrix, we operate with a smaller company mentality than the relatively large company that we are. What do I mean? We focus on results and on delivering—that's all that matters. You focus on getting your work done while also ensuring that you're taking time for your family and your own health, mentally and physically. Work and life happen in harmony nowadays.

As Levy tells us, and as we've seen ourselves in many organizations: "A lot of companies will talk about work-life balance but what that really means is more work, less life. Here's your cell phone or here's a laptop so you can do more work at night."

For Gen Z the lines between work, play, and life are blurred—the idea that you have to be in a specific place at a specific time to work is as foreign as the thought of having to find a pay phone to make a phone call. There is nothing natural about traveling to an office to work, any more than it's essential to work that men wear ties or women wear pantyhose. These are societal norms that ebb and flow over time; it's worth considering what we take for granted as the "normal" way of working.

It's also a common misconception that only start-ups or small companies can handle remote workers. We've spoken with many IBM employees in the last few years about the ability to work remotely in a company of nearly five hundred thousand employees. In the 1970s through the '90s, IBM was jokingly said to have stood for "I've Been Moved" because of the frequent job relocations career IBMers endured. This took an enormous toll on employees and their families, who would move, on average, two to three time every ten years.

In response to increasing pressure from new hires, who were much more open to travel than to relocation, IBM changed its stance in 1995, launching an experiment in Norfolk, Virginia, that allowed for remote work, whether at home or "in the field" at client sites. This was an experiment the company did not take lightly, and it hired a behavioral psychologist to consult on cultural impact, knowing it would be a dramatic shift in the way the company operated. After the initial experiment showed promise, IBM rolled out similar programs to all of its U.S. sales offices, and in 1996 it began expanding the remote work program to international offices as well.

IBM estimates that the shift that allowed employees to work from anywhere led to as much as a 50 percent increase in productivity as well as a $700 million dollar savings in real estate costs, as the company collapsed office space from a 4:1 staff-to-desk ratio to an average 12:1 staff-to-desk ratio. As of 2012, 39 percent of its more than four hundred thousand employees work remotely. Multi-generational impacts have been acknowledged as well.

According to research by the United States General Services Administration (GSA), referencing IBM's results, "In addition, mobile quality-of-life benefits have proven instrumental in retaining and supporting both a maturing workforce and a younger generation of associates."[4]

Ultimately, the biggest challenge in the way a company works is identifying how a company's leadership values "work." Do executives value putting in the hours or getting results? Supporting remote work isn't done because it's a fad or because it's more convenient for workers. It's a cultural shift that changes the traditional metrics of office work and refocuses on what "work" means. Justin Levy illustrated this for us by providing some added context.

> Our company structure is set up for a results-driven culture, or what has become somewhat famous from Best Buy's culture—a "Results-Oriented Work Environment," or ROWE. While we don't officially use Best Buy's ROWE methodology, we are focused on results. What does that mean? If I lay out four to five growth goals for myself or for my team for the quarter, what matters is that I get those done and, of course, any of the other things that come up over the course of that quarter that need to be dealt with. Did I get those done or not? Putting in 100-plus hour workweeks or traveling eighty days—employees shouldn't be judged on those sorts of metrics.

When we hear people debate the merits of working in an office or face-to-face versus working remotely, what we hear are people arguing from different sides of the generational chasm, and using the circumstances that each of them has become accustomed to working in as the basis for their point of view.

With nearly every aspect of work being digitized and networked, the question "Where should I work?" is not one that is limited by technology. Being hyperconnected takes away the physical barriers of the working environment and along with them the broad and often delayed metrics that were used to manage employees. And, as we'll see in the next chapter about hyperconnecting, without these barriers and with the ability of the individual to clearly influence and measure his or her contribution to business results the question changes to "How do I *best* work?"

Put It Into Action:
Chapter 2 #breakinggenerations #GenZ

Learn from Gen Z Leaders

- Robb Webb, chief human resources officer for the Hyatt Hotels Corporation
- The d.school at Stanford University
- Justin Levy, head of global social media for Citrix

Are You Ready for Gen Z?

- How much of your organization is built around the metaphor and assumptions of the population pyramid?
- How much of your career and its trajectory have been built around the classic population pyramid?
- How will your organization prepare itself for the change from a population pyramid to a population skyscraper?
- Do you recognize and try to avoid the generational traps we outlined in this chapter?
- Are you planning for or entering your "Third Act"?
- Are you preparing yourself to remain relevant through your retirement—whatever form it may take?
- When training salespeople and customer service people, do you practice empathetic listening (as Hyatt does)?
- Does your business understand the different ways that employees want to be recognized, as individuals, rather than employing a one-size-fits-all recognition program?
- Do you recognize and celebrate your "Antonios"?
- What's your target for employee engagement? Do you aim for 100 percent engagement, or is your goal lower? How does that translate to the bottom and top lines of your business?
- Are you (or is your organization) involved with remote work?

- Are you (or is your organization) focused on a results-oriented work environment?

Find out whether you're ready for the Gen Z Effect by taking the full assessment at TheGenZEffect.com.

3

Hyperconnecting: From Me to We

Man will see around the world. Persons and things of all kinds will be brought within focus of cameras connected electrically with screens at opposite ends of circuits, thousands of miles at span.

—JOHN ELFRETH WATKINS JR., "WHAT MAY HAPPEN IN THE NEXT HUNDRED YEARS," *THE LADIES' HOME JOURNAL*, 1900

In this chapter we look at the growing hyperconnectivity between people as well as the proliferation of devices and the changing nature of what constitutes a "device." We'll also talk about the Gen Z challenge of living in the two worlds of online and offline experience, with a specific look at Gen Z through wearable devices such as Google Glass. We'll explore the role of reverse mentoring as a way to manage the fast-changing behaviors of Gen Z within an enterprise, looking in depth at the way Cisco is using reverse mentors. Finally, we talk about the importance of visualizing hyperconnected social networks and the often-invisible value they provide an organization through increased productivity. At the end of the book, we've included an appendix with a helpful guide to reverse mentoring for those of you who are working to implement it in your own organizations.

Like it or not we inhabit an incredibly hyperconnected, information-saturated world, and we are suffering from a severe form of global attention deficit disorder as we are incessantly bombarded by more and more information and stimuli.

- There are more cellular mobile devices in use today than there are people in the world.
- 50 percent of us check our e-mail before getting out of bed in the morning.
- 60 percent of us sleep with our mobile devices in or near our bed (79 percent of those under age fifty).
- The number of online contacts in social media and e-mail doubles every nine months, on average, for 70 percent of online users.
- We spend on average of five and a half hours online daily, and an overwhelming 40 percent of twenty-two- to thirty-two-year-olds spend more than thirteen hours a day online.
- 2.7 billion humans now inhabit the Internet.
- We are connected to another fifty billion devices that are attached to the Internet, from surveillance cameras to wearable devices to smart cars.
- Each day 2.5 quintillion bytes (that's a billion billion bytes) of data are created.

That's quite a list, but let's face it, our senses have become numb to overload, and few of the stats we just listed are likely to impress you.

It's easy in that context to try and dismiss much of what is happening to us—like sleeping with our smartphones—by writing it off as quirky behavior, driven by younger generations. While our research showed differences in the degree to which these behaviors are expressed among different ages, the differences were not dramatic. The fact is that the vast majority of the people we surveyed across all ages are adopting new behaviors when it comes to how they use new technology. It used to be that when clients asked us how long it would take for a radical new technology to catch on, we'd quip, "You'll have to wait until an entire generation dies off so they will get out of the way of change." We had accepted, as so many have, that truly radical change could only come with a new generation.

Great ideas have to summit the Everest of accumulated cultural legacy left by the generations that preceded them. Historically, it has taken roughly fifty years for most truly disruptive technologies, such as the radio or telephone,[1] to achieve critical global penetration because it took fifty years for a generation to move out of the way and take their antiquated ideas with them.

One of the most widely circulated myths in the late 1990s and early 2000s was that technology was penetrating global markets faster because it took less time for each new disruptive mode of connectivity to reach fifty million global users. For example, radio, telephone, television, cable, and cell phones were said to have taken thirty-eight, twenty-five, fifteen, seven, and five years respectively.[2] However, when you added a third dimension to this trend line by plotting each technology's penetration as a percentage of worldwide population, you got a daunting and rather depressing dose of reality—of these technologies, only the cell phone had been able to reach more than a fraction of the world's population in the first fifty years of its existence.

It was easy in that context to chalk up the impediments standing in the way of large-scale change to generational resistance in adopting behaviors that could keep up with new technology. That is simply no longer true. As this book is being written, the Internet has achieved adoption in excess of 30 percent of total global population, a number that eclipses any other human phenomenon in the same time frame, even if we include global pandemics! If we look at the trend in figure 3-1, it's easy to gain an appreciation for just how dramatic the impact of hyperconnectivity will be in the coming decades.

In a previous book, *Cloud Surfing,* Tom made the case that the single greatest phenomenon contributing to global growth, prosperity, and social and political change in the past two hundred years is the dramatic increase in connections, in particular the rapid increase in machine-to-machine connections, popularly termed the Internet of Things. At the time *Cloud Surfing* was published, the projection for the number of devices that would be connected to the Internet by 2020 was seventy billion. That estimate did not, however, factor in the connections from an additional three trillion intelligent sensors we estimate will be in existence by 2020. In addition, what we have experienced till now are increases in connections that are separate, localized, and segregated. But what if all these segregated connections were suddenly part of a single, interconnected whole that worked in harmony? As more devices and sensors are connected directly to the Internet the ease of interconnecting them increases dramatically. Devices that were never designed to work together, suddenly are. Your smartphone, automobile, wearable health monitor, and myriad other devices are suddenly able to share data about you and your behaviors.

Nobody designed these devices to work together but that is not to say that there is not an immense and untapped value in their being able to.

The potential connections that can be made among all of these devices are a direct result of the number of devices to be connected. With each new device we are increasing the number of possible connections by the total number of existing devices. In other words, if we have one billion devices and add one more connected device we've just created another potential one billion connections (to and from the new device and every other device in existence).[3] Clearly, the mathematical potential is far greater than the practical number of usable connections (it's unlikely that my toothbrush needs to connect to my pressure sensor in my car's tires) but our point is that we don't yet know how many of these possible connections will, in fact, be practical, useful, or valuable.

When you add a node to a network, every connection beyond the first one is effectively free. In other words, if you buy a cell or smartphone you don't pay based on the number of people you might call. You pay for the phone and your actual usage.

With that in mind, what if we were to shift the focus of our discussion from the total possible number of connections to the number of devices, the real determining variable in the explosion of hyperconnectivity? That's important because devices, unlike hypothetical connections, need to be justified individually—you don't buy a phone or a computer without some reason to use it, even if it is only to play *Angry Birds*.

If we plot the number of user computing devices from the advent of the mainframe to the present, something remarkable begins to emerge. (In order to be consistent we're using the term "user computing device" to represent the number of users that can be supported by a computer. In the case of a mainframe or mini-computer, a single computer can support thousands of potential users. Whereas a personal computer or a smartphone can only support a single user.) **In each decade, starting with 1960, the total number of user computing devices has increased by one order of magnitude.**

If we assume that a computer such as a mainframe or minicomputer that can support χ users is the equivalent of χ devices, while a PC, laptop, tablet, or smartphone is a single device, then the number of computing devices translates into one million devices in 1960, ten million in 1970, a hundred million in

1980, one billion in 1990, ten billion in 2000, and a hundred billion in 2010. By the way, the trend shown in figure 3-1 does not include the trillions of sensors we've discussed or the twenty-five billion microcontrollers—basically chips used in thousands of applications, from automotive to medicine—that were shipped in 2014.

The top line in figure 3-1 looks like a pretty steep curve already, and if it continues on that trajectory we will end up with a nearly impossible-to-comprehend figure of 1,000,000,000,000,000,000,000 (10e21) devices by 2100.

Let's put that into perspective. **There are estimated to be 7.5x10e18 grains of sand on all the beaches in the world—that's less than 1 percent of the devices we're projecting by 2100.**

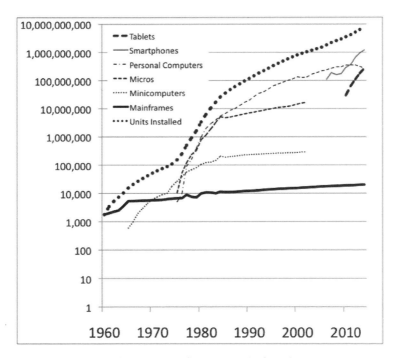

Figure 3-1: Growth in Computing (Logarithmic Scale)

The total "Units Installed" line for all computing devices, including mainframes, minicomputers, microcomputers, PCs, smartphones, and tablets, shows how the number of devices has increased by one order of magnitude each decade, even though individual technologies may have tapered off (e.g., mainframes, PCs) or been eliminated completely (e.g., mini and microcomputers).

That just doesn't seem to make sense. Unless we rethink what the term device implies. For example, how many devices do you currently interact with as part of your daily experience? Most people are shocked to find that they already have hundreds of dedicated devices that they personally own or have embedded in items they own. Take, for example, the list in table 3-1. You likely interact with, on average, more than two hundred devices on a daily basis, most of which you never actually see, such as those in appliances, automobiles, surveillance cameras, ATMs, traffic sensors (which gather data about traffic volumes and speeds), and possibly a personal wearable health monitor. And the estimates we show in table 3-1 are very conservative. For example, if you recently bought a new car, it alone is likely to have two hundred individual sensors. You're not off the hook if it's a used car. In 2001 a new BMW had sixty-plus sensors. What is your tally?

Table 3-1: Types of Connected Devices and Average Number Interacted with Daily

DEVICE Examples of Devices	Average Daily Interactions[4]	Your Daily Interactions
Automotive Onboard computers and diagnostics, GPS, safety, tracking	150	
Home/Residential Appliances, TV, HVAC, lighting, security	20	
Wearable Sensors Fitness, activity, headsets (e.g., Google Glass)	2	
Implantable Devices		
Traffic/Transportation Roadway, tolls, safety, public transport	20	
Cameras/Surveillance Commercial buildings, public spaces, government	20	
Computers PCs, laptops	3	

Mobile Devices Tablets, smartphones	2
Industrial Sensors, Controllers Elevators, nonresidential buildings, parking garages, airport facilities, commercial security systems, or scanners	10
Retail POS, facial recognition systems, traffic flow monitors, eye tracking	5
Banking/Financial/Insurance ATMs, POS, smartcards, insurance tracking	2
Medical Implants, blood sugar monitors, BP monitors, defibrillators,	3
Pets Tracking implants, GPS	1
Communications Network devices, satellite/dish, VOIP	5
TOTAL	243

It's a short step from the sensors on the list in table 3-1, which are not yet connected, to sensors that can talk to one another in real time. If all of this seems overwhelming, consider that if you had told somebody in the 1960s that within sixty years there would be ten billion computing devices, they would have thought you equally absurd—perhaps even more so given the lack of precedent and track record for mobile devices.

Even with all the computers, microcontrollers, and sensors we've talked about so far, we've yet to experience the full impact of hyperconnectivity, in part because most of these devices are not yet connected to the Internet and also because the explosion of connected devices is still at its earliest stages. If you also plotted all of these devices on the chart in figure 3-1, all of the very steep curves in that chart would flatten immediately, becoming insignificant as a percentage of all hyperconnected devices.

If you think that this sudden eclipsing of prior technologies makes the future we are describing less probable, we should point out something that may not be immediately obvious. Earlier we talked about how we are perpetually living on the elbow of ever accelerating growth in computing devices. In chapter 2 we also talked about the effect of multiple power curves, which end up creating an overall behavioral curve that is constantly exponential.

But that wasn't visibly obvious in figure 3-1 because we used a logarithmic scale, a sleight of hand that increases by orders of magnitude—so that an increase of 1,000,000,000 looks the same vertically as an increase of 10 or 100—rather than a linear scale, which we simply couldn't draw in any visually meaningful way since each decade would by itself be a J curve. This behavioral J curve will continue to accelerate. What we do not yet know is exactly how, but the technologies we've listed in table 3-1 are clearly going to provide the fuel for this growth over the next decade.

While our definition of devices may not fit the traditional idea of what a computer is, these devices gather data, process it, store it, and deliver it to a vast array of other devices, providing a level of intelligence among inanimate objects that is foreign in today's context. Describing what this hyperconnected world will look like is challenging because we lack the shared experiences and the behaviors to talk about it. **We end up trying to force fit the future into the present, something that always undermines our ability to imagine new possibilities.**

Those of us who speak multiple languages experience a similar phenomenon when we try to describe something complex for which we do not have the vocabulary in our non-native tongue. This same limitation of vocabulary applies when we attempt to describe the future. **Because we do not yet know the language of the future, we are forced to use the language of the present to describe something we have not yet experienced.**

The result is that we discount the future because it sounds odd, far-fetched, or foreign. In the 1970s Buckminster Fuller attempted to describe the future of education.

It will be possible not only for an individual to say, "I don't like it," on his two-way TV but he can also beam-dial (without having to know mathematics), "I want number so and so." It is also possible with this kind of two-way TV linkage with individuals' homes to send out many different programs simultaneously; in fact, as many as there are two-way beamed-up receiving sets and programs. It would be possible to have large central storages of documentaries—great libraries. A child could call for a special program information locally over the TV set.

While Fuller's use of terms such as "TV set," "beam-dial," and "beamed-up" sound dated, the totality of his quote is amazingly prescient. He had no choice but to use the words of his own time to conjure up images of the future.

Rather than spend the rest of this chapter trying to predict every way in which hyperconnectivity will change our lives and our businesses, we've chosen to focus our discussion on areas where we expect to see the greatest and most immediate shifts in Gen Z behaviors, as well as one of the most powerful methods we've encountered to help organizations create connections across existing generational boundaries, Reverse Mentoring.

IT'S STILL YOUR BRAIN, IT'S JUST MOBILIZED

Of the 2.7 billion global users on the Internet, 1.8 billion are active on social networks. However, what is astonishing is that there are more than 7 billion mobile subscribers globally—that's greater that the world's entire population, so it's clearly not a one-to-one correlation between person and mobile device. Our research found that we average 2.5 cellular-enabled mobile devices per person. Some simple math—dividing the 7 billion cell numbers by 2.5—gives us a rough equivalent of 2.8 billion users of smartphones—amazingly just about identical to the total number of users on the Internet, as shown in figure 3-2. (This includes not only your cell or smartphone but also tablets and wearable devices equipped with cellular numbers.) Clearly, the mobility of our connections has become a central theme in the way Gen Z behaves.

On a recent Amtrak trip from New York City to Boston, Dan had just settled in and taken out his laptop, tablet, and smartphone. At a subsequent stop a young woman boarded and sat across the table from him. She took out her laptop, tablet, MP3 player, and three smartphones. To anyone passing by, the scene must have looked like a Best Buy kiosk. We are not only connected, we

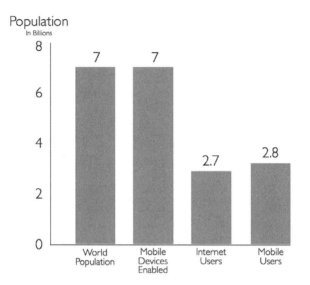

Figure 3-2: Comparisons of Population, Mobile Devices, Internet Users, and Mobile Users

are connected to a multitude of devices simultaneously. This sort of disjointed connectivity does not lend itself to a collaborative set of behaviors. Instead, it forces us to orchestrate an ever increasing and more complex set of connections.

This disjointed connectivity is not just a U.S. behavior. In fact, while the United States has 101 percent penetration of mobile devices, Western Europe has 129 percent penetration, South America has 126 percent penetration, Central and Eastern Europe has 151 percent penetration, and Russia a whopping 180 percent penetration, meaning that there are just under two phones for every person.

According to our research, we currently spend approximately five and a half hours daily, on average, actively engaged on some sort of Internet-connected device. If you look at just the twenty-two- to thirty-two-year-old age group, that number jumps to seven and a half hours, on average. However, an overwhelming 40 percent of the twenty-two to thirty-two age group is online for thirteen or more hours each day.

We are increasingly relying on what science and technology writer Clive Thompson called our "outboard brain" in a 2007 *Wired* magazine article. Our outboard brain is a simple way of thinking about the degree to which we rely on mobility and the cloud to act as an always-available resource for us; it's a staple behavior among Gen Zers. For example, most of us have been in conversations in which a question arises that nobody present can answer. In that instant, the line between who is and who is not a member of Gen Z is immediately drawn based on who reaches for a smartphone to query Google, Bing, or Yahoo for the answer.

In fact, many children born into Gen Z have an annoying habit of constantly fact-checking their parents during conversations; it's like playing a nonstop game of *Jeopardy* with IBM's Watson. One of our study respondents shared with us a story about grocery shopping with his fifteen-year-old son that illustrates this increasingly typical behavior:

> My son asked if he could buy some meat for "steak" tacos. I dutifully reached over and picked up a packet of stir-fry beef. Incredulous, my son looked at me and said, "But that isn't steak; it's beef! The Mexican restaurant we go to serves steak tacos—that's what I want." I went on to explain that steak is beef and that the restaurant was just trying to make its tacos sound a bit more high end by using the term "steak."
>
> My son immediately pulled out his smartphone and started tapping away, no doubt to double-check on my knowledge of butchery. There was no further discussion on the topic so I'm assuming Wikipedia agreed with me.

The same scenario has started playing out in nearly every social context. As subtle as it may seem, this Gen Z reliance on an outboard brain fundamentally alters power structures and implicit assumptions about how we form relationships of trust.

In our own experience, this tendency to query authority figures started playing out in university classrooms years ago when students began showing up with Internet-connected devices. At the time, many professors would disable the classroom's Internet and explicitly state that no browsing, texting, or e-mailing was allowed during class. This was a silly if not outright impossible rule to enforce. However, the attitude on the part of professors was that technology was a "distraction" that took the students' focus away from lectures and conversations.

Fearful of the way in which connectivity might distract students, these professors were themselves distracted from the real effect and the benefit of connectivity in the classroom: the transparency that forms a foundation for trust.

In one of Tom's classes, he experimented by taking a page out of the Gen Z playbook and turning the tables on students. His policy was that they were welcome to use any connected devices as often as they liked—with one caveat. He would periodically throw out a fact or statistic that was blatantly incorrect, and he expected students who were online to promptly take him to task and correct the error.

The approach paid off in ways he never imagined. Not only did students see it as a welcome challenge to correct a professor, but they brought to light all sorts of anecdotes, and some critical conversations evolved from information they found related to the lecture.

For Gen Z, connectivity creates a level of transparency in relationships that makes trust an earned status rather than one bestowed upon an individual or an organization.

We believe that viewing the resulting behaviors of hyperconnectivity as distractions rather than a potential way to increase engagement and trust is a big mistake. Swimming against the Gen Z tide of hyperconnectivity is like swimming against a tsunami—only an idiot does it. If you want to survive the tsunami, you have to ride the wave—it's your only option, no matter how frightening it may appear.

THE END OF YOUR LIFE IN TWO WORLDS

As Gen Z becomes more accustomed to the mobility of a hyperconnected world, they are also increasingly living their lives in two worlds: the three-dimensional offline world of things that can be seen, heard, touched, smelled, and tasted and the online world of desktops, laptops, tablets, and smartphones. Most of us thrash back and forth between these two worlds, trying desperately to integrate one into the other. The fact is that we're fumbling our way through hyperconnectivity because we haven't had much time to establish an agreement about what our behaviors should be when it comes to being hyperconnected.

It's no different with kids. We were discussing hyperconnectivity with a colleague who told us his daughter met her first boyfriend in her freshman year of high school. **He said it was a typical teenage relationship, except for one very odd behavior—his sixteen-year-old daughter's boyfriend moved in with her, in a manner of speaking, on Skype.** Every time he would go into his daughter's room, her boyfriend's smiling face would be there on the laptop screen, propped up on her bed. "They wouldn't even be talking to each other," he told us. "They would just sit there on each other's laptop, sharing the same virtual space." Awkward? Perhaps at first, but that's the thing about behavior; even the most aberrant behaviors, repeated often enough, seem completely normal.

Your first temptation may be to bristle at this type of relationship as far less appealing than what you experienced in your early dating life—relationships are, after all, about human contact. Something must be lost if we reduce them to Skype. But that's the argument made about virtually every new generation of technology. Even writing was seen by some of the world's greatest philosophers, Socrates and Plato, as a step backward and a far less effective way of connecting and communicating.

It's supremely ironic, then, that we only know of Socrates and his work through the writing of his student Plato. In one of Plato's books he recounts a metaphorical conversation between two gods, as told by Socrates.[5] In the conversation, one of the gods responds to the other about bestowing the gift of writing on mankind.

> For this invention [writing] will produce forgetfulness in the minds of those who learn to use it, because they will not practice their memory... You have invented an elixir not of memory, but of reminding; and you offer your pupils the appearance of wisdom, not true wisdom, for they will read many things without instruction and will therefore seem to know many things, when they are for the most part ignorant and hard to get along with, since they are not wise, but only appear wise.

The words are twenty-five hundred years old, and yet they sound familiar—it's the same argument we hear used against myriad other technologies, from electricity, automobiles, and television to electronic calculators, spell checkers, and Google.

We love to perpetuate generational arrogance; in large part because we value what we have learned because of the effort it took to learn it. The smartest people make the best case for holding onto the past; after all, they ended up being the smartest by using the tools of the past in the best possible way. When we fall into these sorts of broad generational traps we severely constrain the opportunities we can imagine; it's just too easy to limit our view of the future by thinking of it in terms of the behaviors of the present—if we've learned anything over the past two hundred years, it's that the future knows no such bounds.

Change is not linear: it's exponential and it's disruptive. It has no allegiance to the past. If we are to stand even the slightest chance of understanding the potential of hyperconnectivity going forward, we need to first examine Gen Z from a neutral vantage point, one that does not impose a historical standard of behavior established in a far less-connected world.

In a Bill Moyers interview, Sherry Turkle, a professor at MIT who has written *Alone Together,* a book that looks critically at the way in which technology takes us away from human connections—as contrasted with online connections—said: "What concerns me as a developmental psychologist is watching children grow in this new world where being bored is something that never has to be tolerated for a moment." Turkle tells Moyers, "Everyone is always having their attention divided between the world of people [they're] with and this 'other' reality."

A post responding to the interview, on Moyer's website, provides a succinct and cutting counterargument:

> We are a herd animal. Any technology that allows us to maintain more efficient contact with the rest of the herd is going to be embraced by its members. Technology will be more and more integrated into each of us as individuals. Google Glass is yet another step in this direction. What scared us about the Borg in Star Trek's *Next Generation* is being embraced by the next generation(s). Technology and communication will be integrated into our very being, and we will welcome it. It appears that this is our future as a species.[6]

We love Turkle's work; it's prosaic and delightful to read, and some of it resonates deeply with us, especially her observations that youth are increasingly losing the ability to be alone and are panicked at the thought of it.

We'd offer her a Pulitzer Prize if we could—at least for the elegance of her argument. But we can't help but believe that her arguments are anchored in the past, in the same intellectual vein as Socrates' disdain for writing. Something is being lost through progress, perhaps, but not everything, and much is being gained. Children who were outcasts and whose shyness locked them into solitude now can socialize in ways that add richness to their lives.

We recall a story shared with us by a colleague we were having dinner with as part of a consulting engagement with a group of large manufacturers. The conversation meandered as we talked about our work and the critical importance of keeping an open mind toward new online behaviors that we may see as antisocial—excessive gaming, for example. Our colleague, Joe, described a nephew (we'll call him Barry) who suffered from Tourette's syndrome, a potentially debilitating neurological condition that causes uncontrollable tremors, movements, tics, and occasional, sudden bursts of disconnected—often profane—language. While the cause and triggers for Tourette's are not well understood, it manifests in such a way that those communicating with someone who has Tourette's may interpret the behavior as, at the least, disruptive and at worst antisocial. Tourette's, unlike stuttering or nervous twitching, is not a modifiable behavior—at least not consciously modifiable. The resulting social stigma can drive those living with Tourette's to insulate themselves from social settings, making education, work, and socializing difficult, if not impossible.

However, Joe told us that Barry, who is an avid gamer and very active on social networks, has no problem when he is communicating or collaborating online. "Of course," we responded, "it makes perfect sense that via a keyboard his condition becomes invisible, allowing Barry to communicate freely without any prejudice on the part of his peers."

"No," said Joe, "I'm not talking about his communication via keyboard. I'm saying that he will use a gamer's headset and talk without any indication of Tourette's. It's as though his brain suddenly finds a way to calm those misfiring neurons because of his ability to be so in the moment. I can't explain it but it is an amazing transformation. Unfortunately, I'm worried that Barry, who is still in school, will not be able to join the workforce in any traditional sort of setting where he has to interact with others face to face."

Here's the beauty of the Gen Z Effect: we don't think Barry will need to interact face to face unless he chooses to. Barry is not broken. What is broken is our way of defining work and the way work "has to be" done—because that's the way it's "always been done." We draw lines that separate work that's face to face in an office setting from remote work that's performed online. We refuse to accept that online can replace in person. But these two modes of working are not in a contest with each other, any more than the written word is in competition with the spoken word.

When we try to pit one behavior against another we create a zero-sum scenario, in which the future is always competing with the past, when what inevitably happens is that the future converges with the past. Like a highway with infinite on-ramps, we are always integrating new behaviors as they join old behaviors. Eventually, some of those old behaviors take an exit while others simply fall behind, fading slowly as traffic accelerates. Most, however, refuel and become part of the way forward.

When the separateness of our worlds could be easily divided into work and play, professional and personal, we could live with generational divides, like solid lines marking the lanes of a highway, and prosper despite them.

For Gen Z, however, and certainly for the children of today's children, there will be no separation between the two worlds Turkle describes. They will not see online and offline settings in competition. Far from being an either-or proposition, the two worlds will be integrated in a way that multiplies people's potential and their opportunities to live, work, and play.

We have already taken the first steps in the amalgamation of offline and online, not only with traditional mobile devices such as smartphones but also with technologies such as Google Glass (Google's wearable device for connecting to and interacting with the Internet). These wearable devices do more than blur the distinction between the two worlds; they begin to eliminate it. That may come across as hyperbolic, but it is only if we limit our imagination by what we have already experienced rather than extend it to catch a glimpse of the future.

In 1876, a cash-strapped Alexander Graham Bell offered to sell his telephone patent to Western Union for $100,000. While considering Bell's offer, which Western Union turned down, officials who reviewed the offer wrote the following recommendation:

> We do not see that this device will be ever capable of sending recognizable speech over a distance of several miles. Hubbard and Bell want to install one of their telephone devices in every city. The idea is idiotic on the face of it. Furthermore, why would any person want to use this ungainly and impractical device when he can send a messenger to the telegraph office and have a clear written message sent to any large city in the United States?

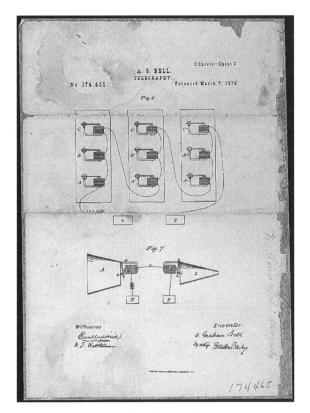

Figure 3-3: Alexander Graham Bell's telephone patent, although one of the most profitable and contested patents of the nineteenth century, was flatly rejected by Western Union.[7]

Laughable, isn't it? However, the problem Western Union had is the same one we all share: **the future never comes fully formed. It is always disguised in a clumsy package that doesn't comfortably fit the behaviors we are accustomed to.**

It's a familiar pattern of behavior.

The first pocket transistor radio didn't fit into a standard shirt pocket. Sony cofounder Akio Morita had to order tailor-made shirts with double-width pockets for his salespeople. Many people thought it was silly to have a personal radio; after all, radio had been built around the expectation of a shared experience. Since its introduction, more than six billion pocket transistor radios have been sold.

Motorola's first portable cell phone, popularly known as "the brick"—although, in fairness, it weighed slightly less—didn't fit neatly in your hand and definitely did not fit in your pocket. At the time of its introduction, even the most outrageous pundits projected somewhere in the range of ten million to one hundred million cell phones in use by the year 2000. We've already said that today there are more than seven billion. That's hardly a rounding error.

The first laptop computer, the Osborne I, introduced in 1981, was larger and heavier than a portable sewing machine of the same vintage and weighed in at twenty-five pounds. In addition to the difficulty of carrying it around, there was the obvious question: "Why would anyone need to carry a computer?"

In each of these cases, it's not that the technology building blocks of the future weren't already in the devices of the present but rather that behavior had not had a chance to form itself around the technology. But when people begin using new a technology they try to use it as direct replacements for earlier technology. However, with a bit of experimentation they inevitably find purposes for which the technology was never intended but where it ultimately has the greatest value. For example, the initial value of radio transmissions was thought to be for person to person communication and not for broadcast to massive audiences, which is where it revolutionized mass communications.

It's that last point that we need to develop and embrace new behaviors in

Figure 3-4: Osborne I Portable Computer[8]

"Osborne 1 open" by Bilby - Own work. Licensed under Creative Commons Attribution 3.0 via Wikimedia Commons -

order to realize the value of a new technology, which is most important to grasp in order to appreciate how radical disruption works and the impact the Gen Z Effect will have.

It's human nature to initially place "new" technologies into old behaviors since we have no other frame of reference. When the first Walkman was introduced, walking around in public with tiny headphones on made little sense—in fact, it seemed weird and antisocial. In an attempt to make the Walkman more "socially acceptable" Sony incorporated a microphone that allowed the listener to press a button and hear the person he was talking with, by channeling the person's voice through the Walkman and into the head-phones. It sounds like a ridiculous feature.

Yet today it is acceptable for people at a dinner table to be staring down at their smartphones rather than at one another. Ridiculous? Indeed, but only in contrast with previous behavior. Ultimately, much of behavior is temporal, defined by the norms and customs of the time. If we are dismissive of these new behaviors we fall back on generational stereotyping, which only reinforces the barriers between people.

THROUGH THE GLASS

What each of the technologies we've mentioned—transistor radios, cell phones, portable computers—had in common was that they were considered an oddity. They simply did not fit into the behavior of the time. The latest disruptive technology to face this hurdle is Google Glass, the wearable computing device resembling a pair of eyeglasses, introduced by Google in 2013.

We talked to some of our study respondents who had used Glass—these were among the people Google called its "explorers," the first group selected by the company to purchase and use Glass in 2013. A common theme emerged from these conversations: something odd happened to many who started to use Glass. Namely, they had no frame of reference for this new way of interacting with the world. It felt disorienting. In the words of a colleague, George Achillias, one of the first Glass Explorers: "I wanted to draw a hard line between offline and online, and I couldn't. Once I realized that the line between offline and online was one that I had accepted as an immutable line of demarcation, I began to think of the experience in a very different way. Glass soon felt oddly natural, as though I had suddenly regained a sixth sense I never knew I had been missing."

Perhaps you're thinking, "But I want to compartmentalize my world and separate the offline from the online. I need that escape. I want to be unplugged. It's just not healthy to be on 24–7!" What is not healthy, in our estimation, is the anxiety created when technology clashes with entrenched behaviors. Inevitably, that initial conflict is resolved as we discover new value that we simply hadn't anticipated. For instance, in our research we found that 65 percent of people who have smartphones sleep with them on or near their beds. By the way, that's just slightly lower than the number of married couples who claim to sleep together.[9]

Some of you are shuddering at that last statistic. Seriously, who would sleep with her smartphone? But, wait, do you still have a landline on your nightstand? If it rings in the middle of the night do you answer it? That, too, would have been considered aberrant behavior during the first half of the twentieth century, when most households had only one phone line, shared

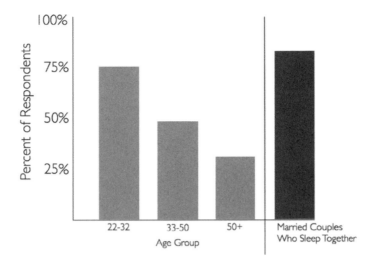

Figure 3-5: Percentage of People, by Age Group, Who Sleep with a Mobile Phone Within Reach Compared with Percentage of Married Couples Who Sleep Together

not only by everyone in the house but also, in the case of "party lines," by the neighbors as well!

We can debate the merits of being connected, but it doesn't change the fact that we are drawn to connectivity and, as a society, have always chosen the path toward increasing the number and frequency of our connections.

Because the sort of change created by new technologies such as Google Glass is so disruptive to our learned behaviors, and the value of the new experience so difficult to appreciate, there is a natural tendency for people to become entrenched in old behaviors. It's then and there that generational lines get drawn. We've only seen and experienced one sustainable way by which to counterbalance this generational reflex: reverse mentoring.

TURNING THE TABLES THROUGH REVERSE MENTORING

In 1994, Delphi Group—the company where we both ended up working and which we grew to an Inc. 500 global player with offices in the U.S., Canada, England, South America, and Asia—was still in start-up mode. The firm was looking for a new hire to take over computer systems, which consisted of half a dozen Apple Macintoshes and DIY four-strand telephone lines running a proprietary AppleTalk network and e-mail system. This was before web browsers had come on the scene, when e-mail was mostly used inside companies but rarely between them, and the Internet was a curiosity for the vast majority of businesses.

The people we interviewed for the position were predominantly programmers from large companies that could afford to staff their computer operations. These candidates knew how to run mainframes or minicomputers and code in now long-forgotten languages such as COBOL and FORTRAN.

We would show them our small, strange Macintosh system and they would look at us as though we had just arrived from another planet. We had just about given up on finding someone to fill the position when a young twenty-something responded to our classified ad in the *Boston Globe*. He had blonde hair that grew to below his shoulders and a degree from the Berklee College of Music, and he played an awesome keyboard, none of which qualified him for the position. But he also knew what a Macintosh was and he seemed to have a passion for cutting-edge technology, including the then relatively new Internet.

Over the next decade, this young man not only built Delphi's information systems to support its multinational business but became a reverse mentor to Delphi's CEO. He was also the person nearly everyone in the company would go to in order to get a glimpse of how new technologies were changing behaviors. In 2001, for example, he noticed the initial rise of a new category of companies that focused on facilitating social connections and he developed a close working relationship with one of the earliest, LinkedIn. At his urging Delphi ran one of the first events on the topic of Social Media, which at the time was considered by most people to be no more than a curiosity. Your authors—Dan, the mentor, and Tom, the mentored—are the "we" in this narrative, and that was our introduction to reverse mentoring. At the time, neither of us had the slightest idea that we were creating a model for mentoring that would be important to Delphi and our clients, or that it would be part of what we would one day call the Gen Z Effect. However, we were not alone.

At about the same time, Jack Welch at GE was putting in place a similar model to help himself and his senior execs familiarize themselves with the rapidly changing technology landscape of the Internet. Other companies such as The Hartford and Cisco would soon do the same.

However, less than 15 percent of the six hundred companies we surveyed for this book have a reverse mentoring program in place, even though 51 percent have cross-generational teams. What is especially interesting is that, of the companies that have a reverse mentoring program in place, 94 percent also have traditional mentoring programs, even though only 56 percent of all companies have such programs. Clearly, while reverse mentoring may be an outlier, it is much more likely to exist in organizations that understand the benefits of mentoring. It's an interesting twist on how we started our own journey down this path, since Delphi had—as one of its founding principles—a traditional mentoring program for every new hire.

The organizations we studied that had a reverse mentoring program in place were also among the more progressive ones in terms of their attitudes toward remote work, wage transparency, and less rigid or flat organizational structures, such as a Holacracies, which distribute decision making throughout teams rather than deriving decisions from the top of a hierarchy.

So what exactly is reverse mentoring, and how does it work?

Let's start with the simple foundation of mentoring. Recall that almost half of the organizations we studied are unaccustomed to traditional mentoring, or have decided it is not a worthwhile use of resources. The notion of the mentor as a trusted advisor who helps guide a protégé and shares life experiences and acquired wisdom fits nicely into our traditional population pyramid. However, it also explains a bit about why mentoring is not as prevalent universally since the traditional population pyramid always has fewer potential mentors than protégés.

Although 56 percent of organizations may have a mentoring program in place, it is less often the case that individuals have the benefit of a dedicated mentor throughout their careers. Few of us are likely to be assigned a wise old counselor to help us learn the ropes. Those of us who do have mentors often meet them through professional relationships.

However we form them, mentoring relationships can be among the most valuable and meaningful professional and life relationships. The premise is simple: experienced individuals pass their know-how, successes, failures, and confidence on to less experienced individuals. But this is where many of the principles of the Gen Z Effect start to turn the tables.

In a traditional mentoring relationship, the mentor almost always picks or is assigned to the protégé for the express purpose of passing on knowledge and experience. The agreement is that the mentor will share what she knows for the benefit of the protégé, in exchange for the satisfaction of increasing the likelihood of her protégé's success. In pop culture it's called "paying it forward."

However, for Gen Z, experience and influence don't flow only from the top of the pyramid; it's just as likely that knowledge and ideas will percolate up from the bottom. Over time, the Gen Z Effect creates a need for mentoring in both directions, up and down. That's the basic premise behind reverse mentoring—experiences change so rapidly that we have to look to those most comfortable and confident in their use of new technologies to help us keep up.

"Keeping up," in the case of Gen Z, is as much about understanding the behavior and value of new technology as it is about using the technology. In fact, the technology is only getting simpler, it's the behavior that is hardest to grasp—if it's accepted at all.

We recall a Cisco meeting one of us attended where a group of young Millennials had been paired off with a larger group of Boomers to discuss the merits of new behaviors in social media. The Millennials represented an extraordinary group of individuals who Cisco had handpicked to help reverse mentor and pass on their perspectives to tenured employees and customers.

During a roundtable discussion, the Millennials were talking about the importance of transparency and openness in organizations. The focus was on how social media helps create a culture of sharing and open dialog, both inside the organization and with the marketplace. One of the Boomers attending was shocked by what he felt was a naïve attitude among Millennials about the risks and downside of such an extreme degree of openness. The back and forth and the level of irritation on the part of the Boomer illustrated just how difficult the process of reverse mentoring can be.

Unlike traditional mentoring, in which the mentor is always a senior individual who can pass on experience without much risk of pushback from the protégé, reverse mentoring provides no safe haven for the mentor, who can easily be trumped by the protégé's position in the organizational hierarchy.

There are only two scenarios we have observed in which reverse mentoring stands a chance. The first is the model popularized by GE's Welch, who issued a direct edict establishing the importance and value of reverse mentoring. Welch not only mandated that five hundred of his executives find a reverse mentor, he did so himself. The second scenario is one in which the protégé suspends her authority and seniority, accepts that her life experience is not a proxy for disproving the radically different experiences of her mentor, and puts up with the level of discomfort required to gain a new, and likely very disruptive, perspective.

The best way to think of reverse mentoring is in terms of how it differs from the objectives of traditional top-down mentoring. While traditional mentoring is often accepted as a natural and valuable way for an experienced and older individual to share her knowledge, the same is not true of reverse mentoring, which might be considered a poor use of a new or younger employee's time. In fact, unless the mentored colleague is the young mentor's boss, it's probably the boss who will have the biggest problem with the distraction it causes the young employee.

THE CISCO STORY: A CASE FOR REVERSE MENTORING

One of the best examples of a formal approach to reverse mentoring comes from our client Cisco. Carlos Dominguez, senior vice president in the office of the chairman and CEO at Cisco, started his experience with reverse mentoring the way many of our clients do, with the need to better engage Gen Z and share its behaviors across generations.

The real story on reverse mentoring at Cisco actually starts way before we did it. We hire a lot of college grads into what we call our Associate Sales Rep Program and Associate Systems Engineering Program. We put them through an intensive twelve months of training to get them ready. We teach them technology, communication skills, even how to hold a fork and a knife and manners; it's a real polishing act and a big investment in our talent.

We were out at one of the events in Raleigh, and I remember sitting and talking to a group of these new hires. I asked them—point blank—"What's your philosophy on life? What are you expecting?" Their responses were along the lines of, "We're not just driven by money. We want to learn, we want to make a difference, and we'll go wherever we need to do that."

The realization for me was that we were spending an exorbitant amount of money on training and educating them, and many of them might leave after a relatively short period of time if we don't give them good reasons to stay. I asked myself, "What does Cisco need to do differently to keep them engaged and onboard?"

The idea we came up with was that we needed to give them a voice, to let them participate, and get them engaged and contributing while also giving them a taste for what the corporate world was like. In the process, we also needed to learn something from them about how they see the world and their values. That simple insight was how the whole reverse mentoring idea came to be.

We started by creating a small group of people that were all on the social media team, which had all the young people—no surprise, right? I simply asked them, "Hey, do you think there's a potential for you folks to mentor some of the executives in the company?" They thought it was a great idea.

The process formally began matching the Millennials with the executives—not every executive participated. It was completely voluntary. We didn't want to force it on anybody.

What I found most interesting was how the relationships formed. Suddenly, a relatively new hire had access to a fairly senior person that they wouldn't have access to otherwise and from whom they too could get coaching, mentoring, and learning—it was clearly beneficial to both parties.

One of the things I've learned is that I don't force reverse mentoring upon our execs. I try selling them on the benefits of being technically savvy or aware.

If you do that, there are some great benefits. I promote that with all of my peers but, frankly, some of them don't want to do it. If they don't want to do it, why put them in a situation where they're not going to grow? Or where it's not going to be successful?

Another part of the strategy for reverse mentoring is to pick an up-and-coming executive who can benefit from reverse mentoring. Start featuring them and highlighting them wherever possible so that everyone else gets the message, "Hey, this is something that I think is important," but you'll always get resistance.

Eventually, we created a very simple app to match mentor and mentee. Once matched, they meet each other to see if there is some chemistry, just like any mentoring program; it's just a basic mentoring principle that the chemistry has to be right. What I think is a little different in the case of reverse mentoring is that in a traditional mentoring relationship, the mentee normally gets a lot more out of it.

In reverse mentoring, if it's done right, I'm not sure who's the bigger recipient of value because they're both getting something really vital. The younger person is, in some cases, mentoring some of the most powerful executives in the world. What they [the mentor] can get as an ally and as a coach is just immense. In turn, the executive is getting an invaluable education through the eyes of someone on the front lines of technology and behavior.

Here's the irony of it all. My kids have been reverse mentoring me in technology for years. I'd always see them on Facebook, Twitter, or Pinterest, and would ask, "What are you doing?" They'd sit me down and walk me through it. But for those who don't have that luxury in an informal setting, reverse mentoring is perfect.

Cisco's reverse mentoring program seems incredibly simple and straightforward, so much so that you have to wonder why more companies haven't put one in place. In our work with dozens of organizations that are instituting reverse mentoring programs, we've found that the idea is still not widely understood, despite case studies dating back nearly thirty years.

We can't help but believe that there is a fear factor on the part of older executives who are wary of being upstaged by younger hires, as well as fear on the part of the younger employees that they will not be taken seriously or that their advice might be interpreted as criticism of a more senior employee.

To help you start a reverse mentoring program, we've included in the appendix a basic guide, which we use with our own clients, to allay some of these fears and educate the organization about the benefits of reverse mentoring.

SEEING THE INVISIBLE SOCIAL NETWORK

You now understand the behaviors of hyperconnectivity, and you're well on your way to creating a reverse mentoring program that will provide the foundation for a shared understanding of how these new behaviors are changing the way you build an organization for Gen Z. What's left? Something that most of us would never think to do: create a way to visualize hyperconnectivity so that you can follow the way social networks are formed and the way they influence your business and the marketplace.

We're not talking just about a network's technology—the wired and wireless connections and the devices that represent each node, often referred to as a network topology. These are just like highways and interchanges. They only tell us how connections can technically be made, not how people actually use them.

The best analogy to use when comparing the visualization of a computer network to that of a social network is that of a static visual map compared with a real-time GPS system, such as Waze, which uses information from fifty million drivers about traffic and road conditions in order to map the fastest route for your trip. The former tells you how you can get to a destination based on roads available while the latter tells you the fastest way based on how people are actually using the roads.

Similarly, the key to leveraging networks in a hyperconnected world is understanding the way they are used, how people communicate and connect socially, what they are saying, and how all this creates an understanding of the way an organization or a marketplace works.

We'll warn you that visualizing hyperconnectivity in this way is going to push the envelope a bit—it's just not something that most of us are familiar with. So let's start with a simple example of why we'd want to do this in the first place.

A Brownie Camera for Social Networks

Around 2001, Marc Smith had a crazy idea: create a way to visualize any network of online interactions so that they were as simple to use as a Kodak Brownie camera, which revolutionized "snapshots" when it was introduced in 1900. With the Brownie, anyone—not just photographers with darkrooms, knowledge of chemical processes, and specialized equipment—could take pictures. The Brownie was the spark that ignited personal photography. Every camera you've ever owned, including the one on your smartphone, rests on the legacy of point-and-shoot photography that the Brownie introduced and promoted for more than eighty consecutive years.

The Brownie made it possible for people to view the world through another's eyes. In many ways, it is one of the cornerstone technologies—along with radio and telephones—that ushered in the age of global connectivity. This basic camera expanded photography beyond the professional arena—with its carefully posed subjects—to harness the power of the crowd and capture the way the world really looked rather than the way we wished it did. The same is true for what Smith is trying to do for social networks.

Using the Crowd to Map the Crowd

Smith's vision is to "illustrate social networks, by allowing people to create pictures of them that show how we really work and communicate. The result allows us to poke into the nooks and crannies of social networks, something no single organization can do." Smith is cofounder of the Social Media Research Foundation and the driving force behind NodeXL, an open source network visualization and analysis tool first funded and created while he was working in Microsoft's Internet Services Research Center. According to Smith: "Only when there is a swarm—a large group—is it possible to map a network's social interactions, in the same way that it would be cost prohibitive, if at all possible, to send a paid photographic team to take pictures of every major event on the planet, you can't capture a complete social network; there's simply no way."

Smith used the example of the Billboard Top 50 to illustrate his point:

The Top 50 presents a recording's position in the list, but it's only a moment in time, condensed to a single number. It's useful but, much like the stereotypes we see when we try to lump all people from a single generation into a single identity, it doesn't provide much context as to why that artist or song is in the Top 50, who is listening to it, or why they are listening to it.

Social network visualization and analysis provides the same sort of overhead view that newsrooms rely on to show the actions of physical crowds. Until recently, we simply haven't had the ability to do that with networks. Says Smith: "After the last several years, you know that when several thousand people gather in a square, that's newsworthy. And yet every day several thousand people gather in a hashtag, or on a message board, or a discussion group, or some form of cyberspace. That is the sociological equivalent of a square, and yet we have no photographs of those squares."

Smith's mission is to provide what he calls "aerial photographs of crowds online."[10] The objective is to show how people are gathering virtually, whether in social media, e-mail, or internal communities, and to do so with the simplicity of point-and-shoot photography. This view will make it possible for human resources professionals, managers, marketers, and salespeople to see and understand a network effect in ways that don't require a PhD in databases or network theory.

Smith believes that the wide-scale use of network analysis tools on an everyday basis is right around the corner: "Every mid-level manager in corporate America is going to have to deal with a network in the next three to five years. Everybody who sits in front of a computer and has a pie chart on their screen will soon have a network chart in front of them."

When used in enterprise conversations and connections, network analysis can reveal both the official and unofficial experts who answer the questions asked by their colleagues, partners, and customers. It can also reveal the bridge makers who connect otherwise disconnected groups as well as uncover an organization's "structural holes," where a bridge or link is needed. For companies involved in mergers and acquisitions, for example, internal social network analysis can identify where there may be difficulty in integrating organizations or specific departments and divisions. It can also identify where early wins might be had, in areas that are socially hyperconnected and ripe for cooperation and collaboration.

The problem is that people don't see the value in mapping social networks because most use of such networks today is considered a personal activity that does not have a place in an organizational setting.

For those who didn't live in the era of the telephone's introduction, it seems curious that people once worried that telephones were a waste of time in the office, and, at best, should be limited to use in specific roles such as executives and their secretaries. You may recall that the same thing happened with e-mail.

All through the history of connectivity and communication, there have been rifts between those who perceive the new technology as distracting or useless and those who recognize its value. The latter group leaps straight to the value, which only later becomes evident and the "new normal" for the naysayers.

However, unlike the journey many of us have taken through generations of painfully primitive technologies to the point where the hyperconnected end game is in sight, the vast majority of humanity, from this point forward, will not gradually make their way down that same path. Instead, as we'll see in the next chapter, they will *slingshot* past the evolutionary phases and end up directly in a hyperconnected future.

Put It Into Action:
Chapter 3 #hyperconnected #me2we #GenZ

Learn from Gen Z Leaders

- Jack Welch, former CEO of General Electric, who initiated a reverse-mentoring program at GE
- Carlos Dominguez, senior vice president in the office of the chairman and CEO at Cisco, who created a reverse-mentoring program accidentally
- Marc Smith, cofounder of the Social Media Research Foundation and the driving force behind NodeXL

Are You Ready for Gen Z?

- How hyperconnected are you, personally? Is that level of hyperconnectivity providing what you want for your social life and for your career? Is it keeping you informed about the world in the way you want?
- Is your organization hyperconnected or disconnected? Is it connected only internally or with external partners and customers as well? Why?
- What opportunities are you missing to connect with customers, partners, and media, given your organization's current state of hyperconnectivity?
- How often do you rely on your "outboard brain"?
- How many computing devices do you interact with on a daily basis?
- How are you taking advantage of these devices in your life and work?
- Are sensors wired into your business's goods and services? Should they be?
- Do you use transparency to build trusted relationships or do you shy away from transparency?
- Is living your life in two worlds something you are able to manage? Are you comfortable in that mode of work?

- Have you noticed ways in which hyperconnectivity is helping children reach a higher potential than they could have in the past?
- Can you think of examples where you have placed new technologies into old behaviors and discounted their value?
- Does your organization use reverse mentoring to bridge generational divides?
- Have you offered to be a mentor or mentee?
- What are you doing to help visualize your social networks in order to better identify opportunities and gaps?

Find out whether you're ready for the Gen Z Effect by taking the full assessment at TheGenZEffect.com.

4

Slingshotting

The further back you look the further ahead you can see.

—WINSTON CHURCHILL

In this chapter we describe the effect of slingshotting, which propels the adoption of technology by a majority. We'll look first at the barriers to technology adoption and how these have been steadily eroding through increased simplification, ease of use, and usefulness for a particular purpose. Part of our discussion focuses on the way in which gamification is providing new paths to learning and embracing technology as we continuously add new technology capabilities. This leads to the concept of the Ideal Final Result, a method of better understanding the trajectory of technology and its ultimate universal global availability.

In a classic science fiction plotline, humans send a manned spaceship off on a long journey of decades or centuries to land on and explore an Earthlike planet in a distant solar system many light years away. While the ship is making its journey the pioneering crew is put into suspended animation. Years pass and the crew are finally awakened from their long slumber to land on the distant planet.

However, they soon realize that their destination is already inhabited by an advanced civilization—namely, humans whose technology advanced so far during the time of our original ship's voyage that they were able to not only get to the destination ahead of our original ship and crew but develop a means to go back and forth and build a new outpost for humanity in that same period of time.

That's the essence of *slingshotting*, the accelerating force of innovation that moves technology forward to the point where those on the slow side of the technology adoption curve (the "laggards") effectively skip multiple generations of technology and instead arrive in the same future with those who suffered through technology's painful evolution.

With most of the technology we use today, the vast majority of issues involving buggy hardware and software, unreliable connectivity, and complex user experience are largely gone. New users can simply step in now that the barriers are removed and use the Internet as easily as they can turn on the faucet and get a glass of water. You don't have to go anywhere special, such as the Internet cafes of the 1990s—remember those? The Internet is simply there, all around us, wrapped around our wrists, attached to our eyeglasses, and in our pockets, bags, and backpacks. It's on our desks, in our kitchens, mounted on the wall in our TVs, and, increasingly, in our cars. Suddenly, a foundation exists and the step of "going online" is nearly gone, which you can easily see in the sheer volume of mobile devices—smartphones, wearables, tablets, and laptops—in virtually every setting.

According to the International Telecommunication Union (ITU), we passed a critical marker for Internet access in 2005: 50 percent of the population of the developed world had access.

By contrast, the number of global online users during the dot-com boom of the late '90s looks like a rounding error. We were just barely getting started at that point, with less than 10 percent of today's users online in 2000.

As shown on figure 4-1, which is compiled from data provided by the World Bank,[2] while growth in the developing world hasn't yet started to accelerate—as we said in chapter 3, we're only seeing 9 percent yearly growth globally—in the developed world, we have risen to the level of exponential growth and are closing in on 100 percent of the population participating online. Steady downward pressure on costs for both connectivity and devices, along with a tremendous reduction in the effort needed to go online—nothing is required other than activating a new device at an Apple or Best Buy store or in one of

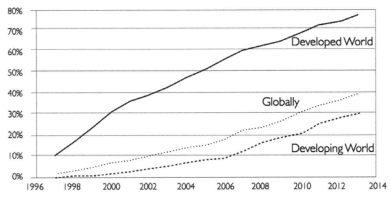

Figure 4-1: Internet Participation[1]

As shown, while the developed world has reached nearly 80 percent penetration in terms of Internet access, the developing world is still at only 31 percent penetration.

thousands of kiosks around the world—has completely changed the parameters for who can and will participate as a member of Gen Z.

When you break it down, three factors enable slingshotting:

1. **Simplification:** The technology available provides a user experience and set of technological capabilities that are finally ready for "normal people," rather than computer scientists and the earliest adopters of what in hindsight were "user-hostile" experiences that required users to type, read, and use very specialized interfaces. The rise of mobile, social, highly visual interfaces, and, more recently, touch and voice controls, together with decreasing costs for both the computing device and high-speed access, has removed most of those early barriers.

2. **Accessibility:** Because of hyperconnectivity and the accessibility of technology, "being connected" is both socially acceptable and technically possible (witness the rise of Wi-Fi access in most cafes, restaurants, libraries, and hotels). As a result, a comfort level with "being online" is spreading among groups of people who have traditionally not participated. For example, grandparents who used to carry photos of their grandkids in their wallets or purses, can now—thanks to Facebook, FaceTime, and similar applications—stay in

touch with their distant families by following, posting, and commenting on their profiles online or by reaching out for a live video call without needing to think about the technology.

3. **Datafication:** The ability to capture the interactions of people with technology, which reveals their actual behaviors for analysis and personalization, makes the vast majority of "free" services—search engines, Twitter, Facebook, YouTube, and most public websites—worth offering because of the value of users' data to potential advertisers. If the product is "free," the product is actually *you*. This has always been true in marketing, but is far more directly applicable to Gen Z.

Let's peel these factors apart a bit. The 2.7 billion global users and 7 billion cell numbers in use—described in chapter 3, "Hyperconnecting"—are the new foundation that allow slingshotting to happen. This readiness, or ability to slingshot, is quite new, and by many accounts was triggered during the recession that began in 2008, punctuated by Apple's launch of the original iPad in 2010. While the iPad initially met with intense skepticism—why would anyone need "an oversized iPhone?"—Apple has since sold more than 195 million iPads[3] and ignited a worldwide expansion of the sales of tablets, which grew from 116 million in 2012 to 195 million in 2013.[4] There are now millions of new users on the Internet for the very first time, users who in many cases had never touched a computer.

The easiest way to understand how slingshotting works is with figure 4-2, which shows the various ways that we can get to the future.

The first of these is to try and go directly from the present (the lower left quadrant) into some distant, disruptive technology and a new set of behaviors. That simply never works. Technology and behavior have to both evolve in lock step. The other path into the future is through the upper left quadrant, in which technology changes but behavior stays relatively stable at first, and then changes over time and through multiple generations of technology. We call this the "Techie Path" because it is a long route that requires fumbling through many new experiences and technologies. It includes, for example, the evolution of the PDA into mobile devices such

Slingshotting

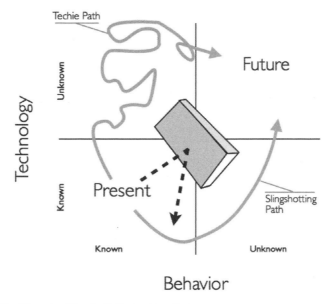

Figure 4-2: Slingshotting's Path to the Future

The lower left quadrant of the diagram represents the known technologies and behaviors of the present. If we attempt to go directly into the future of unknown technologies and behaviors, we quickly bounce back into the present. This is the problem with products such as Apple's Newton PDA and the Sony Data Discman. They attempted to sell into a technology space that was without precedent, promoting a behavior that had not been experienced.

as the smartphone, which happened over two decades with at least twenty generations of technology. Yet once the future technology and behavior are defined and embraced by a critical mass of society, they are now synchronized and the majority of users slingshot into the future via the lower right quadrant. This is slingshotting, and it is ultimately the fastest and least painful way to move into the future. Yet it is also the one most often discounted by both markets and incumbent providers of products and services, as they have taken the long and arduous Techie Path. One of the most vivid examples of slingshotting is the rise of Google. At the time of Google's founding, in 1998, there was already a healthy but fragmented and complex thirty-year-old industry focusing on text search and retrieval. Yet Google was able to slingshot past all of these competitors to establish what soon became the de facto future state of search.

WE'VE BEEN DOING IT WRONG

For those of us who have been online for a long time, it's time to own up. We've been pointing the finger at the "technology luddites" who couldn't be bothered to figure out how to use their computers, when in reality, it's been the technologists, geeks, and inventors who made computers so difficult to use. Simply put, technology until recently has been "user hostile" far more often than it has been "user friendly."

Some long-held myths about who has opted out of hyperconnectivity and why are finally beginning to unravel. The supposedly technophobic Baby Boomer generation and the Mature/Silent Generation have had good reason to delay getting online, and it has far less to do with fear than with simply not seeing the value in it. Studies by the Pew Research Center and the Stanford Center on Longevity have found, not surprisingly, that the "first life" of older generations has plenty of social interactivity and a "second life" online hasn't been worth the effort—until now.

According to Dr. Laura Carstensen, who heads the Stanford Center on Longevity, "It appears that a bigger reason [than complexity] for the failure to use digital technologies is the lack of perceived need. For a lot of older people, they're quite satisfied with their social relationships, their friendships, their contact with loved ones."[5] However, that tide is turning. There are suddenly many reasons to be online: they can connect with distant family members, friends, former coworkers, and schoolmates that they may have not seen or heard from in decades. In fact, a Forrester Research project on "Digital Seniors" shows that 60 percent of all U.S. seniors are online, with 49 percent of them using Facebook.[6] This demographic is also the fastest rising social media demographic,[7] contrary to most of our ideas about who is online and using social media.

Although social media use is currently dominated by the under-thirty-four crowd, according to the GlobalWebIndex,[8] don't expect that to continue. Large chunks of the world's population, around two hundred million yearly, are coming online. We expect that to progress exponentially year over year, leading to full global Internet penetration sometime between 2020 and 2025.

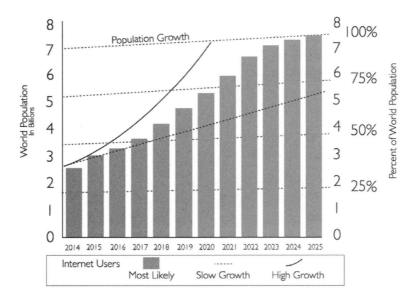

Figure 4-3: Scenarios for Internet Growth Reaching 100 Percent of Global Penetration

THE SLINGSHOTTING CATALYSTS:
USEFULNESS AND USABILITY

All this participation by people who had previously avoided the "new-fangled Internet" shouldn't be a mystery. The timing is finally right, as technologies that are both useful and usable have arrived at price points that make being online no longer a nice-to-have but a must-have with an easy user experience.

We spoke with Dr. Joseph Keebler, a human factors psychologist who studies how to design technology with the human in mind, and who is currently assistant professor of psychology and director of the Training Research and Applied Cognitive Engineering (TRACE) Lab at Wichita State University in Kansas. He described a roughly thirty-year-old methodology for studying the way people deal with new technology, which began with the Technology Acceptance Model (TAM) first created in 1989. The original research, proposed by Fred Davis, now a professor of information systems at the University of Arkansas's Sam M. Walton College of Business, focused on two sets of questions, one about the impact of a technology on our ability to do work (its usefulness) and another about how difficult or easy it was to learn and use a technology (its usability).

Let's pause for a moment here.

If you were to predict whether *usefulness*—a user can see that his work is easier as a result of the technology—or *usability*—the technology is easy to use, including training—had the more significant impact on the actual use of a technology, which do you believe would win out? It turns out that the technologies that were predicted to have high usefulness—to make work easier—are 50 percent more likely to be successful than those that were predicted to be more usable.[9] Of course, we don't live in a world where you have to settle for either a useful tablet or a usable tablet—you can have both, and undoubtedly, that's what you want. It is certainly what companies that are trying to get a new technology into the hands of users want to provide.

The lesson learned? If you're going to target a technology at a group that has never used it before, focus on making sure that technology is useful to your target market. If people don't see a reason to use it, they simply won't. The thrill of the technology itself is not what drives them—it had better be truly useful. Keep in mind we are talking about slingshotting here—how the masses adopt a new technology, not the geeks. If you are prone to taking the "techie path," which we showed in figure 4-2, technology by itself probably does drive you.

Usability, on the other hand, ensures that those of us who aren't geeks don't get frustrated with the technology, hit a wall, and bounce back—which we described earlier in the chapter, in figure 4-2.

The holy grail is, of course, marrying highly *useful* technology with highly *usable* technology, creating novel user experiences that invite in people who previously hadn't seen a reason to participate. More polished capabilities make the technology nearly effortless to use. It's important to keep this ideal marriage of the useful and the usable firmly in mind, as markets do not know how to ask for a product in its future state—they haven't experienced it or the behaviors that make it a necessary part of their lives. The streets are littered with products that did not achieve both usability and usefulness.

We will see this same theme of usability and usefulness echoed as we talk about each of the remaining topics in this chapter: flow, gaming, and the Ideal Final Result. Each relies on the unique chemistry of usability and usefulness to engage and win users. Dr. Keebler provided a variety of examples that demonstrate how companies that do both, taking user experience and the novelty of their solution seriously, have a unique advantage in the market:

> Take Apple TV—the remote is very simplified, with essentially four buttons: play/pause, menu, select, and one button that has a few functions on it to navigate. Now, compare that to your DVR or cable box controller, which probably has a dozen or more buttons on it. In the middle of the night you could pick up your Apple remote and pretty much use every button without even thinking, but try to pick up a standard remote without lighting it and you're lost; it doesn't matter how long you've owned it. Both are *useful* and accomplish the same end goals, but one is clearly more *usable*.

We'd add to Dr. Keebler's examples the advent of voice-operated systems such as Amazon's Fire TV, Apple's Siri, and the Xbox's voice recognition and gesture-driven interfaces. These technologies are all trending toward simplification, which opens the opportunity to slingshot even more users by removing every button and allowing users to interact with their devices more like they would talk to the people around them, rather than have to channel their energy into learning key commands, manipulating a mouse, or using any of the more foreign interfaces that we've seen over the years.

This is also why business users have a near universal hatred of the technology that "corporate" imposes. The technology may be theoretically useful in helping you with your work, but in practice, it is more frustrating and time consuming to use than it should be, especially when it's compared with consumer technologies that use interfaces that require no training. Think about it: When is the last time you bothered to use a manual when opening up your latest consumer technology purchase?

It's not intuitive, but the time and effort people invest in understanding and using earlier technologies is one of the primary reasons that slingshotting is as dramatic as it is. The reason is that after investing enormous amounts of time mastering a technology, the last thing most people want to do is move on to a new one, even when they complain bitterly about what they have. Having been burned once (or multiple times) with painful-to-use new technology, they actively avoid it. This creates a resistance to change that also results in a technology being used long past its useful life.

The problem is that while technology may move forward incrementally, people don't. Most people don't want to change from a technology they are comfortable with until there is an overwhelmingly compelling reason and a much simpler alternative. The result is a pent-up tension—a form of stored potential energy—that ultimately slingshots people into the future in a very sudden manner, once the stage is set so that they can fly past the pain they've experienced or purposefully avoided in the past.

It's a bit of a Rip Van Winkle phenomenon; many people effectively sleep through the painful evolution of technology until one day they wake up in the future. They turn on the TV, see the many ads that show people easily recording family videos, taking photos, playing music, reading the news on a tablet, or playing a game on their smartphone, and suddenly they realize that they have a reason to use this new technology, and it looks awfully easy. Seems simple enough, right? So outside of rare exceptions, such as the iPhone or voice-activated interfaces, why don't we see really useful, highly usable technology every day? Why wouldn't everyone be doing this? According to Dr. Keebler, the reason is that there are fewer than ten thousand qualified professionals who pay attention to usefulness and usability—what is often referred to as user experience (UX) or, more formally, human factors—around the world, making it a relatively rare skill set. And few universities teach the subject.

Bill Gribbons, who runs the Usability Lab at Bentley University, one of the nation's top programs in user experience, believes part of the challenge is that our expectations for user experience are constantly changing: "We live in an 'experience' economy, one where we expect things to be very powerful and deliver tremendous value. Over time, we expect things to be even more beautiful and deliver better and better experiences. And that's true of everything in life, from relationships to products. What pleased us five years ago will not please us today. Although it drives manufacturers and producers crazy, it's what fuels innovation."[10]

Companies such as Apple, Microsoft, and Google regularly snatch up students in the user experience field—and, given the popularity and use-fulness of the products these companies design, is it any wonder they are as successful as they are? If you are a technology provider and you design user experience well, you can go beyond slingshotting and *catapult* a large portion of humanity forward in one fell swoop.

For example, Apple introduced the first iPad on April 3, 2010, and within ninety days of its initial release, the iPad managed to penetrate 50 percent of Fortune 100 companies.[11] Along with the strong demand for the iPad, from first-day sales of three hundred thousand units, the growth of apps for Apple's iOS devices (iPads, iPhones, and iPods) grew from fifty billion downloaded by May 2013 to sixty billion in October 2013, and to sixty-five billion by January 2014.[12] These were among more than one million available apps in Apple's App Store created by nearly three hundred thousand iOS developers working on iOS apps as of early 2014.[13] This kind of growth is almost incomprehensible for such a new device. That's the power of the potential energy that slingshotting unleashes, which fueled not only the revolution of iOS devices, but also the entire industry of nontraditional "app developers" that have sprung up around these devices, which we just talked about.

One of the biggest mistakes you can make is to blame slow technology adoption on a generational divide by assuming that an entire generation shares the trait of technology avoidance; this is exactly what we have done historically when we stereotype "older" workers by saying that they don't "get" technology. That puts the blame on users, when, as Pogo (*Walter Crawford Kelly Jr.*'s iconic comic strip character) said, "We have met the enemy, and he is us."

That concern of generational stereotyping was evident in a number of the comments in our Gen Z study. One of the respondents, who works for a large global company, said: "We have found too many older workers look down their noses at younger people, while the younger workers don't believe older people have anything of value to offer. We follow Peter Drucker's advice and encourage everyone to challenge his or her assumptions. We also offer internships, education/training, and reverse mentoring." Another respondent commented: "My fear is that each generation will not let go of stereotypes and will continue to leave talent on the sidelines and this will impact the future of not only these individuals, but the company's success."

These are very real issues that will not just resolve themselves; they have to be dealt with proactively by leadership in order to prevent them from driving a generational wedge into the organization. The lines we've become comfortable with drawing to delineate the traits of various generations are arbitrary. It's not chiefly fear of technology or lack of skills that prevents people from picking up a technology; more often, those we label as "technophobic," regardless of age, just don't see a reason to use that technology—yet.

At the same time, to balance the conversation, there are many people who have had to take the long route to learning technology through all of its many generations—from mainframes to smartphones—who, with more than a tad of smugness, don't want to believe that those who haven't been technology savvy can adapt to it. As one of our middle-aged study respondents said: "I don't know why people my age are bitter about the older generation slingshotting—as you put it—instead of embracing the idea that technology puts us all on the same page. There are a lot of technology martyrs who want to remember when we had Commodores, dot-matrix printers, and dial-up modems. 'Woe is us. We had to put up with it and so should they.'"

Even though smartphones and tablets may be the initial entry point for someone slingshotting into the modern Internet, that doesn't mean that the ability to win new users' hearts, minds, and more importantly, their time, money, and attention, is guaranteed. The most useful and usable apps work to remove the barriers that get in the way of people simply using the device. Today, developers are increasingly aiming for "seductive" or "addictive" experiences—what snack food producers call "crave"—taking apps to an entirely different level of both art and science—and this is a measurable phenomenon, according to Mihaly Csikszentmihalyi. In his 1997 book, *Flow: The Psychology of Optimal Experience*, Csikszentmihalyi, professor of psychology and management at Claremont Graduate University and founding codirector of the Quality of Life Research Center, unveiled his theory that people are happiest when they are in a state of flow. **Flow is the state of mind we experience when we remove most of the obstacles in the way of us being fully engaged in an activity.**[14] Business and consumer technology providers are beginning to realize that helping people achieve a level of "flow" is what they should be striving for.

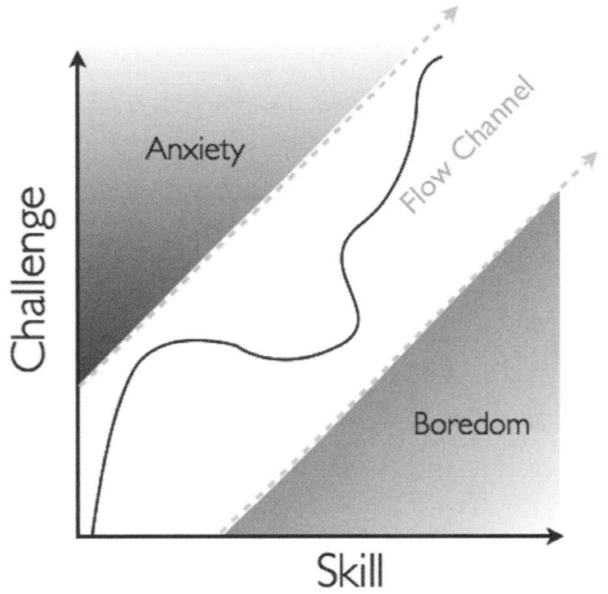

Figure 4-4: Staying in the Flow Channel

Flow is best described as a channel that balances the level of challenge and the skill required to perform a task or activity. If the challenge or skill does not fit our abilities we will end up either anxious or bored. This is critical to understand in any learning environment since staying in the flow channel allows us to progressively learn and develop our skills and take on greater challenges.

One of the key concepts behind helping people effectively apply technology for gaming, education, or enterprise applications, is keeping them in a state of flow. Flow is similar to a Goldilocks Zone—that place where all of the variables for success are just right—where they are neither understimulated and bored, nor overstimulated and anxious. Over time, a person in a state of flow feels increasingly challenged as her skills improve.

Flow might seem like a pretty abstract and hard-to-achieve condition, but this is where datafication (measuring behavior and collecting behavioral data) and what is known as gamification (turning data into actionable information) come into play. Why? Because we're not looking to create flow only because it's a great state of mind, but because it makes people more interested in doing whatever it is they're doing.

GAMIFICATION

Gamification, a term that's surfaced in recent years, is a set of techniques designed to track and increase engagement of consumers or employees. It's an area of intense focus despite the first impression that it's only for game designers, a myth we will be obliterating in chapter 6, "Adopting the World As My Classroom."

Defined by Rajat Paharia, CEO of Bunchball, one of the earliest providers of gamification technology:

Gamification is about motivating people through data. That's it.

We've all turned into walking data generators, and more and more of what we're doing at work or buying and using as consumers is being mediated by technology. This throws off "Big Data" that can be tracked and leveraged to motivate people by making it visible and acting on it.

Examples could be creating competition among salespeople to sell more than others on the sales team, to sell earlier in the quarter, or to insert a certain number of leads into their sales funnel.

In a customer call center it can be used to motivate people to hit specific metrics for customer satisfaction, like a high Net Promoter Score (a common marketing measurement used to measure customer loyalty; it asks customers how likely they would be to recommend a company, product, or service), while also keeping call times low.

Gamification is sometimes described as "the use of game mechanics in non-game situations, to drive user behavior," which leads to the question, "If I'm not a gamer, how does this apply to me?"

As you might expect, this is a question that Paharia has answered thousands of times since the launch of Bunchball in 2007:

People often ask us, "I can see how this works for kids, but why would it work for senior executives?" Well, I'll bet your senior executives care about their status on the airline that they fly, and are very proud of that status, right? They get upgraded to first class, get to board first, they show up on the early boarding screen, and are treated better than the average traveler.

You see similar behavior in the military, where people care very much about their rank; it's no different with senior executives. If you went up to them and said, "You know what, I'm not going to change anything else about your job, you're going to have the same reports, the same salary, the same responsibilities, I'm just crossing the senior off your card, and so now you're just a VP." How would that make them feel? You've taken away nothing of any "real" value but you've clearly taken away something that's valuable in their eyes, right? It's called status.

"Status" is an intangible by itself, this indication of my seniority in the community, my commitment to it, my experience in it, and the kind of benefits and perks that accrue with it. That's how gamification works. It doesn't matter what the age group, this is general and typical human behavior and it motivates people, regardless of their age.

The point to keep in mind with gamification is that the most engaging and attention-capturing experiences are those that give you guidance, make it clear where you stand, show how far you have to go, and nudge you to toward a state of flow, where you are challenged enough to keep progressing but not hitting a barrier that causes frustration to set in.

Some of the most successful gamified apps and technologies are those that take a highly personal approach. How many people used to measure their heart rate multiple times a day? Now there are smartwatches like Basis that track heart rate, perspiration, number of steps taken, stairs climbed, and calories burned. Incidentally, Basis was one of the most financially successful crowdfunded smartwatch projects when it launched—with more than $1 million raised in presales—and the company was acquired by Intel in early 2014.

A similar device, the Fitbit bracelet or belt clip, shows how many steps you've taken, how close you are to your daily goal, and your level of exertion during that day (how often you raised your heart rate to a meaningful level). You can challenge friends to track their progress with you or join communities that have undertaken a joint objective, for example, to collectively walk enough to circle the globe in a certain number of months.

There are other apps, such as MyFitnessPal, that allow you to scan the bar codes on most commercially produced foods and drinks to automatically track and calculate your calorie consumption each day, with trends shown over time—again, plotting where you started and whether you are on track to meet your dietary goals, as well as tracking your weight, percentage of body fat, and percentage of water weight.

In most cases, it's barely harder to do any of these of these things than to not do them. Rather than monitor your exercise on your own, you simply wear a sensor that is tracking you all the time, feeding into a fitness app. Rather than note everything you are eating or drinking, you simply point your smartphone camera at an object's barcode and it enters itself into your diet app.

Dr. Keebler described these gadgets as cognitive aids, described as "an outboard brain" in chapter 3. This idea of self-tracking is often called the "quantified self" movement, which includes a growing number of people who are measuring just about everything in their lives, health metrics in particular. When you combine direct monitoring of your behaviors with a social support mechanism, such as friends or a peer group, the results can be quite dramatic.

For example, in a WeightWatchers study, of the people who lost weight and kept it off, 80 percent had social support; of those who lost weight and then regained it, only 30 percent had used social support.[15] WeightWatchers has since expanded their in-person support system in the over five decades of their existence, with an online social community of mutual support with members from around the world, acknowledging the new found capabilities of hyperconnecting which augment traditional social support with the social tools that now sit in most people's hands.

The "one-two punch" of data and social support fits directly into the expectations of Gen Z, who believe that life is all about constant feedback and social engagement, regardless of the situation.

Digital health is one of the newest and fastest-growing areas of interest, with "smart devices" out in front. A 2013 CEA survey found that 33 percent of mobile device owners had used their devices to track some aspect of their health in the previous twelve months. The January 2014 Consumer Electronics Show—"the world's gathering place for all who thrive on the business of consumer technologies"—experienced 40 percent growth of the digital health footprint (physical space used by vendors and sponsors) at the show, compared with the previous year.[16]

The Pew Internet and American Life Project's report, published in January 2013 and based on data gathered in mid-2012, found that 69 percent of adults in the United States keep track of at least one health indicator—weight, diet, exercise routine, or symptom.[17] Contrary to what a gamified application or wearable device does, 49 percent of those respondents track the progress "in their heads," 34 percent keep notes on paper, and 21 percent use technology such as a spreadsheet to track their own health data. However, all of these methods require intervention to do the tracking and are done after the fact, rather than measuring automatically while people exercise, eat or sleep, leaving the digital health market wide open for competition and innovation in making health tracking and feedback a nearly invisible and "always on" tool for those who care about their health habits.

As Dr. Keebler summed up in our conversation:

> The scientific background for what you're describing as slingshotting would be a mixture of technology acceptance and optimal experience. There are people who just shut down when they run into new technology, and others who are willing and have the capacity to try it, and may jump at it immediately or just need a nudge. You could say there's a capacity there to "slingshot," to jump on board and try something out to see what it can do, and that really makes a difference. Then once they get engaged with it and realize, "Oh, I can do this with it, I can do that with it," it becomes a very cascading effect.

This cascading effect is the marriage of hyperconnectivity and slingshotting—where both the connectivity of the Internet and the devices to participate are more than "good enough." They allow anyone, with relatively low investment and almost no effort, to get online in ways that are useful and relevant to *him*.

How do you do that? You try to remove every barrier between what the person is trying to do and the way he does it with the technology in question. Aim for the most ideal, "blue sky" version of the technology that will help him.

WORKING TOWARD THE IDEAL FINAL RESULT

It wasn't long ago that sharing video meant recording on videotape, digitizing that tape with special equipment, editing it for size and content, exporting it as finished video file, saving a smaller/compressed version to post online, and then, *finally*, e-mailing a copy to your family and friends. This process and the equipment required easily cost thousands of dollars and could turn a thirty-minute video of a child's recital into a multi-week effort worthy of an Oscar nomination—or at least a "Best Dad" trophy. If you still have 8mm film footage or VHS tapes of family outings, think about how often you've shared those videos with anyone outside your home—we're willing to bet it is not very often.

Capturing and posting a video today is one or, at most, two steps, whether you are working directly within Facebook, Twitter, or the camera apps of a smartphone or tablet, which allow you to share instantly via a Multimedia Messaging Service (MMS) to other cell phone users, via e-mail, or by posting to YouTube, Facebook, or Vine, with minimal configuration. This simplification of technology has its basis in a concept called the Ideal Final Result, used by innovative companies such as Apple, Google, Samsung, LG, and GE. It is not commonly known, despite being employed for more than sixty years by a growing segment of the business world, from refining factories to nanotechnology companies. The Ideal Final Result is a description of a solution free of the constraints of the original problem. The solution to a problem such as, "I want to share home videos with my family and friends," moves from a long, drawn-out, expensive, and complex process to one that has almost no steps aside from point, shoot, and share on a single "connected" device.

You can see this trend toward the Ideal Final Result in many areas. For example, for thousands of years, washing clothes meant whacking them against rocks in a river. Then, in 1797, the process of laundering clothing moved to manual scrubbing on a metal board and later on to the hand-cranked rotary washing machine of 1858, then the electric washing machine in 1908, the more modern and recognizable washing machines with agitators and automated dispensers of the 1940s, through to front-loading, steam-cleaning washing machines of the twenty-first century, which use 77 percent less water and 81 percent less energy[18] than a traditional top-loading, agitator-driven model, and—in a nod to hyperconnectivity, notify you on your smartphone when the clothes are done.

Compared with previous generations of technology, the technologies we have access to now—and which represent the epitome of slingshotting—are radically reducing the effort it takes to accomplish just about any complicated or manual task. Things that used to require significant effort today take almost no effort at all. Consider the wearables we've mentioned, such as Fitbit and Google Glass. These are clear examples of aiming for the Ideal Final Result. Because they are literally "always on"—both on your body and electronically—they fade into the background and become a "natural" part of your experience, just as regular glasses or contacts have been for decades.

The other aspect of technologies that move toward the Ideal Final Result is that they integrate what used to be multiple devices or operations into a single seamless experience. However, the concept of an Ideal Final Result is a bit of a misnomer, as the result is not a final destination. Instead, it is a continuous path toward ever-increasing integration and simplification.

Slingshotting is accelerated, and its effect is magnified by the integration and simplification of technology over time. This is an ongoing process, because technologies mature over different periods of time. An example is the integration of multiple devices, such as still photography, video, audio recording, music players, GPS, health monitors, flashlights, calculators, and computing capability in smartphones. This trend toward creating technologies that move closer and closer to the Ideal Final Result (figure 4-5) has been accelerating, and each new innovation or improvement cycle builds on the best of the previous cycles, further enabling the slingshotting phenomenon. For example, the iPad, iPhone, and iPod of today—collectively, the iOS line of products from Apple—barely resemble the first iPod, which debuted on October 23, 2001.

In the course of ten years as a product designer at Apple, Tony Fadell led the team that created the first eighteen generations of the iPod and three generations of the iPhone. That represents twenty-one total generations of devices in a ten-year time span. Even given that many iPods and iPhones are nearly the same device—different only by whether they included cellular technology—that is a remarkably compressed time span.

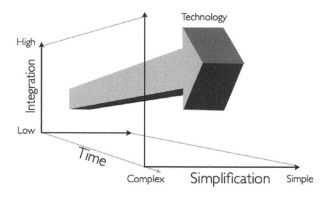

Figure 4-5: Moving Toward the Ideal Final Result

By contrast, Microsoft is well known historically for operating on three- to five-year life cycles for new product introductions,[19] such as Microsoft XP, introduced in late 2001, Windows Vista, in 2006, Windows 7, launched in 2009, and Windows 8, which launched in late 2012.

While the ever-increasing impact of slingshotting continues to build new bridges between what were distinct generations, you can't assume that *everyone* will take on the characteristics of Gen Z. As we saw with reverse mentoring, a cultural catalyst is also required to influence the shift to a new behavior.

Part of the challenge then, is answering the question, "What can you do to magnify the influence of your colleagues who already represent Gen Z (by birth or choice), and help those who do not *yet* represent Gen Z take the steps that will enable them to jump into a new way of operating?"

That is the shift from affluence to influence, which represents the single biggest societal shift impacting consumer purchasing, political movements, and activism of all kinds since the pre-Internet days of Civil Rights and the anti-war activism of the 1960s and '70s—and which we explore in depth in the next chapter.

Put It Into Action:
Chapter 4 #slingshotting #GenZ

Learn from Gen Z Leaders

- Dr. Laura Carstensen, head of the Stanford Center on Longevity
- Dr. Joseph Keebler, assistant professor of psychology and director of the Training Research and Applied Cognitive Engineering (TRACE) Lab of Wichita State University
- Bill M. Gribbons, founder and professor of the Design and Usability Center at Bentley University
- Mihaly Csikszentmihalyi, professor of psychology and management at Claremont Graduate University
- Rajat Paharia, CEO of Bunchball
- Tony Fadell, founder and CEO of Nest

Are You Ready for Gen Z?

- How much of the technology that you use at work (or which you may develop and deliver) is user friendly versus user hostile?
- Can you think of examples of slingshotting that you have been part of or have witnessed up close?
- Do you subscribe to the belief that older generations are simply technophobic and will therefore never "get" technology?
- If you create consumer-focused (rather than business-focused) technologies, how obsessively do you focus on user experience (UX)? Have you hired experts in the field of UX?
- On a scale of one to ten (with ten being the best) how simple and accessible are the technologies you use (or produce)?
- How often do you find yourself in a state of flow with the technologies you use? (Answer from a user perspective if you develop and deliver technology.)
- Do you use gamification to engage employees and users?

- What goods or services are you using that do as much as possible to move your (or your users') experience toward the Ideal Final Result?
- How is your business using the Ideal Final Result to simplify the world for your customers? Do you use it to bring in new customers who may have been waiting for you to take that next step so they can slingshot forward?

Find out whether you're ready for the Gen Z Effect by taking the full assessment at TheGenZEffect.com.

5

Shifting from Affluence to Influence

The past influences everything and dictates nothing.

—ADAM PHILLIPS

In this chapter we take on one of the most critical, and perhaps most controversial, Gen Z issues, the shift from affluence to influence. We'll start by discussing the ways in which Gen Z is using hyperconnectivity to shift power toward networks and communities of influence, creating what we term elastic influence. Then we take a look at some previous work done on the way influence is exerted through psychologist Robert Cialdini's six principles of persuasion. Our focus then shifts to the persuasive mechanisms used in marketing and how they are changing for Gen Z from "paid" media to "earned" media—and how earned media's effectiveness can be measured. We'll also take on the use of influence inside an enterprise and the role it plays in engaging Gen Z employees and measuring their performance. Lastly, we look at the role of big data in understanding Gen Z behaviors.

As the Gen Z population pyramid stretches upward and outward, taking on the shape of a skyscraper—and with its transformation shattering many of our assumptions about the way the world works—the relationship between two of our most basic frameworks, affluence and influence, is undergoing a profound change. The power to influence the masses has always been a critical part of how society and commerce operate. Until the 1800s, however, influence was a highly localized activity, limited by the lack of modern transportation and communications. Keep in mind that even the telegraph and the steamship did not come into existence until the early 1800s. It wasn't until the advent of both these technologies, along with the expansion of railroads, broad circulation print media and, ultimately, the introduction of radio and telecommunications in the early 1900s, that influence became a purchasable commodity through which an individual or entity could reach the masses and shape opinions.

This set the stage for the modern-day vehicle of influence, which for the past one hundred years has resided mostly in the large-scale media empires that have acted as a megaphone for some of the most affluent and influential people in modern history. One of the earliest and best-known examples was William Randolph Hearst, who took over publishing the *San Francisco Examiner* from his father in 1887 (amazingly, ownership of the *Examiner* was won by William's father from a gambling debt; if not for this somewhat random

Figure 5-1: William Randolph Hearst
Hearst's advertising model defines paid media for the better part of the twentieth century.
Photo Credit: Library of Congress Prints and Photographs Division

acquisition, much of William's career and the model of modern-day influence may not have evolved quite as it has).

Hearst extended his media empire to more than two dozen newspapers, making his organization the source of news for one out of every four Americans, ultimately expanding into the radio business in the 1920s and the TV business in the 1940s. Hearst's net worth at its peak was by some estimates $30 billion, making him many times wealthier than Bill Gates in today's dollars. In fact, from the standpoint of raw purchasing power Hearst had the equivalent of $5 trillion in today's dollars, or about one third of the U.S.'s current annual gross domestic product. Hearst lived in a world in which affluence drove influence, which was made possible through the massive and expensive distribution networks that were involved in physically getting media into the hands of the masses.

Mass distribution of print media on this scale was revolutionary. In many ways, this distribution network was a crude analog form of early hyperconnectivity, one that required massive resources and large amounts of money to broadcast a thought from one person to many others. Yet it formed a foundational business model for media, which is still in use today: first buy an audience, then get advertisers to buy the opportunity to influence that audience, then go back to step one and repeat, in a cycle of ever-increasing influence.

However, we have come quite a long way in the redistribution of influence from the days when only a few owned the content and the medium for its delivery to today's content-rich society with nearly a billion websites and four hundred million daily blog posts. **Democratization of media is one of the cornerstones for the way Gen Z is altering the relationship between affluence and influence.**

INFLUENCE AND OTHER WEAPONS OF MASS DISRUPTION

Affluence is easy to understand—its signs and its effect on the world are all around us, and it's the basis of most of the messages bombarding us on a day-to-day basis. Influence, however, remains a bit of a mystery despite the fact that it has been studied formally for more than thirty years, starting with pioneering work in the field by Dr. Robert Cialdini, known as the "Father of Influence." Regents' professor emeritus of psychology and marketing at

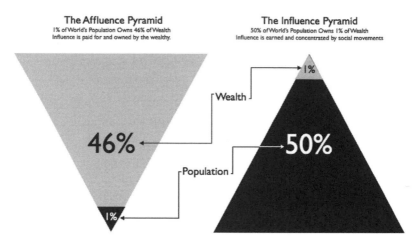

Figure 5-2 The Affluence and Influence Pyramids

One percent of the world's population owns a staggering 46 percent of wealth and, historically, holds the vast majority of influence, while 50 percent of the world's population owns only 1 percent of its wealth. Yet, if the 50 percent are able to connect and coordinate their efforts, the sheer magnitude of their influence will structurally alter the way businesses and governments operate and make decisions.

Arizona State University, Cialdini is the author of the 1984 book *Influence: The Psychology of Persuasion*. The book, updated and rebranded as *Influence: Science and Practice*, is now in its fifth edition and has sold more than one million copies over its thirty-year history.

Social influence has typically been associated with the masters of persuasion: marketers, salespeople, and politicians. These people are so good at pushing our buttons that often, before we know what has happened, we react and empty our wallets before we come to our senses. This is not, however, where Cialdini was going with the notion of persuasion. His view emphasized ethical persuasion that helped both parties in a conversation.

Cialdini took influence to an entirely new level by looking at it as a science, boiling down the most consistent principles of persuasion and influence into six items that work—in true Gen Z spirit—regardless of the age of the person or the geography/culture she lives in.[1] As we look at Cialdini's six principles of persuasion—which combine to form the basis of influence—keep in mind that our focus is on how these can be used to create bonds of trust and community.

1. Reciprocity—the principle that people tend to return a favor, such as purchasing a product after receiving free samples. This includes "paying it forward" and giving and receiving personal favors.

2. Commitment and consistency—the principle that if people commit to an idea or goal, whether orally or in writing, they are more likely to follow through on that commitment because of the cultural expectations to "do what you say," particularly when the promise is made publicly. Oaths of loyalty, as well as the public stating of goals at company meetings or in support groups, are examples.

3. Social proof—the principle that people will do things they see other people doing, even when they wouldn't typically be the first to jump in to any given situation and may, in fact, be morally opposed to what the group is doing. In one experiment, one or more participants would look up into the sky. Bystanders would then look up into the sky to see what the others were seeing, the result being a growing crowd, all staring into the sky at nothing in particular, because of the pull of group behavior.

4. Authority—the principle that people tend to obey authority figures, even when asked to perform objectionable acts. This includes benign examples such as patients not questioning their doctors because of a fear of offending them, as well as other instances of obedience to authority. Advertisements featuring actors dressed as doctors offer an example of people "dressing the part"; the white coat and stethoscope lend authority to people who are clearly *not* doctors.

5. Liking—the principle that people are easily persuaded by other people they like, such as celebrities, who are given more leeway to "behave badly" simply because of their popularity. It is the principle behind the sales strategy of companies like Tupperware, which relies mainly on women to sell to their friends and family. It is no accident that the primary activity on Facebook is "Liking," which is a micro-step in the direction of following a crowd of similar people who all "like" the same ideas, politics, music, or products.

6. Scarcity—the principle that things that are perceived as rare or "scarce" appear to be more valuable. Advertising that offers are available for a limited time only often encourages sales. Companies and individuals who constantly push this persuasion button often find, however, that "false scarcity" undermines them in the end.

In Cialdini's view, these principles are more important than the age group people can be lumped into. They are part of a revolution in understanding behavior at both the individual and the group level.

ANALYZING AND AUTOMATING INFLUENCE

As part of the shift toward more scientific methods of recognizing the effect of influence, marketing algorithms and experimental campaigns are beginning to factor into persuasion techniques. This allows marketers to personalize messages based on constant testing of the influence techniques that work for each prospective customer.

In our own work with companies, especially those in the consumer space, we've found personalization to be one of the most powerful tools in building a sense of trust. It leads to persuasion that is considered ethical and valuable to both the buyer and the seller. By measuring the response of people to various persuasion principles, companies can build a "persuasion profile" at an individual level, which allows them to understand a potential buyer in ways that are remarkably portable across online and in-person behavior.

Arjan Haring, vice president of marketing at Science Rockstars in Amsterdam, which uses Cialdini's six principles of persuasion as the basis for building and measuring persuasion profiles, told us: "Some people are persuaded by scarcity, and if they are persuaded by scarcity in shopping at a book store, for example, then they are more likely to be persuaded by scarcity when they book a flight online, and so on across categories. It's a stable personality trait."

While Cialdini's six principles stem from research based on in-person sales, phone solicitations, and traditional marketing, Science Rockstars has taken these principles into the digital world by building data-driven persuasion profiles that can be applied online but also in real time. This has radical implications for marketing to Gen Z. While persuasion profiling is operating purely online as of this writing, there are early trials being run in retail stores; these tests are feeding persuasion profile information to in-store salespeople, so they are aware of how repeat customers react and can reduce the friction of in-person selling.

For example, RetailNext—a provider of Big Data solutions to retailers such as Bloomingdale's, Brookstone, and Family Dollar—is measuring the behavior of more than eight hundred million shoppers per year by collecting data from more than sixty-five thousand sensors (Wi-Fi, video cameras, point-of-sale systems, Bluetooth, and other sources). **Amazingly, a single shopping trip will generate an average of ten thousand data points, which means that RetailNext now analyzes eight trillion data points annually.**

According to George Shaw, vice president of R&D at RetailNext:

Retailers today have massive appetite for fact-based insights about the physical shopping world. We work with 120 brands and retailers to improve staffing, store layouts, fixtures, or marketing campaigns, based on what they learn about human behavior in their stores. We're not looking at traffic counting or sales data alone—it's the collection, correlation and analysis of so many disparate data sources that makes RetailNext powerful.[2]

Gen Z is starting to expect this sort of intimate understanding of their behaviors and the resulting precision, which allows retailers to provide them with an experience that aligns with their needs, values, and behaviors. We know at this point you're likely thinking, "Wait, that's just creepy! Why would I want you to know how to best persuade me?" This is where we need to look at the issue of influence in a new way, getting past the manipulative connotation it has had in the past.

Imagine you are buying a new kitchen appliance; let's say it's a refrigerator. You may be online or in an actual store. In either case, it's easy for retailers to apply just a few of Cialdini's persuasion principles and make the experience more meaningful to you. Knowing that you are most comfortable buying what your most active social network friends have also bought (liking); that you have a hard time deciding on major purchases and do so mostly when a sale is ending or a model is being discontinued (scarcity); and that you have shown an interest in manufacturers that are giving back to your local community (reciprocity) allows the retailer to guide you to a decision that is aligned with your values and that you feel good about.

Again, we can anticipate your concerns: "I don't want retailers to know any of that about me!" But your credit card company already knows. Data about your buying habits exists. It's not that your behavior isn't being captured; it is, to the tune of ten thousand data points per shopping experience. What does not exist is the connectivity to make sense of it. We know it sounds Orwellian to have behaviors tracked in this way, but the goal is not to convince you that you need a refrigerator—you've already made that decision—rather, it's to find which one best fits the pattern of behavior you've already exhibited.

If you're part of Gen Z, you will look to the retailers that can do this for you as those that best understand your needs and interests, and can be most trusted. In fact, we'd go so far as to say that you will be distrustful of retailers who are too lazy or primitive to "get" you, just as you'd be a bit upset if a local merchant you do business with regularly forgot your name or the color of your house after you'd just purchased twenty gallons of colonial white paint from him.

Influence-driven digital marketing is focused entirely on what is termed evidence-based marketing and on understanding which data have predictive value over time. This is very different from broadcasting the same TV ad to a mass audience or A/B testing—comparing one advertisement to another—to see which ad produces better results. This mass approach often chases broad-based trends that have short lifetimes and demographics that put people into buckets rather than thinking of them as individuals.

Think about it in this way. If you had the option, who would you rather go to when you buy something—a person who has known you for years and understands your values, likes, and dislikes and wants to keep you as a customer by getting to know you better or a stranger who is just trying to sell you what he has? Pretty easy answer, right? That's exactly what we're trying to get across.

We don't necessarily fear marketers understanding our behaviors; what we fear is being misunderstood by technology. However, the fear of technology is something Gen Zers don't bring to this discussion, because their lives have always been made transparent by technology.

While this focus on evidence-based marketing may seem new, in many ways it is a return to the initial discipline of direct marketing (sending postcards and targeted mailings to prospective customers), which was pioneered by Claude Hopkins. In the 1920s he wrote, "The time has come when advertising in some hands has reached the status of a science," and, in a nod to hyper-personalized, influence-driven marketing, "We must get down to individuals. We must treat people in advertising as we treat them in person." This concept is nearly one hundred years old. It's just that now we have the technology to make it practical.

By the way, it's important to note that the traits found in persuasion profiles have nothing to do with age, showing again that we are breaking generations as a workable model. As Science Rockstars' Arjan Haring told us of his work with persuasion profiling, "Looking at age—just like looking at your postal code—doesn't have much predictive value." So far, Haring has found no sign that the response to any of the six persuasion principles is tied to any particular generation. As Cialdini proposes, these are just basic human responses to influence cues. By contrast, while location may be useful in targeting mailings to the appropriate area, and knowing the income of a household may indicate the types of goods or services worth offering, data about age does not, in and of itself, indicate whether the recipient will respond in any particular way to a specific marketing or sales message, while their behavioral response to the six principles of persuasion that Cialdini indicate, are age independent.

Influence-based marketing and marketing automation is still in its embryonic stage, and marketers have much to learn about how various forces interact with individual consumers. Haring's recommendation, if you are interested in pursuing this in your own marketing, is to focus on the persuasion principles of social proof, authority, and scarcity. These are the most easily implemented and clearly understood, making them pragmatic steps toward leveraging influence for your own purposes. However you approach persuasion profiling, it is just the tip of the influence pyramid.

POEM, AN ODE TO MARKETING

Our next stop in understanding the evolution of influence is POEM. It's not an ode to the power of marketing but more like a nod to the Gen Z marketer's understanding of how to influence her prospective or existing customers. POEM stands for Paid, Owned, and Earned Media.

Paid Media

Outside of the sort of viral influence we've started to see on the web through YouTube, Twitter, and other such media, influence has been bought and paid for by affluent people and companies, creating what is, not surprisingly, called "paid media." It's what most of us know as TV and radio commercials, newspaper and magazine ads, billboards, and banner ads.

During the last two hundred years of mass media, you had to pay for influence if you wanted to grow your company in any serious way. Outside of newspapers, magazines, TV, and radio there simply were no options that could provide large-scale reach for a company looking to influence the marketplace. Companies such as Coke, Nike, Pepsi, IBM, Anheuser-Busch, Procter & Gamble, and myriad other brands, have had a tremendous advantage in the market because they have been long-term players and have enormous advertising budgets. **In fact, P&G.'s v. U.S. ad budget of $3 billion is greater than the GDP of twenty-nine countries, and its global budget of $9 billion tops the GDP of fifty countries.**[3] By the way, about 35 percent of the company's U.S. budget is spent on digital marketing, according to P&G . As a result of this incredible bombardment of advertising, these brands are known around the world. So much so that a study conducted by the Amsterdam School of Communications Research showed that even two-year-olds could typically identify eight out of twelve major global brands.[4]

That sort of recognition puts brands in a position that any new company would love to have but clearly can't afford to pay for by going head to head with the advertising spend of mega brands. You would think that, after decades of being imprinted on our collective psyche, a brand such as Coca-Cola could sustain itself without the need for paid advertising. Does the money really need to be spent? Any advertising executive worth her Madison Avenue address would say, "Of course! Otherwise, your competitors will step in and quickly eclipse your brand."

The high priests of advertising, Al Ries and Jack Trout, wrote the gospel on modern advertising with their 1981 book, *Positioning.* Their constant refrain was that repetition of the tagline was the best weapon in the influencer's arsenal, and it clearly remains one of the most significant sources of advertising spent for traditional businesses.

However, you can't "own" somebody's mind, despite Ries and Trout's claims to the contrary. Massive advertising has simply been the best and only means available until recently. In the absence of anything better, it became the default method for every company that wanted to build a brand. Recognizing this simultaneous power and weakness of paid media is key to understanding the switch from affluence to influence that is now under way.

If you still think the only way to keep your brand, goods, or services in people's heads is to pay to put it there, your business is in more trouble than you might realize. The problem with influence from paid media, whether it be billboard ads, press releases, TV ads, or the like, is twofold. The first is that once you start using paid media it is extraordinarily difficult to stop without creating the impression your brand is fading. Research conducted by Ad-ology during the recession of 2009 uncovered that 48 percent of adults in the United States see a reduction in advertising as a signal that a business is struggling.

Our own research surfaced a completely new phenomenon as well. **In the under-thirty-two demographic, the success of a brand that promotes itself primarily through, or with significant assistance from, social media—think of the viral effect of YouTube videos—was ranked twenty-four percent higher in terms of its overall value.**

We're not saying paid media is going away. The lesson is that if you want to reach Gen Z you have to meet them on their terms, creating value that aligns with their belief that the community decides what's important and true rather than an ad agency. We will revisit this later in the chapter when we look at how Free the Children focuses on genuine conversations and meaningful media.

One of the best examples of meeting customers on their own terms, and the influence it unleashes, is Dove's Campaign for Beauty. Rolled out in 2004, the campaign started what has become a beauty and fashion revolution by making the point that media manipulates us (especially women) to aspire to images of beauty that are unattainable and unhealthy. Now, let's be clear, the campaign was spearheaded by Ogilvy & Mather's very expensive creative team, so this was paid media. However, some of its most successful ads were distributed only through social media and were done on a budget small enough to be a rounding error in the mega brand ad industry.

One of the most powerful pieces of the campaign was a YouTube video called "Evolution of Beauty," which showed a young woman transformed through layers of makeup, lighting, and Photoshop into a billboard model. The YouTube video fades to the end with the simple white on black text, "No wonder our perception of beauty is distorted." The video created a firestorm of attention on YouTube and in all forms of broadcast and print media, with well over three hundred million views across all channels. Yet the entire budget for the video was $135,000 dollars. Just to put that into perspective, $135,000 wouldn't buy you four seconds of a Super Bowl ad, and that's not taking in account production costs. By its own estimates, Unilever, which owns the Dove brand, generated the equivalent of $150 million dollars of paid advertising. But what it did most effectively was connect with an audience by showing that the company cared about its customers' values and challenges.

Another problem, and this is also key for Gen Z, is that paid media is "interruptive." For example, commercials that interrupt your favorite show for eighteen to twenty minutes out of every sixty, pop-up ads that prevent you from reading what's behind them, and "interstitial" ads—pages that interrupt the normal hyperlinking that advances you from one page to another by inserting an ad page you have to view before continuing—are the kiss of death for a company trying to reach Gen Z.

But here's the kicker. If you present an ad that fits the persuasion profile of the viewer—in other words, it's personalized and actually meaningful to them—you suddenly have gone from advertising to influencing; the holy grail of earned media. But, before we move on to earned media there is an interim step we need to talk about: owned media.

Owned Media

With owned media, you are not simply repeating taglines, jingles, or the same advertisement and message over and over. Instead, you are creating what is essentially a community-owned yet company-branded experience, website, social media campaign, mobile app, or retail store. Apple's retail store, for example, with its brand-controlled experience yet customer-focused use of space and high employee-to-floor-space ratio, is an extreme example of owned media.

However, owning the real estate doesn't necessarily mean you're creating an experience. When Apple opened its first store in 2001 at Tyson's Corner, Virginia, it was lambasted by press as a poor use of Apple's resources—but Steve Jobs understood the value of creating an immersive customer experience that reinforced the cultlike community of Apple owners. Today, Apple has more than 400 stores worldwide, 250 of which are in the U.S., and it is increasing its number of stores by 10 percent yearly. Compare that with Sony, which opened its first retail store in 2004 and has announced it is closing twenty of its thirty-one remaining U.S. stores.

The same principle of owned media exists in the online world, where businesses create branded experiences. For example, Doritos has a dedicated Facebook page and a microsite to promote its "Bold Mission," which solicits ideas for Super Bowl commercials. The company sends participating customers on "missions" to demonstrate their dedication to the brand. There's also Tiffany & Co.'s "What Makes Love True" site, which was built to allow customers to share their engagement and wedding stories alongside other Tiffany customers' experiences.

However, owned media and the experiences built around them tend to be quite expensive to start and maintain. They are typically supplemented by high-cost and high-effort campaigns using paid media, not unlike our earlier example of Dove's Campaign for Beauty. In addition, owned media efforts are often targeted at very specific demographics, including age segments. This means these campaigns tend to not scale well across age groups, making it that much more expensive to expand across generations. Exceptions to this rule are rare, but they are important examples to understand.

Apple and IKEA stores, for instance, are among the best at crossing wide demographic boundaries. Step into any Apple Store and you will likely find people between the ages of four and eighty similarly engaged. This is the ultimate expression of the Gen Z Effect, which draws generations together through the simplicity of technology.

You've probably heard people quip that that the sense one gets from this sort of shared community experience is cultlike. That sounds cute, but there is something more to being an Apple user than owning the technology; Apple users have a sense of belonging to a group with aligned interests. And that's why our final category, earned media, is so important to Gen Z.

Earned Media

The high point on the rising tide of influence for Gen Z is "earned media"— the online equivalent of people talking about you at the water cooler or around town. If you can (and we believe you most definitely can) tap the power of earned media, your dependence on paid or owned media to buy mindshare is radically altered. **You know you have "street cred" when you are no longer forced to buy attention.** This sort of respect from the marketplace creates a demand that brings you more influence through which you can grow and expand, based on the trust you have earned with your customers and fans.

Earlier generations did not have the ability to form communities and to influence the behaviors of society in the way Gen Z will. Stephanie Fischer, president and CEO of the Global Retail Marketing Association, put it well when she told us, "Meaning is the new money. These kids care about the DNA of your organization, you really have to be able to do things that are meaningful to them. They influence each other more than any generation out there because they're always connected. If you're a businessperson and you're having a very meaningful relationship with this generation, they're going to be your best brand advocate. They'll be your best marketers."

We would add that, conversely, if you don't do well by them, they could also be your worst nightmare. Previous generations had the option to demonstrate against or to boycott a product or company—even a government—but only if they could effectively enlist the media in their cause. Gen Z doesn't need to win over the media gatekeepers; they have the ability to wreak havoc on companies and even governments through the influence they wield as a hyperconnected community.

One of the greatest success stories we've seen in this area of hyperconnected community comes from the nonprofit Free the Children, a global organization whose mission is to create a world where all young people are free to achieve their fullest potential as agents of change. In just under two decades Free the Children has had an enormous global impact, with 2.3 million youth members between the ages of twelve and eighteen in forty-five countries. The organization has built 650 schools and schoolrooms, delivered more than $16 million worth of medical supplies, and provided one million people with clean water, health care, and sanitation, all without spending a single penny on paid marketing.

The story behind the organization is the stuff Gen Z is made of, and as inspiring as its achievements are, we'd guess that you've never heard of the organization. Craig Kielburger started Free the Children in 1995 when he was just twelve years old. As Craig tells the story, one morning he was flipping through the *Toronto Star* in search of the comics when he came across an article that caught his eye. It was about a courageous boy his age named Iqbal Masih who had been born in South Asia and sold into slavery at the age of four. For the next six years Iqbal was chained to a carpet-weaving loom. After being freed, he captured the world's attention by speaking out for children's rights. Iqbal's actions also caught the attention of those who profited from debt slave labor and who wished to silence him. At twelve, Iqbal lost his life defending the rights of children.

Kielburger was so moved by Iqbal's story that he gathered together a small group of seventh-grade classmates, including his brother Marc, and Free the Children was born. We talked to Marc Kielburger about some of the dramatic shifts he is seeing in Gen Z through the unique lens of what has become one of the most influential Gen Z nonprofits in the world.

Kids are more communal than ever but their community is not local anymore; it's global, and they have a global outlook, a global perspective. **The interesting thing that we find in our interaction and engagement with young people is that community to them is probably the single most important piece of their identity.** It's much more important and significant than with previous generations; to them community is a sense of belonging, purpose, meaning, and acceptance—and their community, of course, is very much online. Young people will most support the communities they've decided to belong to. It's their decision as opposed to it being thrust upon them.

When you stop to think about the degree of connectedness that Gen Z has been born into, it makes perfect sense that community would be such a central part of their lives. It's not that community in some form has not always been important. The difference with Gen Z, however, is that the community is a conscious choice that comes from within rather than something that is imposed from the outside, and they are drawing from a much larger, global set of communities. For those born into Gen Z, though, a far more transparent and connected culture has been their default condition, making the issue of "conscious" choice debatable, at least during their childhood.

Marc Kielburger also echoed the themes of influence that we've described as percolating up from younger members of Gen Z.

> First, kids today feel more empowered than any other generation. They know that they don't have to wait until they're eighteen to vote to have an impact. They know that they can have impact now.
>
> Second, it's no longer about trying to simply market to kids. It's about starting a conversation with them to make yourself part of their community, whereby that young person can actually have a conversation about the brand or the values of the brand.
>
> Third, is the influence that they have with their parents. The reason this is relevant is that they're more tech savvy, they're more knowledgeable, they're more likely to speak up, they're more empowered.

He is passionate about the fact that Gen Z kids have much more influence with their parents than generations before them ever had, and he sees this as critical for companies to understand, whatever age they are trying to influence.

> These kids are on a level playing field with their parents because they have access to information, and they have access to technology, and they know technology better than their parents do. I feel these parents actually constantly defer to their kids because the parents don't have the same level of understanding as their kids probably do.
>
> So, if I were a car company assessing the impact of advertising on my consumer, I would be marketing to teenage girls to push their parents to

buy a hybrid. I wouldn't be marketing to their parents. The impact of a teenage girl saying, "Mom and Dad, don't you care about the world I'm going to inherit?" is going to be much more significant than just about anything else I could do.

We asked Kielburger to help us see the issue of loyalty through the eyes of the kids he works with, and he talked about one of the most significant aspects of developing trusted relationships with Gen Z.

> **The whole concept of traditional loyalty is dead, and what we need to do is specifically focus on "How do we build mutual understanding within the goals of this generation?"**
>
> The reason is that if brands aren't aligning in a genuine way—and I can't stress the word "genuine" enough—with causes, or issues, or campaigns, or things that they care about, or values in the community, young people will go to those brands that are.
>
> We say to our young people [Free the Children volunteers and members] all the time that, "You vote every single day with your wallets, not your ballots," and they get that. I don't think a lot of brands get it.
>
> We have the largest Facebook cause in the world now. The reason being that we recognize the power of young people to have genuine conversations with each other.

This sort of indirect metric of influence works in others areas as well. For example, in the venture philanthropy space we've worked with many large funds, especially in health care, that similarly measure the impact of their investments in terms of ultimate cures. If you're seeking to cure a particular type of cancer, or Alzheimer's, or multiple sclerosis, it's exceptionally hard to find intermediate points of influence for your investment. Either you create a therapy that works or you don't. There is no return on investment for research that does not create long-term tangible results.

However, the ability to measure intermediate results is a critical part of the way for-profit businesses determine the effectiveness of their influence through marketing. This ability to measure and use the resulting "Internet of influence" has only surfaced in the last twenty-five years with the rise of the web and social apps, despite the Internet having existed for more than forty-five years. Measurement of influence has become one of the principle drivers in the shift from affluence to influence, as it provides mechanisms for precisely identifying how influential all points on that spectrum really are.

MEASURING INFLUENCE

At its core, the shift to earned influence has come about because of the way in which we can now track influence as it spreads across a population. Perhaps the best-known example of a company whose business model is built on measuring commercial influence is Google, quantifiably one of the most-recognized brands in the world, just behind Apple, and in front of Coca-Cola.[5]

Despite Google's early home page being as stripped down as a web page could possibly be—a design that remains to this day—it was neither what you searched for nor the text Google had "spidered" from millions of websites that made its search results better than the competitors of the time, including Yahoo, Lycos, Excite, AltaVista, and a host of others (mostly long since dead). An utterly simple and straightforward technique, Google's PageRank, was the linchpin of the revolution in the way we measure influence. PageRank measures the influence of any given site or page and brings the "best" results to the top of the search results page. It was a unique approach that was impossible to accomplish until the web came into existence.

By connecting the dots (the hyperlinks between sites and pages) from the influencers who wrote content that best described their ideas and opinions, and businesses, goods or services, to the people searching for them, Google inadvertently flipped the affluence pyramid upside down by exposing previously unseen realms of influence. This flip empowered those who were either naturally gifted or who had learned the skill of creating content that could reach into people's heads and touch their innermost desires and cravings and jump in front of their more affluent competitors who are used to the high cost, low return of traditional paid advertising.

In fact, in the early days of Google, the company did not even allow paid advertising on its site, a nod to the recognition that affluence was no longer as powerful as it had been and that it could corrupt Google's core mission of organizing the world's information. Clearly, Google has since changed its stance on paid ads, which now account for 97 percent of its nearly $40 billion of annual revenue.

However, even Google's paid advertising model, AdWords, explicitly recognizes influential ads. The "best" ads (those that are clicked most often) cost less than those not clicked as frequently. To be number one on a list of competing AdWords costs less on a per-click basis than those appearing beneath your ad, which may come as a surprise to some. The reason is that the more effective your ad—the more often it gets clicked on—the more relevant you are to the reader. Google acknowledges that by increasing your ranking independently of what you are willing to pay as an advertiser. Unlike earlier paid advertising models from Overture.com and Yahoo, as well as most other competitive bidding models, which ranked the order of ads purely based on who was willing to pay the most to be on top, AdWords explicitly rewards those who understand that the ads which influence people to take the next action are the ones that benefit both advertiser and searcher.

Google is a prime example of the way the spectrum from paid to earned media is not a zero-sum game, where the two extremes are in competition. In traditional media, advertising and editorial ran side by side and reinforced each other, and the same is true of search results in Google. The difference, and it's a big one, is that anyone can write, record, speak, or perform whatever they want to be indexed by Google, earning their right to be found based on the value of the content rather than the size of the budget.[6]

Google's success in this area is in large part due to the fact that you, as a marketer, can easily measure the influence of paid advertising by tracking the path a customer takes from an online ad, which you place with Google, right through to the sale of a product. It's why Amazon spends more than $55 million per year on Google's AdWords.[7] It's also why State Farm plunks down $43 each time you click on a State Farm ad, which shows up because you searched for the term "self-employed health insurance." By the way, that $43 dollar price point is not set by Google, but instead established by a bidding mechanism that pits advertisers against one another to determine the price based on demand for the term. **The bidding model has turned paid media on** its head, since it's not the media owner who sets the value of advertising but the advertisers.

While traditional media, such as TV, radio, magazines, and newspapers will still claim that ratings, based on the number of viewers or subscribers, is a proxy for market demand and reach, it is far more primitive than the direct series of links between an online ad and a sale. All of this has put enormous pressure on large companies such as Procter & Gamble to become more precise in the way they track value and return on their traditional investment of advertising dollars.

To be clear, it's not that companies don't already do that by tracking advertising with sophisticated marketing mix models that look at every nuance of their many marketing campaigns and how they relate to product sales. The difference between these empirical measurement methods of the past—however sophisticated the science involved—and the behavioral influence models we are moving to is like the difference between bowling with earplugs in and the lights off and reviewing your performance later on infrared video versus turning the lights on to see and hear the immediate result of your actions.

You are probably realizing by now that the power switch we mentioned at the outset of this chapter is not just a switch from paid to earned or from off-line to online advertising. Instead, it is a switch from the darkness that used to cloak influence to the full light of day, which exposes the workings of influence.

An example of this sort of transparency is a relatively new start-up Upworthy, a site self described as "viral with a purpose." Upworthy, launched in March 2012, shows just how fast a company can go from zero unique visitors to, as of this writing, a peak of nearly eighty-eight million monthly unique visitors in November 2013.[8] The site's purpose is curating and promoting material oriented toward social good.

The growth of Upworthy is not accidental. Its three cofounders are Eli Pariser of MoveOn (a progressive social movement site), Peter Koechley (former managing editor of the long-lived satirical news site, *The Onion*), and Chris Hughes (one of the cofounders of Facebook and, perhaps most famously, the coordinator of online organizing for Barack Obama's 2008 presidential campaign, the first true social media–powered campaign of its kind). Simply put, these fellows know the power of online crowds well, and they know how to influence them to click, watch, and share. They know who they're looking for, how to find them, how to motivate them, and how to get them to vote on videos—a surprisingly difficult task given how infrequently voting happens. They know that the power of social media as a way to tap social proof and liking has a significant impact on building an "Upworthy" site.

Upworthy drives traffic by posting attention-catching headlines such as "You'll never believe how (fill in any topic)" or "This woman did (something) and you won't believe what happened next" with curated content—images and videos they did not create, and are simply referencing or highlighting. It's a relatively simple concept that wouldn't seem to be all that powerful, and yet the growth and impact are undeniable.

While the long-term success of Upworthy has yet to be determined, its rise from an idea to one of the forty most visited sites on the web in less than two years demonstrates the founders' deep understanding of human behavior. As a result, Upworthy has become, as of this book's writing, the fastest-growing media site *ever* on the web.

THE FUTURE IS FEEDBACK

Organizations need to engage Gen Zers instead of merely employing them, providing them with a very different type of mechanism for feedback than that used for earlier generations. The increase in the rate of change has made the importance of feedback central to success.

The dreaded employee performance review—one of the most loathed and despised aspects of corporate life for the vast majority of us—is perhaps one of the greatest anachronisms of the employer–employee relationship, no matter how we try to dress it up. In light of the constant learning that Gen Z expects, it's time to rethink annual reviews. A hint at what we're about to discuss: improving the performance review process involves many of the mechanics of gamification—which we discussed in chapter 4, "Slingshotting"—as a way to take micro-measurements of the working relationships among employees, managers, and a far wider network of participants.

Jeetu Patel, General Manager and Chief Executive of Syncplicity, a Silicon

Valley company owned by EMC, experienced hyper-growth in 2013, and has the unenviable challenge of building an organization with the brightest minds in an industry and location where competition for the best talent is fierce. He explained to us that working with Gen Z means changing the way we look at some basic aspects of retention. Foremost among these is the classic annual review. He gave us an example of what not to do if you want to hold onto Gen Z. Dan Pink was among those who inspired his thinking.

> At a fundamental level, the way that large companies operate and the feedback that they give people is typically far from instantaneous. **These kids are used to consistent and constant feedback almost in real time. If they don't get the feedback, they think there's something fundamentally broken in the model.**
>
> So let's say we hire someone (from Gen Z), call her Toni, and we put Toni in a feedback deprivation chamber—aka the annual performance review. Here the manager gives Toni feedback referring to an activity that occurred nine months prior, to offer up ideas on what Toni could've done better. Toni's immediate instinct is to wonder why her manager didn't just give her the feedback in the moment.
>
> It's very much like Hollywood, where the ratings of your movie in the first few days determine whether your product is successful or not, rather than waiting for the first year to see whether or not your product has revenues.
>
> This behavior, ironically enough, is starting to move upstream to previous generations, causing us to have to adopt a very different model for how we provide feedback and recognize people.

The phenomenon that Patel is describing is not limited to his experiences at Syncplicity and, as he's found, it's not just for those who are Gen Z by birth. It turns out that better and more frequent professional feedback is welcome whatever the employee's age—we simply didn't have a measurably useful model to provide that for knowledge workers on a daily or weekly basis until recently. If you worked in a factory or production environment you would typically have metrics that provided real-time feedback about quality, volume, throughput, or other such measurable aspects of your job. As a knowledge worker you took for granted that such metrics simply made no sense. Instead you relied on periodic reviews of your performance that were often based on a large dose of retrospective analysis. Even if you were in a sales or direct billable role there was often much more that went into your performance feedback than just hard numbers, such as relationship building, team work, managing others, attitude, and professional growth. We've just taken for granted that these things could not be measured in anything other than a subjective yearly or semi-annual performance review. That's not the way Gen Z wants to work. They have been raised with an expectation of instant feedback in the way they game and socialize. If your Facebook post gets zero likes there is nothing subjective about the fact that it's a lousy post.

We caught up with Daniel Debow, a senior vice president at Work.com—formerly known as Rypple, a company he cofounded in 2008 and which was acquired by Salesforce.com in 2011. Work.com provides just this sort of ongoing real-time feedback for knowledge workers.

> We started Rypple by focusing on what non-HR people needed to do every day to manage and coach their teams on a regular basis, and how we could make that more efficient and easier for them in much smaller time commitments than the once-a-year, annual performance review process.
>
> The mind-set that we've taken is that we trust people and that people want feedback. They want to get coached. They want to develop. They want to learn. Traditional annual performance reviews are often feared by employees and dreaded by managers, which makes them much less useful than they could be, and there had to be a better way.
>
> The analogy I use is that it is like going to the dentist. If you go to the dentist once a year and you never floss or brush, it's not a very fun experience. You dread doing it. That was the performance review. If you floss and brush all the time, you're doing regular maintenance, and at the checkup it turns out you're in great shape—it's the same idea.

Work.com uses many of the mechanics of gamification, such as progress indicators toward a goal, badges that show that a certain level of experience, expertise, or skill has been attained. The system also uses social commentary and feedback similar to what you see on Facebook or LinkedIn, but in this case colleagues and managers provide public feedback on a job well done or encourage people toward meeting their publicly stated goals.

It is probably no surprise that technology start-ups were some of Rypple's earliest customers, but it has since moved well beyond tech. Debow says:

> Facebook became a big customer and an early partner in developing the products, as well as Mozilla and LinkedIn. They were asking, "How do we manage the workforce of tomorrow? Because they're here today. They're in our offices now."
>
> We saw Silicon Valley was a kind of cultural canary in a coal mine, because what happened there has spread out into society five years later. Now thousands of companies are using our approach, not just companies in the Valley.
>
> More importantly, much more traditional, mainstream companies like The Home Depot and 1-800-Flowers have come to the point where this just seems like it's the next step in how they manage and engage their employees.

Work.com's model is really about behavior management, not technology. If you're interested in better performance from Gen Z, Debow suggests redefining the role of managers. While middle management, in particular, is often seen as part of the problem in traditional, hierarchical businesses, these managers can be the ones who lead and ensure that the changes your business wants to put in place are done on a regular basis. According to Debow:

> As a company, to get rapid adoption of new behaviors, you have to say, "We need our managers to engage in these behaviors. We need those behaviors to happen repeatedly, consistently, and scalably through the organization. We need people to be onboarded effectively. We need people to consistently have a person to speak to them and talk to them about what's going on in their life, their career, and their job. We need people to have goals that are aligned with what the organization wants, but also what they want.

Those are behaviors that people engage in and they're simple behaviors. When I say simple behaviors, I mean very simple things like "We want people to express gratitude when other people do a good job," which is validated and scientifically proven to reinforce the behaviors that companies are looking for. "We want sales managers to coach people rather than crush them," which is also proven by behavioral data analysis to result in a better sales organization.

By the way, as Debow confirmed, desire to be coached isn't limited to younger people. **A core premise of the Gen Z Effect is that, while you can be born into Gen Z, you can also choose to be Gen Z by your attitude and behaviors because, at the end of the day, this is really the new face of human behavior.**

Debow says:

Initially, there's no question that younger people understood us and, generally, older people were skeptical. Now, six years later, the level of skepticism is much lower, which is just the nature of how people adopt innovation. We have hundreds of pragmatic proof points from companies in almost every industry that are using our approach and seeing results like sales volume going up because of better and more frequent coaching of the sales team.

Work.com is not the only one seeing a disconnect in the way companies have traditionally handled employee–manager feedback. We also spoke with Survey Analytics president Vivek Bhaskaran, who launched a new offering centered on employee feedback, called FlashLet, in early 2014. Survey Analytics is a cloud-based company that has a long history in providing online survey capabilities for a variety of purposes, but this is its first "purpose-built" application designed to address the problem of getting useful employee feedback.

Bhaskaran has a philosophy about feedback similar to Debow's: feedback needs to be an ongoing process. He also has taken a novel approach to employee satisfaction ratings by creating a system that takes the pulse of an organization on a regular basis:

There is a bit of a conundrum in feedback. We are pushing toward increasing the frequency of feedback, but frequency is usually inversely proportional to the depth. You can't really ask somebody to spend twenty minutes every week providing feedback. They'll always find reasons to avoid it. Alternatively, you can ask them to invest twenty minutes of time every quarter, or maybe every six months, but that gives you old data.

We asked Bhaskaran about the very popular 360-degree evaluations, where peers all fill out detailed feedback surveys on one another in order to provide a comprehensive view of how each employee is perceived by others. These have been a standard for decades in many organizations. He told us, "People no longer want 360-degree evaluations. Everyone we've talked to tells us they are close to useless in such fast-moving organizations; people turn over too often; the dynamics of their problems change week to week."

So, what solution has Bhaskaran come up with?

I believe you can ask somebody to spend one minute each week to click on one link. Just like they would to do a "like" on Facebook. That's a relatively innocuous thing to do, but you'd be amazed at how much data you can get out of that over time. You're not getting a lot of deep data but you do get broad data that can be very useful and is close to real time.

So what I'm suggesting is that you do a weekly "pulse" survey. It's almost like going to a clinic if you're not feeling well. They always do certain things no matter what your condition. One is to take your temperature. Temperature alone isn't going to tell much, other than the fact that there's something going on with your immune system or your body's ability to regulate itself. It's a symptom, an indicator. That's what weekly pulse surveys do; they point to a problem. It has to be easy, quick, and anybody should be able to do it.

Employee engagement has to be a top priority, especially with Gen Z. If your employees are not engaged—don't feel engaged—then it doesn't really matter how smart they are.

If you assume that employee engagement is going to make or break the business, then the first thing you need to do is to somehow create a baseline for measurement of employee engagement and satisfaction.

Ask Gen Z how the last year was and you might as well be asking them to drive by looking in the rearview mirror. They want instant feedback, and I'd claim they need it in order to perform in a world where managing in real time is the only way to successfully respond to threats and opportunities.

At Google, the feedback process takes a very specific route via what the company calls upward feedback surveys (UFSs), which are filled out by employees to measure their managers. Those surveys are seen by the manager's manager as a way to collect actionable feedback that flows both up and down the company's relatively flat structure. This began as "Project Oxygen," which was intended to answer the question, "Do managers matter?"

The surveys address twelve to eighteen different facets (shown in table 5-1), including whether managers treat their employees with respect, give them clear goals, share information with them, and so on.

Table 5-1: The Project Oxygen Eight Behaviors for Great Managers[9]

A good manager...
1. Is a good coach
2. Empowers the team and does not micromanage
3. Expresses interest/concern for team members' success and personal well-being
4. Is productive and results-oriented
5. Is a good communicator—listens and shares information
6. Helps with career development
7. Has a clear vision/strategy for the team
8. Has key technical skills that help him/her advise the team

This sort of feedback demonstrates whether managers are engaged in the process of actively managing their teams. By providing feedback to their managers, associates have an opportunity to influence the organization.

The measures are tracked across the company, and trends are followed over time to gain a broader picture of the quality of Google's people management, including performance profiles of managers themselves. This method measures teams and the company as a whole rather than focusing solely on individual-level employee reviews, which are the only measure of performance done in many organizations. An explicit set of measurements for managers also makes workers' satisfaction with their managers a foundational element of Google's strategy for managing people within the organization. While the raw data itself will not ensure great managers, both the data and the cultural environment that provides improvement-focused feedback—rather than penalty-driven feedback—mean the demise of the "pointy haired boss" syndrome (for *Dilbert* fans), with bosses who are clueless about the negative impacts they have on their teams.

This trend toward measuring management and teams is another example of the pyramid being flipped upside down. Traditional human resources, or HR, is often the "compliance" arm of an organization, tasked with making sure that employees are doing what their bosses told them to do. Gen Z flips this model so that managers are held accountable to their own team and, as warranted and evidenced by feedback, are required to correct their own behaviors.

In traditional hierarchies, people are often pushed into management positions when they have no interest in, natural talent for, or training for the role—the classic outcome of the Peter Principle, which assumes we all rise to the level of our own incompetence. It's another danger of the affluence pyramid, where the only way to progress in your career is to climb the ladder into territory where you may not want to be or are thrust into a role you are not suited for.

Conversely, if you don't learn and adapt in your current job, you may fall victim to a Gen Z variation of the Peter Principle, *according* to Gary Burnison, CEO at Korn/Ferry International:

The Peter Principle, which asserts that employees will continue to get promoted until they reach their level of incompetence, has evolved. Today, employees don't need to get promoted to become incompetent. They will become incompetent in their current jobs if they don't grow, adapt, and evolve. **If you stop growing and learning, your job will** outgrow you. **If you grow and learn faster than your job, employers will always want you.**[10]

BIG CROWDS MEAN BIG DATA

The final step in our journey from affluence to influence has to do with the flood of information that is being created by all of our social interactions. It's what has come to be called Big Data, and it will lay bare Gen Z behaviors in ways we are just beginning to understand.

Big Data is the understanding of behavior and influence "under the hood." For the vast majority of us, Big Data is invisible. But the ads and promotions we see as consumers are often the results of Big Data; for example, ads that target our buying preferences and interests (at least supposedly) show up on web pages we visit based on our behaviors elsewhere on the web. The science that underlies these targeted messages is one of the most important aspects of influence, because it's the basis for how virtually everything we've talked about so far, as it applies to measuring influence, can be used to develop a deep understanding of our behavior.

THE LOWE'S STORY: BEHAVIORAL LIFECYCLES

Kevin Davis is former enterprise business intelligence director at Lowe's Companies, Inc., a Fortune 100 home improvement company founded in 1946 that serves approximately fifteen million customers a week with more than 1,800 stores and 260,000 employees. Davis characterizes the shift toward analyzing data to understand customers' behaviors in this way:

> When you look at just the purchase data itself and you see movement, what you see is people buying items at Thanksgiving simply because it's Thanksgiving, or you see increases in purchases based upon some kind of flyer; you really just see the after effect.
>
> But when you start looking at behavioral data, especially when you get information that's not purchase related, such as trip data about whether

a customer is in the store or online, or where they are in their life stages or a purchase cycle, it paints a whole different picture."

Making sense of the behavioral data sources we've been capturing in recent years has been a monumental challenge, with companies focusing the majority of their consumer behavioral analysis on simply trying to get the data into a coherent structure so that it can be analyzed. As Davis describes it:

> I remember in 2006 at Lowe's, the consumer research team was five people: one statistician, one director, and three analysts. Eighty percent of their job was data collection and data preparation to get data to a point where they could actually tie it together in a meaningful way. To me, Big Data is the technological advance that automates collection and preparation so that we can dig deeper and spend time on analysis versus prepping the data.
>
> So how does that move things forward? Well, now you've got people looking at analytics so you can start interpreting different buying patterns. At Lowe's we actually did an online anthropology of consumer buying.
>
> We studied the behaviors, the discussions, the blogs, the tweets, the Facebook posts, the Jimmie Johnson [a NASCAR driver that Lowe's sponsors] fan clubs; any time that people mentioned "Lowe's" or "Lowe's shopping," we tagged it to figure out the motive of what customers were doing. We called that online anthropology. We took all that information, got together in a room, and asked, "What is this behavioral data telling us?" We realized that in that data there's a certain path to purchase for Lowe's customers, with seven discrete stages.
>
> Why was that important to us? Because we can determine that between stage two and stage three, 33 percent of the people drop out of the buy process because they typically don't have the budget. Well, maybe we can send them some kind of incentive to help them with that specific challenge.
>
> **Behavioral targeting helped [Lowe's] drive more buying, and actually drove a better consumer experience across the board.**

As Lowe's discovered, Big Data is allowing us to understand massive crowds at the individual level, pointing out many breakdowns in our assumptions about how and why people buy.

ANONYMITY LOST IS UNDERSTANDING GAINED

Where is the shift from affluence to influence leading? There is no doubt that it is already leading to a far more transparent society in which our behaviors are mined and analyzed continuously. That is a frightening prospect for many of us who are accustomed to some level of anonymity. It's difficult to see beyond the fear of losing that anonymity, yet there is a deep and often ignored value that comes with the power to exert greater influence: namely, greater ability to challenge the status quo and to participate in establishing global priorities and agendas for all types of organizations, from private corporations to nonprofits to governments.

One of the most surprising, and more positive, ways we see this playing out is in the challenges being made to our existing educational models and institutions. Who teaches? Who learns? When, where, and how? We used to know the answers to these questions, but they are no longer quite as clear as they once were.

Gen Z is rethinking the institutions and even the process of learning. Of the people who are currently engaged in transforming the way we learn, many are unlikely players. Some are accidental participants.

In the next chapter we'll see how "learning everywhere"—in every part of the world—is influencing behavior not merely with respect to schooling but also with regard to marketing, sales, hiring, and retention of talent.

Put It Into Action:
Chapter 5 #a2i #GenZ

Learn from Gen Z Leaders

- Kevin Davis, former director of enterprise business intelligence at Lowe's
- Dr. Robert Cialdini, Regents' professor emeritus of psychology and marketing at Arizona State University
- Arjan Haring, vice president of marketing at Science Rockstars
- George Shaw, vice president of R&D at RetailNext
- A.G. Lafley, chairman, CEO, and president of Procter & Gamble
- Dove's "Campaign for Beauty"
- Apple Store
- IKEA
- The Doritos "Bold Mission" campaign
- Tiffany & Co.'s "What Makes Love True" campaign
- Craig and Marc Kielburger and Free the Children
- Google's PageRank and AdWords
- Upworthy and its cofounders Eli Pariser, Peter Koechley, and Chris Hughes
- Jeetu Patel, president of Syncplicity
- Daniel Debow, senior vice president at Work.com
- Vivek Bhaskaran, president of Survey Analytics
- Google and its upward feedback surveys

Are You Ready for Gen Z?

- Is your business leveraging the concept of an influence pyramid? What will you do to increase the attention you pay to influence over the next five to ten years? How do you see that changing your marketing and sales efforts?
- Does your career currently depend on the affluence pyramid or the influence pyramid? If you shift more towards using the influence pyramid, what would you expect your career to look like in five to ten years?

- Does your business use a mix of POEM (Paid, Owned, and Earned Media)?
- When advertising, do you target the direct buyer or someone in her influence chain?
- Do you measure the Net Promoter Score of your business? If so, what do you do with the information?
- Do you use the six principles of persuasion in your work, business, or life?
- What are you doing to engage Gen Z members of organizations such as Free the Children?
- How does your company handle employee feedback? Do you solicit it annually? Quarterly? Monthly? More frequently? Never?
- Has the frequency and style of feedback changed in recent years, or do you expect it to? Why?
- With employee feedback, does your company focus on employee engagement, business results, or both?
- Do employees rank their managers? What are the results of that ranking?
- Does your company target marketing and sales efforts based on behaviors, demographic data, or both?
- Has your company identified buying patterns or stages of the buying life cycle through the use of Big Data?

Find out whether you're ready for the Gen Z Effect by taking the full assessment at TheGenZEffect.com.

6

Adopting the World As My Classroom

Tomorrow's illiterate will not be the man who can't read; he will be the man who has not learned how to learn.

—FROM AN INTERVIEW OF HERBERT GERJUOY BY ALVIN TOFFLER, AND REFERENCED IN *FUTURE SHOCK*, 1970

In this chapter we dig into the changing nature of education and the progress toward universal availability, a foundational force of the Gen Z Effect. We look first at the evolution of MOOCs as a way to better align education with the way Gen Z works, lives, and plays. That will take us to the nuance of gaming as a behavioral shift in the way Gen Z views both engagement and education. We'll explore a variety of ways in which education is changing, discussing approaches taken by organizations such as Google, with its peer-to-peer learning, and Ubisoft, with its Rocksmith video game, which showcases a radical new approach to learning guitar.

If we had to pick one force that is most responsible for casting the generational mold, it would have to be education. **Education is not only the process through which we gain knowledge about the world, but also the process through which we define our own identity.**

Whether it is at home, in a classroom, or on the job, what we learn is what we use to add value to the world. School, whatever form it takes, is where we form the closest bonds with others, where we find our cliques and our peers; it is where shared experiences define our community and, until now, the generation we belong to. It is the place where we gauge our aptitude and measure our capabilities relative to those of our classmates. In short, education is the single most important factor in separating or uniting us. If you accept that education is that important, then you must also accept that, as the world changes, it is critical to understand just how dramatic the changes to educational approaches can and will be.

From the classroom to the enterprise, changes to education are altering, at the most fundamental level, our understanding of the way generations interact with one another. Over time, these new approaches to learning will create a common set of skills and behaviors that further erode generational differences.

What's amazing is that, while the changes we will talk about are already at work bridging generational gaps, many people, especially those most vested in old forms of learning, are still rabidly against modifications and disruptions that threaten traditional ways of learning.

In a wonderful satire on how traditions hold back the evolution of education, Harold R.W. Benjamin—using the pen name J. Abner Peddiwell—wrote a book in 1939, *The Saber-Tooth Curriculum*, that told a fictional story of

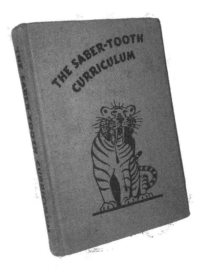

Figure 6-1: The Saber-Tooth Curriculum

J. Abner Peddiwell's 1939 satire on the state of education is just as applicable to most classroom learning today.

how we get stuck in the trap of believing that the education we had is the best method. This sort of academic arrogance surrounds us and creates a fortress of seemingly rational reasons against change.

We forget that our capacity to deliver formal learning on a large scale is a relatively recent phenomenon, which took off in the mid-twentieth century. In fact, the U.S. illiteracy rate in the late nineteenth century was 20 percent, relatively high for a fairly developed country and school system. Even more striking, however, is the fact that only half of all school-age children at the time were enrolled in grade school.[1] The picture had improved only slightly by 1940, when just over half of the U.S. population had completed eighth grade, and a meager 5 percent of adults had completed four years of college. These are startling numbers when you consider how far we've come since that time.

Boomers, unlike their parents—the majority of whom did not complete high school—are well educated, with nearly 70 percent attaining some level of post-secondary-school education and 25 percent graduating with at least a bachelor's degree. Much of this is due to the G.I. Bill of 1944, which laid the foundation for one of the greatest influxes of college enrollees worldwide up until that time. In fact, in 1947, 40 percent of college admissions in the United States were veterans!

Globally, higher education gained increasing prominence on the social agenda in the twentieth century, most notably in the post-WWII era in many of the countries that underwent massive rebuilding after the war. For example, at the turn of the nineteenth to the twentieth century, enrollment in Japanese universities was less than 1 percent of the population aged eighteen to twenty-five; by midcentury enrollment had risen to 4 percent and by the year 2000 to nearly 25 percent.

This same trend can be observed in almost every developing nation during the last hundred years. The result is that today nearly 90 percent of all primary school–age children and over 60 percent of all secondary school–age children globally are enrolled in an education program.[2] While the greatest investment of the twentieth century was in bridging the global education gap in primary and secondary education, the focus of the twenty-first century will be on doing the same with post-secondary education.

Research by UNESCO has shown a remarkable trend in the world's ability to educate. **During the next three decades, the number of graduates will exceed all of the graduates from every educational system since the beginning of recorded history.** This movement towards universal education is foundational to the evolution of the Gen Z Effect because it closes one of the most dramatic gaps that separates generations: their level of education.

Educational disparity creates enormous chasms of understanding between generations, as distinct as the layers of sedimentary rock that define eras in a canyon.

As this gap closes and eventually disappears, it takes with it one of the most profound impediments to our ability to communicate and collaborate based on a common level of education.

YOUNG OR OLD, LEARN OR BECOME OBSOLETE

Globally, education at the college level will continue to provide growing opportunity for skilled workers in developing economies. In many ways, education is the arms race of the twenty-first century. Our ability to move work—without regard to bandwidth, location, or cultural or demographic barriers—will only further this progress.

For Gen Z, every gap—geographic, cultural, and generational—is closing rapidly. Increasingly, it doesn't matter where you are or who you are, and it doesn't matter how old you are either: value is value. If you can participate and produce you're valuable, and this is where universal access to education—free education at all levels from K-12 through university—will have a profound effect on the rapid increase in our ability to innovate and take on some of the world's toughest challenges.

A word of caution here: it's tempting to think of Gen Z as a localized phenomenon that applies only to developed countries that have established institutions for higher education. That's true only if we ignore the trajectory of higher education. Many people, for instance, are surprised to learn that the country with the largest number of colleges and universities is now India, with more than 8,500 government and private universities, 30 percent more than there are in the country with the second-largest number of universities, the United States.

Mind you, we're not saying all of those universities deliver the same quality of education. According to the governor and chancellor of India's state universities, S.C. Jamir, speaking at the eighty-eighth All-India Vice-Chancellors' Conference at KIIT University: "Quality of education in our universities is obviously an area in which our higher education system lags behind. It is quite disheartening that none of the Indian universities finds a place in the top two hundred universities in the world. Expansion without quality improvement serves little purpose. We have to place more emphasis on quality." Even so, the trend and momentum are clear. There is a global agenda to educate on a scale never before attempted.

So, how do we embark on the massive task of educating every human being to her full potential? As with so much of the Gen Z Effect, new modes of learning start with creating new connections outside of the box that has traditionally confined education—the classroom.

The education we are going to talk about is not happening in classrooms, at least not of the sort many of us have become accustomed to. It starts outside the classroom, through myriad alternatives that are reshaping education from the outside in.

ENTER MOOCS

In the fall of 2011, three Stanford University professors opened up Pandora's box when they offered their classes, at no charge, to anyone who wanted to access them online. One of these classes, "An Introduction to Artificial Intelligence," had 160,000 registrants, 23,000 of whom stuck it out and completed the class.

The class, which was taught by Peter Norvig and Sebastian Thrun—both of whom also worked at Google—now ranks as the most widely attended online university class in the world.[3] Thrun went on to cofound Udacity, a major provider of massive open online courses, or MOOCs.

MOOCs are not just online learning. They change the traditional top-down power–knowledge transfer of teacher to student into a very different, hyperconnected model where the lines between teacher and student, and those among students, are less about a hierarchy of power and more about joint learning, exploration, and discussion.

The basic idea behind MOOCs is not as new as it might seem. In the 1920s, well before Thrun and Norvig launched their Stanford class, an alternative to the cost and inconvenience of universities and trade schools was offered through the U.S. mail. These were called "correspondence schools," and they were one of the first alternatives to traditional, formal education. Interestingly, Dick Drew, who secured his first job with 3M as a full-time engineer and is credited with moving 3M from abrasives to adhesives, got his engineering degree through a correspondence program that advertised on the back of a matchbook. At a time when very few people were pursuing a college education, it mattered far less where you got a degree than that you had one. However, as the affluence of developed nations grew, along with the demand for skilled knowledge workers, so did the capacity of universities to produce more graduates.

So what are MOOCs? First, they are "massive," in contrast to traditional education. Getting a handle on the actual number of attendees, courses, and universities is exceptionally difficult because of the groundswell of activity. As of early 2014, more than ten million students had enrolled in MOOCs, which collectively offered 1,200 courses, given by 1,300 instructors from two hundred universities.[4] But when you start adding in the courses being offered outside of universities and traditional learning institutions, such as those from Khan Academy—which we will talk about later in this chapter—the numbers explode by a factor of two to five times.

By the end of 2014, we expect there will be well over one hundred million course visits of both enrolled and exploratory students using MOOCs.[5] Class size is potentially unlimited, although many MOOCs, such as the University of the People (one of the only accredited degree-granting online universities offering MOOCs at no cost) limit class sizes to twenty to thirty people.

One of the reasons MOOCs scale so well is that they often use automated assessments to test students' comprehension. We'll talk more about this in a bit.

"Open" means the courses are not closed off behind the ivy-clad walls of a college or other institution, and they are, theoretically at least, open to anyone. That said, open does not always mean free, particularly if you are seeking credit for completing the course.

Many degree-granting institutions with traditional brick-and-mortar classrooms have invested heavily in MOOCs. The MIT–Harvard joint venture EdX ran up a tab for the two partners of $30 million in start-up costs. Platforms such as Udacity budget about $200,000 per course for a MOOC. So, while the content may be consumed by anyone with an Internet connection, a degree is still going to require anywhere from a few hundred to tens of thousands of dollars.

Most MOOCs are still owned, meaning that their core content is developed and delivered by an instructor. So they are not "open" in the sense of "open source" (freely modifiable and reusable), although there are universities such as MIT, Carnegie Mellon University, Brigham Young University, Notre Dame, Open University, Stanford University, Yale University, and others that have made many, if not all, of their classes freely available. The majority of academic institutions offering MOOCs—unlike the University of the People—are not stating that you have graduated with a degree simply because you've taken their online courses.

For students who cannot afford to attend these institutions, or who live on the other side of the planet, a degree may not be the objective. Whether that is good or bad is an open question and the subject of debate, particularly given the dramatic rise in the cost of higher education over the past two decades.

Bill Gates, Richard Branson, Larry Ellison, Michael Dell, Roman Abramovich, Ted Turner, Ralph Lauren, Steve Jobs, and Mark Zuckerberg—multibillionaires all—did not graduate from college, so clearly the lack of a degree does not spell certain doom in "the real world" of work. And, of course, success after obtaining a degree is not guaranteed either.

The "online" aspect of MOOCs is obvious, and benefits from both hyperconnectivity—socially and technologically—and slingshotting, providing access to learning from anywhere and at any time, as well as the ability to scale in ways that aren't possible given the physical settings that restrict traditional education models.

"Courses" is also self-evident. If the "course" being offered is simply a thirty- to sixty-minute video lecture, it's not really a MOOC; you could just as easily find that content on YouTube. MOOCs are delivered as a series of short classes over time. The best way to think of a course in a MOOC is as a series of lessons that accomplish a specific, verifiable learning objective. The terms "series" and "verifiable" are the key. A MOOC needs to have some mechanism by which learning can be gauged and tested as students progress through the course in order to make sure they have indeed learned something.

CHALLENGING ASSUMPTIONS

We have assumed since the mid-nineteenth century that traditional schooling for children takes thirteen years, from kindergarten through twelfth grade. We have assumed that a bachelor's degree takes four years, that an MBA degree takes two years, that a corporate workshop takes four to five days. But what is all of this based on? Not quite two hundred years have passed since the concept of education for any but the wealthiest of the world's population was first taken seriously. **The fact is that the basis for our current school system is not an immutable law of nature. It's a recent development in human existence.**

What if the technologies we now have allow us to start creating value much earlier, as was the case for Suman Mulumudi, the fifteen-year-old first mentioned in chapter I? What if our careers last well into our twilight years as they continue to change, as is the case for the sixty- and seventy-year-old graduate students we mentioned? What does that do to the structure of our education system?

One thing the scenarios we've been discussing is very likely to do is create learning that is more suited to *just-in-time delivery* rather than to *just-in-case delivery*. *Just-in-case delivery* is how we've become accustomed to being educated. We learn for a brief time and then get ready to apply all of that knowledge for the rest of our lives. By contrast, *just-in-time delivery* flips that concept around: we learn for the rest of our lives so that we can constantly reapply our knowledge. This lifelong approach to learning means that given practical realities learning has to happen in smaller chunks that can be interspersed throughout a lifetime. This chunked approach distinguishes MOOCs from every other type of learning, from the classroom and eLearning to traditional tutoring, as shown in figure 6-2.

MOOCs are not just a new way to deliver knowledge, they are a new way

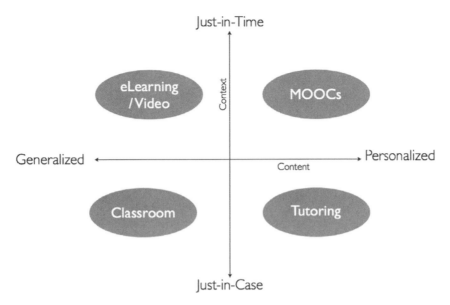

Figure 6-2: MOOCs—Personalized and Just-in-Time Learning

to integrate education into Gen Z's lifelong cycle of learning, unlearning, and relearning.

In the United States, the coursework for an MBA typically takes two years. In many universities outside the U.S., an MBA can be completed in a single year of coursework. Why? Are MBA students in other countries getting ripped off with only half the material? We doubt it.

In recent years we have begun rethinking whether the traditions of education still make sense. **Mass education, like mass manufacturing and mass marketing, is yielding to more personalized, and accelerated, methods of learning.**

Even the role of the instructor in the classroom has changed significantly, as Eric Tsui, a professor at the Hong Kong Polytechnic University, told us: "For decades, if not centuries, traditional education was pretty much delivered by one too many lectures. You can imagine the revolutionary effect of technology; that now we're starting to realize that you don't have to come to the same location to listen to the professor or lecturer. Not only that, but I can learn from my peers as well, not just from the instructor." Professor Tsui is describing a blended form of learning, where each aspect of the learning experience, from classrooms to mobile delivery to global interaction, is tuned to its strengths.

We spoke with Kevin Werbach, an associate professor at Wharton, whom we have known for many years, and who has always been on the cutting edge of new technological innovations in both media and learning. He gave us his description of a MOOC and how he goes about creating one. "One mistake people make is that they assume MOOCs have to be heavily produced for hundreds of thousands of dollars; not true, it's about quality of the content, not the presentation. For example, I've taught a gamification MOOC that has sixty or so video segments. Each video segment is roughly five minutes."

It's important to point out that, while Werbach's approach downplays the cost of producing a MOOC—consider our earlier statement that Udacity budgets $200,000 for each MOOC—every online course is different in terms of its production value and complexity, the value of the instructor's time, and the specifics of testing and certification.

MOOCs essentially start with the best of what has always worked in education: a teacher with a passion for his topic and the ability to communicate to people who want to learn about it. They combine that with the realization that a five- to twenty-minute attention span is not just a result of the popular, but unfounded, belief that "Millennials have ADHD and can't focus," but is simply the way we humans are wired to best absorb knowledge.

We asked Werbach about this phenomenon, as he is plugged into the structure of Wharton, a long-standing traditional university, while also living and teaching online through the Coursera MOOC platform. He said:

Why are small [video] segments needed? Attention.

From the viewer's side, we can talk about generational shifts, and of course you can overgeneralize and oversimplify, but I think that while video isn't replacing textbooks, it is becoming much more prevalent. The students that I have in college now are much more comfortable watching a video segment than reading the equivalent in a textbook. No one has attention to sit and watch someone talking for an hour. They don't have attention to watch me do it in a classroom; we know this from all kinds of studies.

Attention span is not just generational. There are roughly fifty years of research about why lectures are problematic. One of the main reasons is that no one can really stay focused and pay attention for an hour—no matter how compelling the lecture is—and recall the material. **It's not "kids these days and their short attention spans!"**

That being said, Linda Stone coined this term "continuous partial attention" a few years ago, which she presented at my Supernova Conference. There is something about the world today where there are so many interruptions and information sources, and we get used to this constant going back and forth. As a result, I think it is more challenging for today's college students. Traditional classrooms are more out of step with how they live their lives.

Short segments are not simply about retaining the viewer's attention, however, and don't let the idea that they are short fool you into thinking they are less work to produce. The effort that goes into a short but effective course is reminiscent of Blaise Pascal's 1657 statement, "I have only made this letter longer because I have not had the time to make it shorter."

Interestingly, MOOCs are rarely delivered in real time, despite the rising tide of live video-streaming and faster networks. This comes back to the "massive" piece of the MOOC; scale is best handled by allowing students to learn at their own pace, without being tied to a specific schedule.

This is a Gen Z trait that assumes we can "time-shift" whatever it is we want to do, whether that is learning, working, or buying. This assumption was first signaled by the rise of TiVo and other digital video recorders (DVRs), which were just coming to market when the first Gen Zers were born. Time-shifting also sets the stage for an expectation of instant gratification, an expectation set for Gen Zers as children, in part to save the sanity of their parents and grandparents, as time-shifting allowed both young and old to juggle entertainment schedules to meet their own needs. In other words, if you still find yourself waiting for a commercial break to run to the bathroom, you may want to check out that pause button on your remote.

The Accidental Birth of the MOOC

The essentials components of MOOCs were predicted with amazing prescience back in 1962 by one of the twentieth century's foremost thinkers and futurists, Buckminster Fuller, when he said about the future transition from live classroom lectures by professors:

> We are going to select, instead, the people who are authorities on various subjects—the men [and women] who are most respected by other men [and women] within their respective departments and fields. They will give their basic lecture course just once to a group of human beings, including both the experts in their own subject and bright children and adults without special training in their field. This lecture will be recorded... They will make moving picture footage of the lecture as well as hi-fi tape recording. Then the professor and his faculty associates will listen to this recording time and again.

While the analogies that Fuller used in 1962 seem dated—hi-fi tape recordings—most of the foundation of MOOCs can be seen in his quote, namely, that the value of educational material is not simply in its presentation and robotic repetition, but in quality information from a master in the subject, delivered with time for the student to absorb and apply it.

Teaching Out Loud

As with all profound shifts, the timing for MOOCs was right. To paraphrase Victor Hugo, nothing is more powerful than an idea whose time has come. And if there is an example that epitomizes that saying as applied to MOOCS, it has to be that of Salman Khan.

One of the most amazing and best known MOOC success stories has been the rise of Khan Academy, something that surprised no one more than its founder, Salman Khan. Khan began posting short math classes on Yahoo's Doodle Notepad as a simple teaching aid for his cousin Nadia, who was having trouble with basic math problems such as converting kilograms to pounds. Khan, who has three degrees from MIT and an MBA from Harvard, was living in Boston and working for a small hedge fund in 2004 when he began tutoring Nadia online. Soon, Nadia's brothers, relatives, and friends wanted to join as well. To keep things simple, Khan began to record and post his videos on YouTube, and the fuse was lit.

It is providential that Khan happened to use YouTube as the platform for "teaching out loud" to his cousin; it was simply a convenient and free way of distributing his lessons. But had he chosen to make the lessons private, which he had initially done when he was using Yahoo's Doodle Notepad for one-on-one lessons with Nadia, it's unlikely that Khan Academy would exist as it does today—much as William Randolph Hearst's nearly accidental takeover of his father's first newspaper eventually changed the world of news and media.

The hyperconnectivity that Khan tapped into is what we mean by teaching out loud—teaching is no longer confined to a classroom or private tutoring session but is captured and broadcast broadly. As Khan has said, "If you're watching a guy do a problem [while] thinking out loud, I think people find that more valuable and not as daunting." His approach enabled other learners around the world to find him, and it was this serendipity that drove Khan Academy's growth.

Early on, Khan stumbled onto the benefit of feedback and constant corrections in learning, which remain one of the key differences between Khan's model and earlier online learning models. According to Khan:

Imagine learning to ride a bicycle, and maybe I give you a lecture ahead of time, and I give you that bicycle for two weeks. And then I come back after two weeks and I say, "Well, let's see. You're having trouble taking left turns. You can't quite stop. You're an 80 percent bicyclist." So I put a big C stamp on your forehead and then I say, "Here's a unicycle." [With Khan Academy] our model is to learn any topic the way that you would learn a bicycle. Stay on that bicycle. Fall off that bicycle. Do it as long as necessary until you have [achieved] mastery. The traditional model—it penalizes you for experimentation and failure, but it does not expect mastery. We encourage you to experiment. We encourage you to fail. But we do expect mastery.

Mastery is not simply about receiving information, but about applying the knowledge gained rather than just reading, writing, or talking about it.

The goal of Khan's lessons was not to create a company, let alone an internationally known nonprofit funded through the likes of the Bill & Melinda Gates Foundation, Ann and John Doerr, the Lemann Foundation, and Google. Khan Academy's mission is "to change education for the better by providing a free world-class education for anyone, anywhere," much like Google's mission is to organize the world's information and make it universally accessible and useful. Unlike Google, it seems clear that Khan is dedicated to its nonprofit model.

After Khan provided the initial tutoring to his cousin and the growing crowd of followers, he pivoted and expanded as a K-12 educational platform on an at first slow-growing, but long since accelerated, set of learning resources on topics as varied as math, physics, chemistry, civics, economics, art, and history. By our estimates, Khan Academy today accounts for nearly half of all MOOC courses and students.

Going back to Victor Hugo's quote, all of this could not have come at a better time. Despite disturbingly high unemployment, certain areas of the market are facing a considerable lack of available, qualified talent. Consider the following testimonial (among thousands)[6] from Khan Academy's site:

From Darren, June 27, 2012

Yipeeeeeeee!!!! I just received my Professional Engineering License thanks to you in a large measure. I am a 53-year young guy who attended junior college out of high school, worked, then went back to college to receive a BS degree. However my major was not an accredited engineering program so I could not take my EIT (FE) exam when I graduated. After 30 years I decided to pursue my PE license. I had not taken many of the core engineering courses such as Fluids, Thermodynamics,

Electrical Circuits. I only had taken up to geometry in high school. I only took one math class in all college—Calc. 2 (integration). I took my FE on Friday and my PE on Saturday and I passed (after failing both the previous year). Without the help of the Khan Academy I may not have been able to pull this off. Very helpful and an oasis of hope in a world where it can be hard to find.

Darren is the quintessential Gen Zer, a "53-year young guy" who has figured out that learning is a lifelong journey.

Education is not about picking a career for life; instead, a career is about picking education for life. Subtle? Perhaps, but in that subtle shift lies the mechanism by which we will continuously reshape education in order to continuously reshape society. Our biggest mistake, when it comes to large changes to education, has been thinking that we can retool the educational system en masse once every several decades for the next generation of work and technology.

In the past that was possible only because big changes happened far less frequently, although it may not have seemed so at the time. Tectonic technological shifts were separated by enough time to retrain educators and rebuild curriculums, but that is no longer true. Going forward, such delayed reaction to change would be like chasing a dirt bike with a locomotive; no matter how fast your train, you will never be able to lay down tracks quickly enough to follow the dodging and weaving bike.

This lack of agility is also at the root of the problem of unemployment. If we do not recognize the sort of agility that educational methods and institutions need, we will never be able to re-skill people fast enough for tomorrow's organizations.

Let's use as an example a topic near and dear to us in discussing Gen Z: the issue of trained and available data scientists. Data scientists are today's equivalent of computer programmers in the 1980s and '90s. The difference was that in the '80s and '90s universities were churning out programmers like a factory assembly line. The software revolution had been ramping up over a period of three decades, and the programming languages of the time—Assembler, BASIC, Fortran COBOL—were fairly standard and long-lived. There was time to build courses and degree programs around them because the lifetime of those computing language was measured in decades, not years. The computer language S curve hadn't yet accelerated so dramatically that educational institutions were easily left in the dust, as they are now.

Increasingly, however, that challenge of keeping up with the need for new technical skills has become harder and harder. As programming languages have multiplied, you're much more likely to find good programmers who learned on their own or on the job rather than through a school. To this day, if you ask a room full of developers what they went to school for, relatively few will tell you computer science.

Have schools stopped educating developers? Of course not. The question is, are they educating developers for what is currently needed? In our experience with the tech giants we work with, the answer is an emphatic and definite "No." While you can find any number of contradictory reports about the state of affairs in tech employment—from McKinsey and Gartner pointing to millions of open positions that we will not be able to fill over the next few years to the *Atlantic* in a 2013 article claiming that the tech shortage is a myth—the point we are making is that tech education is not about the ability of schools to issue degrees but rather about their capacity to keep up with the sorts of skills students need.

That inability to keep up is why the lack of educated data scientists is a serious problem, which needs to be scaled to meet the needs of the organizations that want people with specialized skills for analyzing Big Data and developing the behavioral insights we talked about in the previous chapter.

A 2011 McKinsey report estimated that by 2018 there will be a shortage in the United States of 140,000 to 190,000 people with deep data analytics skills, as well as a shortage of 1.5 million managers and analysts who make business decisions based on Big Data.

This need for individuals with a new set of skills to deal with data analytics isn't simply a matter of wanting to be on the cutting edge; you will need it just to keep pace with the market. According to Matt Ferguson, CEO of Career-Builder, technology skills depreciate at about the same rate as physical assets. Our own opinion is that this is much too generous a time frame. We'd go so far as to say that technology skills are likely the fastest-depreciating asset of any organization. As the pace of technology accelerates, skills fall behind quickly as the slingshotting effect not only pushes the technological cutting edge forward, it just as quickly eliminates the need for older technology skills.

While slingshotting works to your benefit as a consumer and user of technology, and to the advantage of suppliers and sellers to the new waves of users entering the market, it does not benefit those who want to deeply understand and advance the state of the art. In other words, the fact that the user interface and technology experience are easier does not mean the underlying technology is less complex. In fact, just the opposite occurs; the rate of underlying technological change increases.

The bottom line is that our educational model is clearly unable to keep up. Learning can no longer be focused on what happens in the classroom. The new reality is that anyone, at any time, anywhere is a potential student, and in fact, *must* be a student.

So, have we solved the problem by using MOOCs as a primary vehicle to deliver education outside of the classroom? Not entirely. MOOCs are simply the platform. The question that still remains is, how do we change the behaviors of Gen Z so that the motivation for continuous learning is always present? The answer comes from one of the most unlikely places: how we play.

Getting Onboard with the Gaming of Education

When we're asked how we think Gen Z will learn and work, our standard answer is to look at the way they game. By gaming, Gen Z is learning valuable lessons about collaboration through massive online communities they need to interact with and education from the real-time learning that they have to adapt to in order to be effective gamers. There are no extensive users guides or long-winded tutorials in these games. Learning happens primarily by observing and by doing. However, in the gaming world it's not called learning, it's called onboarding. Onboarding is the use of videos and interactive examples that invite you in and guide you out of the land of the "n00b" (pronounced "new-b"—gaming slang for a new user) by rapidly developing your confidence and capability.

Even a simple game, such as the hugely popular and controversial *Flappy*

Bird—from late 2013—makes the effort to show you, in three steps, exactly how to play, despite the fact that there is only a single control and the game is about as obvious as can be.

Much more complicated games, such as those from the best-selling *Call of Duty: Black Ops* series, go into far more depth, making sure you are likely not just to buy the game and not just to try it once, but to rapidly "level up" to the competence that makes you want to spend more time getting better and better, particularly when playing against others.

While many players of "first-person shooters" (FPSs) like *Black Ops* are already familiar with the controls and objectives of these games, the first ten minutes or so of the game are spent giving you plenty of opportunities to understand both how to use the physical controls in your hands—how to run, jump, shoot, and reload or change weapons—and how to understand the "heads-up" display that shows your health, amount of ammo left, the radar/map indicating friends and foes, time left in a round of the game, and so on.

By default, these games don't assume you know anything, and do assume that early "hand-holding" will help you get over the initial fear of looking stupid or feeling incompetent. They draw you into the flow, ramping up your comfort with the game as you spend more time. There are often goals, such as finding a hidden object, using a weapon a certain number of times, or using a particular skill successfully a set number of times, that "unlock" new capabilities or further goals that demonstrate you are ready for the next level of complexity.

Great games are extremely good at knowing the right moments both to challenge you and to keep you within a comfort zone that prevents you from getting frustrated. And there is a good reason they know these learning curves so well—they test the playing experience over tens of thousands of hours with new and seasoned gamers to see exactly where frustration sets in. They don't guess, and they certainly don't wait until the game has hit the market before they think about how players are going to react.

In fact, Microsoft, through more than 100 million unit sales of its Xbox gaming systems, has calculated that the typical gamer spends about two and a half years of cumulative time gaming by the time he graduates from college. The enormity of that experiential data collection—about 750 million potential gaming hours in total—provides hard evidence about how people learn.

Just as with the evidence-based marketing we discussed in chapter 5, "Shifting from Affluence to Influence," evidence-based learning, whether in a game or "traditional" learning experience, is the key to modern learning. The lesson is, don't be lulled into thinking something has to be a "game" in order for the principles of gaming to apply, whether in an academic setting or within an enterprise.

THE GOOGLE STORY:
LEARNING ON THE JOB

What if we could build on what we've already learned in this chapter and apply it to an enterprise setting, allowing MOOCs, gaming, onboarding, and engagement to replace at least some of the brown bag lunch and water cooler learning that exists in most companies today? This is exactly what's practiced at Google, with its Googler-to-Googler (or g2g) learning program.

Google's often touted "20 percent time"—in which engineers, in particular, are expected to spend 20 percent of their time on "undetermined" projects, a practice started by 3M early in the twentieth century—is specifically designed to unleash internal innovation. It has been extended into the entire learning realm within Google through the g2g program, which, outside of the Google context, we would call peer-to-peer, or P2P, learning.

Google's challenge was to enable and deliver enough ongoing training opportunities to allow it not only to continue innovating but also to set the stage for a workforce empowered and up to speed on a broad variety of topics. Some training is led by knowledgeable employees in roles that would not normally be associated with learning or teaching, and some by those in the more traditional employee development areas of human resources (HR) and learning and development (L&D).

Google discovered it was nearly impossible to scale up instructor-led training quickly and widely enough to fit the demands of the company, so it turned to g2g as a more Gen Z-like alternative to traditional learning programs. **Fifty-five percent of the courses within Google are taught by employees outside of HR and L&D, with topics ranging from engineering-specific courses to unexpected offerings like firebreathing—yes, firebreathing!** More than two thousand of Google's roughly thirty-seven-thousand people have created and led g2g courses, an enviable engagement level given the general fear most people have of public speaking and the traditionally rare enthusiasm for teaching or learning in corporate settings.[7]

THE EVENTBRITE STORY: EMPLOYEE-LED TRAINING

Using a model of P2P learning similar to Google's, Ty White, founder of Pepperland Labs and former product manager at Eventbrite—an online ticketing service founded in 2006 that allows event organizers to plan, set up ticket sales, and promote events online via social-networking tools—described how the company began with employee-led training in 2011. Eventbrite's P2P model revolves around Brite Camps, which are typically hour-long, in-person, interactive sessions run by employees on a variety of topics. As in Google's program, Brite Camps are not limited to "just work" topics. White described the birth of Brite Camps to us:

Brite Camp started because I saw the need of a coworker who had been an educator previously and joined Eventbrite to do customer support. She was frustrated by the fact that people who understood all the technical stuff that she didn't understand surrounded her and yet she didn't have a straightforward path to learn from them.

We realized that we had smart, well-spoken people around us who could easily teach interesting topics and who would jump at the chance to learn what's put in front of them, if it's convenient and happens in a relatively compressed amount of time.

We started just with a single Brite Camp on Python (a popular programming language). We thought, "If five or ten of us have interest in this we'll be happy." About 40 percent of the company showed up; we were very shocked! By the way, these were not folks who intend to become programmers someday. They just wanted to learn enough to understand what's going on and find some way to make that relevant to their life.

At the very least, all they've given up is an hour to satisfy their curiosity. So, even if it's a failure, not much is lost. If not, then it's a great gain for them! We've continued down that path and curated the vast majority of our Brite Camps based on suggestions that we got from our coworkers.

Another early Brite Camp was on sales strategy. At that time, we probably had about a hundred people at the company. That represents a hundred people who could be selling the company to everybody that they meet.

We hire people who are social, articulate, and can potentially talk to people about the company and convince them to use the product, but they don't necessarily know how to sell it. So we had some folks from the sales team come over and teach everybody how to sell. Again, we were blown away. It worked great.

We rolled out more Brite Camps on design, competitors, finance, forecasting, raising funds, SEO, and marketing. It really became a platform for internal folks to share the stuff they were working on and what they did on an everyday basis. That's what made it sing as something that not only the employees could get behind, but bosses as well.

At this point, Brite Camps have been around for almost three years, and have expanded as a way for anyone who wants to talk about a topic that others want to hear about. It's an hour-long presentation that is self-run and self-led by the employees and happens on a weekly or every-other-week basis. Managers would even ask employees who had big projects to make one of their quarterly goals to give a Brite Camp explaining their work to the rest of the company.

The most important thing when you're doing this is to be inclusive. It turns out that if you have smart people who have interesting things to say, giving them a platform is all you really need to do.

THE ROCKSMITH STORY:
DYNAMIC LEARNING FOR MUSIC

Let's wrap up our discussion of the revolution in learning with an example that sets a very high bar for effectiveness in modern learning methods and shows that the goals students need to meet in order to "level up" their learning can be quite low indeed. Best of all, you can easily experience this for yourself to see exactly how it works.

One of our favorite examples of the way Gen Z is redefining the learning process is *Rocksmith*, a game that teaches you how to play a real guitar—unlike the simulated plastic guitar or bass used in earlier games such as *Guitar Hero* or *Rock Band*—giving the user a completely customized, personalized learning experience. After sessions with *Rocksmith*, you could unplug and jump onto the stage, or at least the living room sofa.

The simplest of tasks, such as plugging in the instrument, as well as more complicated ones, such as tuning (which can be very difficult for those students who do not yet have a sense of pitch or any prior knowledge of how to tune the guitar), are laid out explicitly as part of the onboarding process.

Traditional guitar instructors would expect you to buy a digital tuner, plug in your guitar, and painstakingly tune your guitar to the standard notes of a traditionally strung guitar. *Rocksmith*, however, features on-screen instruction and a built-in tuner that show you exactly how, and in which direction, to turn the tuning pegs of your guitar. It also presents a visualization of how far above or below the perfect tuning you are.

In fact, you cannot even begin to play *Rocksmith* until you have proven that your instrument is tuned. Just as Salman Khan believes it's inappropriate to learn to ride the unicycle until you've mastered the bike, *Rocksmith*'s creators think that if your instrument isn't tuned correctly, there's no point in learning to play it. You'd only be learning to play it incorrectly from the very beginning, which would be a terrible habit and a poor foundation for your knowledge of the guitar.

One of *Rocksmith*'s biggest breakthroughs is similar to the principle that Khan Academy has built directly into its learning system, and that's the idea of adaptive or dynamic learning. Simply put, as the user you have to demonstrate a baseline knowledge before you are allowed to continue on to more complex material. This may seem demotivating at first, but the process is actually quite rapid. In *Rocksmith*'s case, the game assumes you have absolutely no idea how to play any given song. As a result, it only shows you a minimal number of notes, allowing you plenty of time to react to each new note that is "flying" at you on the screen. As the song progresses and you demonstrate you are able to keep up with a note every few measures, the game adjusts the notes, chords, strumming/picking patterns, and other techniques it presents to you, based on the proof it "hears" from your playing. It then either "levels up" (increases the difficulty, number of notes, or techniques such as muting or bending strings) the pieces you should attempt to play or "levels down" (reducing difficulty), in order to keep you in a zone where you are challenged enough to learn and adjust, but not so much that you become overwhelmed and quit. This is truly remarkable—even with in-person, live, world-class musical instructors, this does not happen. To have a dynamic, real-time learning experience like this is another technology and behavioral slingshotting moment.

One of us is a musician (you can find out which one by visiting TheGenZEffect.com) and started studying music at the age of seven, eventually attending and graduating from the Berklee College of Music. Believe it when he says, **"This is a revolution in learning to play an instrument that makes traditional musical education seem like it's stuck in the grunting stage of caveman storytelling."** This is not marketing hype from Ubisoft, nor simply our own enthusiasm for the game. An independent national study by Research Strategy Group found that *Rocksmith* is the "fastest way to learn guitar."[8] This is in large part because the program tells you what you did wrong and allows you to learn the way you want to learn, rather than through the often demotivating exercise of repeating scales or chord progressions that aren't tied to a song you might actually want to play.

We caught up with another Berklee alumnus—Nicholas Bonardi from Ubisoft, the makers of *Rocksmith*—to uncover how the game came to be and what he's learned from the more than one million players of the game:

> I loved *Rock Band* and *Guitar Hero* long before I got involved with Game Tank, the company that created what is now *Rocksmith* by Ubisoft. I absolutely loved those games. They came to me at a time when I was jaded with guitar—at this point, I've been playing guitar for seventeen years. They came to me at a time where I thought, "I play guitar enough. I'm just over it. I don't feel like I'm being creative with it anymore." Then I started playing *Rock Band* and *Guitar Hero* and I fell in love with the dream of being a rock star again because that's what that game was selling.

I remember at one point doing these rock star moves just intrinsically and thinking, "Man. What the heck is with this plastic instrument? What is up with me?" I started playing guitar a lot more after that.

With Game Tank, we had one very basic idea: to make a game with a real guitar, and we had three employees including me. Basically, make *Guitar Hero* with a real guitar. End of story.

Jake and I started to do that because he wasn't a musician at all. He hired me for the musician side of it. That's where we started exploring, "Well, what's the best way to learn?" We started doing intense research and development and came up with ways that would allow us to maximize how someone can actually learn a song from the game. When talking to potential users, we asked "Well, why do you want to play guitar?" The answer was pretty simple: "I guess I want to play guitar to learn a song."

So, everything about the game was getting you to be able to play a song as fast as you possibly could. We had an independent research group study *Rocksmith*, and what they came back with were scientific results that showed that 95 percent of people who played *Rocksmith* and hadn't played guitar before actually learned how to play and saw significant improvement in many areas. They compared it to traditional methods, too, and the response was that *Rocksmith* is the fastest way to learn how to play guitar.

As we said earlier, one of us is a musician by schooling. When he arrived at Berklee, he was first and foremost a keyboard/piano player, but had also played trumpet, baritone horn, rhythm guitar, and bass in front of small groups as well as thousands of people. He trotted off to Berklee with a stack of equipment, mostly keyboard-related, but also with an electric guitar, amp, and associated effects. Within the first three months at Berklee, he sold all of his guitar equipment. It was clear to him that he would never be as good as the dedicated guitarists all around him, and it seemed impossible to even come close to their level of mastery.

Fast-forward many years to the arrival of *Rocksmith*, and within two weeks, playing perhaps three days a week for thirty to sixty minutes at a time, he had far exceeded the level of technical skill he had ever had, despite having taken guitar lessons for years prior to attending Berklee and having played piano and other instruments for ten years before to that.

Will either of us be the next guitar legend? It's unlikely. Has one of us rediscovered the joy of guitar and a feeling of competence and confidence with guitar that he had never achieved previously? Absolutely.

For years, we've been contrarians in our workshop and consulting engagements, where clients wanted to "raise the bar" for creating change. **Our argument has been that we should be lowering the bar enough that people could trip over it. Taking that first step is the hardest, and making it even harder does not promote change.** It creates greater fear and uncertainty that prevents people, teams, and larger organizations from moving forward—and that doesn't have to be the case.

That sort of thinking is exactly what *Rocksmith* set out to do, according to Bonardi:

We wanted to take out all of the hurdles to learning to play. So, we made it so that when you plug in your guitar, there is sound. That sound is going to be the sound that should be on the album, because when you're playing something correctly with the correct sound it actually sounds like it does on the album.

Our first goal is just to get someone to play anything at all from a song they've chosen. We just need them to play the smallest, simplest notes. Something so that we can get them participating immediately, on the lowest level... You don't have to worry about the tone, tuning, catching up to the speed of the music, or knowing what to play. A lot of the unknowns are taken out of it. You just have to focus on being able to do one note. And then once you do that, you're motivated to keep going. Self-motivation is important, because, realistically, many more people have given up on learning guitar than are actually playing guitar.

Rocksmith is taking advantage of the relatively new understanding of behavioral modification and modeling that tells us that changing behavior is not simply about willpower or "putting in 10,000 hours," but rather about creating and repeating many small habits that replace old ones. The result is quickly and visibly "leveling up" skills and behaviors in ways that traditional learning methods ignore and assume are essentially impossible, which Rocksmith and other dynamic learning environments are demonstrating are long-held myths.

When you're looking at how to build learning into your work or life, consider that the motivation to start and continue learning is actually *more* important in many ways than the content itself, because if you can't get someone on the path to learning about a topic, they will certainly never "level up" their knowledge or skills.

Between the examples provided by looking at Khan Academy, Brite Camps, and games such as Black Ops or Rocksmith, consider using smaller segments of learning that can be easily consumed and applied in hours or minutes rather than days or weeks, and provide much faster feedback, whether from a game tutorial, mobile app mini-tutorial, mentor, or coach. If you're covering theory or detailed material such as regulations, policies, or procedures, quickly find ways to apply the theory so the learner can see it in action.

We have become complacent in expecting that adult learning, in particular, is long, drawn-out, and boring; that no longer has to be the norm, whether in the classroom or the boardroom.

The bottom line—education is no longer optional. When done right, continuous learning is baked right in. Everywhere. All the time. Think small, and experiment with these ideas in your own company.

As Elon Musk, founder of Tesla Motors, has said, "Any product that needs a manual to work is broken."

Put It Into Action:
Chapter 6 #TWAMC #GenZ

Learn from Gen Z Leaders

- Peter Norvig, professor at Stanford University
- Sebastian Thrun, CEO of Udacity, research professor at Stanford University
- Salman Khan, founder of Khan Academy
- University of the People
- Kevin Werbach, associate professor at the Wharton School
- Coursera
- Eric Tsui, professor at Hong Kong Polytechnic University
- Matt Ferguson, CEO of CareerBuilder
- Ty White, founder of Pepperland Labs and former product manager at Eventbrite
- Nicholas Bonardi, lead audio engineer for *Rocksmith* at Ubisoft
- Elon Musk, founder of Tesla Motors

Are You Ready for Gen Z?

- Have you personally used MOOCs to learn? If not, what topic of interest could you experiment with in an online course?
- Does your business offer or use MOOCs?
- How do you keep employees up to speed on topics of interest?
- Do you provide opportunities for employees to teach and learn "out loud"?
- Have you tried any of the new games or gamelike experiences, such as *Rocksmith*, to see if you can learn a new skill more rapidly and easily than you might have expected?

Find out whether you're ready for the Gen Z Effect by taking the full assessment at TheGenZEffect.com.

7

Lifehacking: A Playbook for Gen Z

In anything that has to do with knowledge, fear will produce only resistance.
—PETER F. DRUCKER

In this chapter we explore one of the most fascinating and disruptive aspects of Gen Z, its propensity to work around or "hack" the system. We'll talk first about the benefits of the hacking mind-set and then focus on three hacks that we believe will most shape the Gen Z landscape and the future: crowdfunding, 3D printing, and changing attitudes about intellectual property and patents.

The City of Honolulu's website needed a makeover—a big one. The quote from a local software developer detailed a two-year $9.3 million project. When local citizens, a few of whom knew a bit about web development, caught wind of the price tag they had some obvious choices: sit back and watch $9.3 million in local taxes go to waste (and wait two years for the website to be completed) or take to social media and start a movement of outrage to force the city to take a closer look at the excessive cost. They chose neither option. Instead, they "hacked" the system.

Code for America, a nonprofit action group based in Chicago, posted a challenge to developers: build the same website, with a focus on the citizens' needs, and get a $9,300 prize if your approach is selected. The $9,300, representing one-tenth of I percent of the outside bid, was clearly no coincidence.

Within a few weeks, hundreds of new site designs had been submitted. Code for America then ran a daylong session with Honolulu citizens to determine the questions the city's website needed to answer. The thousands of questions were used to build a website driven by an incredibly simple front end that allows a visitor to ask a question and then be presented with all of the resources needed to answer the question.

The citizens of Honolulu saved $9,290,700.

It's an example of what Catherine Bracy, director of community organizing for Code for America, calls *civic hacking*.

THE BRIGHT(ER) SIDE OF HACKING

The Honolulu example captures the essence of hacking, in the best sense of the word: it's the ability to break through barriers and focus on making meaning and purpose the center of our personal and professional experience.

While not every hack is "civic," what we have observed is that questioning accepted or entrenched behaviors is fundamental to the mind-set of a hacker. Hackers want to find ways to circumvent the status quo. That might mean doing something in less time or at less cost, or it might mean taking on challenges that are seen as overwhelming and insurmountable. Hacking is also directed at the most fundamental and granular level of the problem being addressed, the objective being to change the underlying system and not just eliminate the symptoms or cure their cause, as shown in figure 7-1.

Although hacking has carried a mostly negative connotation for some time, it is like any other approach to creative problem solving in that it provides us with an ability to do good as well as to do harm.

In the context of the Gen Z Effect we use the term *lifehacking* to describe two aspects of hacking. First, it refers to the undaunted mind-set of the hacker; second, it recognizes the positive impact brought about by the ability to connect people, mobilize communities, and drive positive outcomes that would otherwise be impossible.

Gen Z and the generation that has preceded it—Gen Y or Millennials—have been viewed as having a sense of "entitlement." The popular interpretation

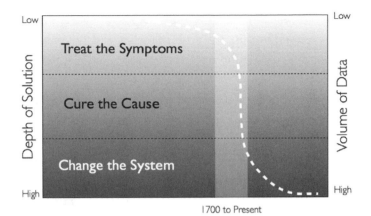

Figure 7-1: The Evolution of Solution Finding

For the vast majority of humankind's existence, we've solved problems based on empirical evidence—if the solution seemed to work in a repeatable way then we addressed the symptoms of the problem. As the scientific method evolved during the last three hundred years, we were able to gather increasing data, allowing us to identify the cause of a given problem and address it with a deeper level of understanding. Today we are making a transition to more systemic solutions based on knowledge of the underlying mechanisms in a given system. It is this lowest level of solution that we regard as "hacking," since it attempts to change the most basic building blocks of a system. For example, medicine, moving forward, will be working directly at the level of the genome to alter the most basic mechanics of how our bodies prevent and repair disease.

of this phenomenon is that these generations have been raised in households where children were encouraged to march to the beat of their own drummer, rarely criticized for failure, and always celebrated for their efforts—the colloquial philosophy that every child is a winner.

We believe that this characterization of behavior, especially when directed at Gen Z, is simply inaccurate. We'd like to offer a different interpretation. Our observation from studying and being involved with organizations that focus on adolescents and teenagers, such as Free the Children (which we profiled in chapter 5) and Destination Imagination, a global nonprofit dedicated to building creativity skills in K-12 students, is that the attitude is less one of entitlement than it is one of extraordinary confidence.

If these kids are seen as being far too sure of themselves and of their capabilities, it is necessary, because the problems they will take on are going to eclipse anything the world of commerce, education, and government has had to deal with so far.

When we look back at the amazing accomplishments of humankind—from those of the Greatest Generation, who lived through the Great Depression then saved the world from tyranny, to those of the Boomer Generation, whose innovation built the World Wide Web—we do not think of arrogance and undeserved confidence. Instead, we take pride in their heroic and brilliant acts that moved civilization forward. We'd like to suggest that Gen Z shares the same spirit of courage for the daunting challenges that we will face over the next century.

So, let's not mince words: it's a damn good thing that Gen Z is confident and comes to the world believing in their ability to take on the challenges of climate change, income disparity, lack of universal education, unemployment, financial crisis, energy needs, limited access to clean water, and poor sanitation. These are not challenges for people who do not have a deep and abiding belief in themselves and their capabilities to innovate.

In 2011, we saw this spirit play out on a global stage in what has come to be known as the Arab Spring. During a nine-month period, starting in Tunisia in January of 2011, protestors organized themselves using social media to demonstrate and protest injustices. This was a grassroots uprising that ultimately toppled the governments of Tunisia, Libya, and Egypt, as well as disrupting nearly every country throughout the Middle East.

Protests are clearly not new. However, these social media–enabled movements were built on the ability of participants to connect quickly through technology, bypass the traditional channels of power and influence, and effectively wreak havoc on government and commerce by mobilizing with a scale and sophistication that would otherwise have required substantial investment in organization. That ability, to circumvent the system in order to achieve a meaningful goal, is lifehacking.

THE THREE MOST DISRUPTIVE HACKS

While there are an infinite number of ways that the hacker mind-set can, and will, be applied to solving the big challenges that lie before us, there are three that we believe will be the most disruptive and meaningful in altering the way we accelerate innovation to keep pace with the challenges ahead: funding, manufacturing, and the protection of intellectual property (IP). These hacks act as a bridge in the gap that stands between ideas and their impact; and in the case of each one, we see hacking the status quo as crucial to building a sustainable future.

We've also picked these three areas because they present the greatest conceptual hurdles when it comes to explaining the future to those outside of Gen Z. The challenge of reimaging funding, manufacturing, and IP lies in the fact that each of these areas is entrenched in existing models and frameworks that have a long and deep history in the present-day landscape of commerce. The ability to raise capital from wealthy institutions and individuals has been a necessary fulcrum of success for nearly every scalable business. The history of the twentieth century is one of invention and protection of ideas. Henry Ford's Model T was not a revolution surrounding his product but one of manufacturing—the moving assembly line. The patent and trademark system is the fortress without which it would be impossible for brands such as Apple to exist—to thrive, the brand requires legal protection for everything from its logo to its devices. In short, we can't imagine today's world without these three cornerstones of free enterprise.

In many ways, changing these institutions of the nineteenth and twentieth centuries is tantamount to changing the canons of a religion. But that is exactly what we need to do. The discussions we are about to have will at times feel like sacrilege; you will bristle at the suggestion that these systems are broken, and even more so at the notion that there is a different way to go about these tasks. That's good. We want you to dig deep in trying to reach new bedrock on which to build the future.

THE FUNDING HACK

In chapter 5 we talked about the changing nature of influence in marketing and in the enterprise, and we made the case that influence is a foundational force driving the Gen Z Effect because it opens the door to disruptive ideas and innovations. However, the biggest shift in influence and the greatest accelerant for innovation will come from breaking through the biggest barrier any new idea faces: funding it.

It's here, again, that the Gen Z Effect is turning the tables on tried-and-true models of raising capital and bringing new ideas to market. One of the reasons that changes in funding are so critical to Gen Z has to do with the changing attitude toward small business and the critical role small business will play in future economic prosperity.

Small business is a critical part of sustainable economic growth. In the United States, the majority of net new jobs created during the past two decades came from small businesses with less than 500 employees. While there is debate over the exact number the Bureau of Labor Statistics' puts the actual percentage of net job growth contributed by small business for this period at about 60 percent and gross job growth at closer to 70 percent.

In addition, beyond the employment contribution, small businesses are simply more innovative, with a much higher average number of patents per employee than large firms. On average, according to a 2014 report by the Small Business Administration,[1] small firms of less than 500 employees produce sixteen times as many patents as firms with over 500 employees. But firms with fifteen or less employees produce an astounding 134 times as many patents per employee as do the largest firms with more than 83,000 employees.[2]

Diminishing the role that these engines of the economy have would be like throwing the plankton out of an ecosystem: it may take some time, but eventually every organism, including the ones at the top of the food chain, will suffer. In fact, the growth of the largest organizations in nearly every industry comes from acquisitions. Innovation needs to be planted first in the protected space of an uncluttered mind that is devoid of the many good and rational reasons why the new idea won't work.

But scaling innovation requires a much different engine, one that enables economies of scale that simply aren't available to small business. The importance of scaling innovation is reminiscent of a conversation we had with the CEO of one of the world's largest tech companies. When confronted with his company's apparent lack of organic innovation he responded, "I do not see my job as that of an innovator. Let somebody else educate the market on why their product is worth buying. My job is to have the capital and the capability to acquire them once they do."

Indeed, the risk of experimentation is far too great for most large companies to take on when compared with the risk of acquiring a proven success—even if a significant premium over inventing the same product is involved. This is exactly what we are seeing with the current trends in mergers and acquisitions; it's better to buy innovation than to build it.

However, that leaves us in a bit of a predicament if the rate of innovation within small business can't keep up with the appetite to acquire innovation on the part of larger businesses. Effectively, we have built a global economy of behemoths that are developing an insatiable appetite for acquired innovation. This means that if start-ups and small businesses flourish and grow, the positive impact on the economy is considerable; if not, then the economy stalls.

The surprising news in our research for the book—which points to a profound shift in attitudes toward small business—is that nearly 50 percent of Millennials, and those born into Gen Z want to start their own businesses. This means securing funding, but, increasingly, funding requirements are much lower than the threshold expected by many professional investors and at a volume that far exceeds the number of investments from traditional sources such as angel investors and venture capitalists. In 2013, for example, a total of just under 5,000 funding deals were cut in the United States. Angel investors accounted for only 884 deals, which totaled $1.1 billion in overall funding.[3] Venture capitalists cut 3,995 deals, for a total investment of $29.4 billion.[4]

Compare those numbers with the fact that more than 500,000 new businesses are started each month, a number that has been steadily rising since 2006.[5] While only about 30 percent of those businesses have more than one employee and less than 20 percent will survive their first year, that still leaves just under four million new businesses each year that are bootstrapping without any outside funding. Are they all entrepreneurial ventures destined to become the next Facebook, YouTube, or Apple? Of course not, but if only 1 percent stand a chance, that's still thirty-five thousand business that do not have access to outside capital—*seven times as many as do get funding*.

Given the rising interest in starting businesses, we see the level of available funding from traditional sources as unsustainable for promoting long-term economic growth. The result is what is often termed a "translational" gap in the marketplace—this gap is a dead zone that ideas cannot cross because entrepreneurs lack the funding to get them from concept to proof-of-concept.

But what if you could test your idea on the market at zero cost, other than your time? If the idea meets the market's approval, what if you could scale it immediately with the funding already in place?

The lifehack is called crowdfunding, and we believe it will be one of the greatest accelerants of new business and innovation in the coming decades.

Owning a Small Piece of a Big Future

There are two basic ways crowdfunding can work. The first is equity crowd-funding. Although raising capital through investors who get equity in exchange isn't a new idea, it had been heavily restricted for the past eighty years, during which time entrepreneurs could not do what is termed a "general solicitation" of investors. In other words, you were limited in who you could reach out to because you had to first register all equity and securities offerings with the SEC. In addition, you could only take funds from "accredited investors," which meant that the investor had to have a net worth of at least $1 million (excluding their principle residence) or a yearly income of at least $200,000 for the past two years ($300,000 if married).

As of September 23, 2013, the first of these restrictions for general solicitation was eliminated, meaning that you could advertise to the general public for investment through crowdfunding platforms such as RockThePost. By the time this book is published, the second of these restrictions for accredited investors will also be modified to include virtually anyone who wants to be an investor. Although there will still be restrictions on how much you can invest based on your income, the change radically expands opportunities for new businesses to raise capital and for investors to participate in growing start-ups.

Assurance Contracts

The second way that crowdfunding works is by tapping into masses of buyers or simply individuals interested in being part of a new idea on platforms such as Kickstarter and Indiegogo, which allow you to preorder a product or service from a start-up, or simply be recognized as a contributor by virtue of something as simple as getting a T-shirt or a coffee mug with the company's logo or simply the joy of contributing.

Most of these transactions involve what are referred to as "assurance contracts." An assurance contract is nothing more than an agreement by the company raising the money that if it does not reach a minimum threshold of funding the funds committed will be returned to the investors. The reasoning is that, if a base level of funding is not reached, the venture cannot produce and deliver the product or service. There are other forms of crowdfunding in which there is no minimum threshold and the start-up can keep the money raised even if it does not meet its goal, although the penalty is steep (9 percent on Indiegogo.com).

The Hidden Billions

If you're thinking that crowdfunding is a passing fad, think again. As of March 3, 2014, more than $1 billion has flowed from a crowd of 5,708,578 people to projects on Kickstarter alone. More than 1.6 million of these individuals have backed more than one project, with more than 15,000 of them backing fifty or more projects.[6] The total value of all crowdfunding transactions is estimated at well over $2 billion. RockThePost's equity funding is approaching $25 million as this book is being written.

What's even more amazing is that it took Kickstarter slightly less than five years to reach this point, from its first day on April 28, 2009, when it seemed like a "crazy idea" to most people, especially traditional investors and banks. Kickstarter's early days were humble, with forty people signing up to spend a total of $1,084 on seven projects on the first day. The peak, so far, on March 13, 2013, included commitments for $4,029,585.45 for the day.

Simply turning to the crowd is not a guarantee of funding, however, and the majority of crowdfunded offerings never meet their funding goals, regardless of how small or large they are.

If the crowd isn't enough, and your product isn't enough, what's missing? Celebrity!

The Gen Z Celebrity

We are entering an era of rampant entrepreneurism, and a perfect storm of ideas, funding, and hungry global talent is creating a stream of opportunities without precedent.

The question is, how do you stand a chance of creating something new that can rise above the noise and get noticed? You do it by building a solid base of rabid fans who want your new product before they can have it, maybe even before they know they need it, and who channel their social influence into the network to create buzz in ways that traditional marketing and advertising can't, at least not for start-ups.

This seems to be developing as a core competency for many Gen Zers, who purposefully build and steer their own brand and influence. For example, on July 13, 2007, Justine Ezarik (known online as iJustine) posted a short video clip in which she unboxed her three-hundred-plus-page iPhone/AT&T bill,[7] which was viewed more than two million times in the first ten days alone. That video propelled Ezarik out of relative obscurity as an early lifestreamer who kept her video camera on nearly 24-7.

When we covered Ezarik's story in 2007, it was clear to us that she was part of a new breed of media star who was thrust into the limelight by the sheer power of influence. The sudden attention created by iJustine's video also caused AT&T to change its default method of sending physical bills of hundreds of pages to its customers, a relatively early sign of businesses listening to their customers' complaints.

Many more examples of both YouTube video stars and companies paying attention to social media have occurred since 2007, although the perceived value of YouTube and video content by most businesses remains remarkably low. The stranglehold of "professional video" for the TV and movie industries appears to be firmly lodged in the old affluence pyramid mind-set.

Some of the most visible examples of Gen Z celebrity influence are in the entertainment industry, where talent has been catapulted past the quagmire of intermediaries that typically stand guard at the gates. At the age of sixteen, the relatively unknown Lorde posted her music to SoundCloud, the audio-only equivalent of YouTube; at a glance, SoundCloud might seem as necessary to music as YouTube was to video, which is to say, not at all! She quickly found a huge following, was picked by the record label Lava Records, and became the most viral music star of the year.

In Lorde's case, the record label used crowdsourcing passively, by simply watching her rise to the top and picking her out of the masses, bypassing the traditional talent scout. What was once seen purely as an art—talent scouting—has been augmented, and in some cases replaced, by analytics that search for a signal against the background noise, finding the most popular of the original music content being generated all around the world.

Crowdfunding Inside the Enterprise

At this point you may be thinking that crowdfunding is only for start-ups in the early stage, independent musicians, or consumer-facing projects. Or perhaps you're falling into the generational trap of thinking that crowdfunding only works for hot new companies or over-caffeinated twentysomethings. Not true.

Ultimately, the greatest contribution of lifehacking is the ability to innovate the way we innovate. Historically, innovation, especially within large organizations, had to follow a fairly linear track, moving from the idea stage through review committees, internal funding, and budgeting, on to proof of concept, prototyping, testing, and finally into production. What would happen if we compressed these activities into just two steps: idea and production?

While there are plenty of public crowdfunding examples that have gotten a great deal of visibility and Internet buzz, there are also many early experiments in internally focused, enterprise crowdfunding projects, such as IBM's iFundIT project, which hacks the traditional model of internal enterprise innovation. We see these activities as critically important to large organizations that are rich in ideas but which have corporate processes that may be impossible to navigate when it comes to finding funding for those ideas.

Creating this sort of internal analog for crowdfunding is essential for Gen Z, which is constantly exposed to the success of public crowdfunding. **Not having the capability to fund new ideas in an enterprise setting would be as frustrating to Gen Z as giving them a typewriter to use rather than a**

computer. Perhaps more so, because they can always go out and buy their own device. They can't, however, fund their own ideas.

THE IBM STORY: CROWDFUNDING INSIDE THE ENTERPRISE

We spoke with Michael Muller, PhD, past lead of the invention development team for the collaborative user experience group and an IBM master inventor, about IBM iFundIT, IBM's approach to internal crowdfunding;

> iFundIT started with a vice president of research, who wanted to do something very different from IBM's Innovation Jams™, which began in 2003. Jams are two- to three-day events run every two years on a topic that's carefully designed by management to spur new innovation. Any one of the roughly 400,000 people in IBM can participate to present an idea for five minutes. It's a nice mechanism for a very broad group of IBMers to inject ideas into the corporate thought process. Jams and projects like iFundIT are grassroots innovations; it's a big part of how IBM keeps itself vital, outside of pure research activities.
>
> IBM iFundIT was a natural progression to take Jams to the next level by putting in place a way of getting people who have ideas to carry them out. It's basically crowdfunding inside of IBM. For our first iFundIT, we invested $50,000 in the project, which looked enormous to us at the time. There were five hundred people in the organization of a Research vice president, and each person got $100. It doesn't sound like much when you break it down, but what we found is that it doesn't have to be.
>
> Participants had a month to propose an idea, promote it to their colleagues, and get it funded in their local organization, such as the T.J. Watson Research Center in New York. Since the groups were geographically co-located, the promotion activities happened in the hallways and at lunchtime.
>
> We had pledges at roughly 50 percent of our budget and participation of around 40 percent of the people who could participate. This was really solid participation and we considered it a roaring success.

However, that was just the beginning. Every iFundIT trial since then has done even better.

One of our favorite iFundIT ideas that made the cut was a project to put a 3D printer onsite. At the time we didn't have one at IBM T.J. Watson Research Center. The people behind that idea got very creative and put up signs next to the conventional laser printers saying, "Don't you wish you were printing on a 3D printer now?" Not surprisingly, they had a very easy time getting it funded.

After that, IBM's Almaden Research Center in San Jose wanted to do the same thing and so we ran their trial. They had a similarly broad focus but what the vice president there wanted were tech-specific proposals. The VP simply said, "Here is a space in which we need technical innovation," and asked people to think creatively.

Roughly at the same time that the Almaden Research Center was trying iFundIT, the CIO's office—which runs many of the innovation programs for IBM—also wanted to run a trial. Unlike the Watson Research Center or the Almaden Research Center, the CIO group is radically decentralized, with people in dozens of countries. This was a really interesting challenge for us because there were no hallways or lunchrooms that people shared. You couldn't just stick your head in your colleague's office and say, "Hey, would you support my proposal please?" People had to persuade each other online and, in most cases, people they'd never met.

Yet, both Almaden and the CIO's team tripled our original budget and spent just about all of it. In fact, there was one moment when they were in danger of overspending. While we [at the Watson Research Center] got pledges of 41 percent of budget in the first trial, they got pledges of 100 and would've easily had pledges of about 110 percent of budget if they hadn't pulled the switch. They've run two more successful campaigns, and it's becoming part of their normal innovation operation, not just in the CIO organization but across IBM as well. We no longer control it, which is a great sign that we have been successful internally at transferring the project and creating a transferable capability within IBM.

Given the size of IBM, we asked Muller about the participation in IBM iFundIT across generations. IBM officially does not allow demographics such as age to be tracked, partly because of the concerns of the European countries that they operate in, which have strict laws against that type of data gathering. Anecdotally, Muller mentioned that generational biases and differences seemed to be minor:

> Of people I know personally who proposed ideas in iFundIT, their age ranged all over the place. One was a young colleague who I used to say was "half my age, twice my IQ." At the other end of the age spectrum, one of the IBM Fellows proposed a project and it wasn't funded, so it wasn't that people bowed down before authority. Maybe the idea wasn't good enough and, despite the IBM Fellow being extraordinarily smart and having changed the business in very important ways, they didn't get their project supported. The crowd said no. We saw over and over again that the crowd exercised a form of crowd wisdom. Some projects got funded. Some projects came close. Some projects were nearly dead on arrival. That's the way it goes.

Muller stressed that diversity from within IBM and the idea that nobody is necessarily smarter than anyone else, certainly not all the time, is a keystone of initiatives like iFundIT: "One of the big IBM sayings—for decades—is that 'none of us is as smart as all of us,' because difficult problems require diverse intelligences and lots of different perspectives. So a good way to get people to contribute under those circumstances is to give everybody the same chance, same budget, same standing with their peers, so that's what we did."

While IBM has not done formal social network analysis—a visualization of the social network—the company performed a much more straightforward analysis by asking a set of questions of each proposer about his or her relationship with each of the people who funded the proposal. Muller says:

> We made a list of all the funders for each project and we sent it as an e-mail to the project proposer. One of the questions asked if the person who invested in the idea was "not known to me"—in other words, a complete stranger. In our original trial, 40 percent of the funders were

unknown to their proposers. In the CIO trial, the number jumped to 70 percent. It's the strength of the idea rather than personal relationships that seems to be the most important factor. People also crossed country lines, organizational lines, working group lines in order to fund ideas that looked important to them.

People were also funding ideas which they knew would be good for another group or good for IBM's culture even though they wouldn't benefit directly from it. We've seen that in many, many different cases.

What's also interesting is that we just haven't found the downside. One of the things we wanted to know was if your project isn't funded, do you leave? Is it a bad experience? There's no evidence of that either.

Knowing your audience intimately is one way to up the odds that your crowdfunding initiative will be successful. In the case of enterprise crowdfunding, Muller recognized that, at least in IBM's experience, focusing ideas on the goals of the company was the key to long-term success.

I think it's very important that the funding executive or funding group clearly explain the focus of the project to proposers and investors and provide a conceptual "envelope" inside which people are free to innovate. You can't make it a free-for-all, that sets people up for too much rejection. For example, in one case, somebody realized a little bit too late that the theme that was being targeted was technology when they had proposed a morale-oriented project—they actually went back and increased the target funding to make sure they would fail because they didn't want to do something that wasn't addressing the organizational need.

This person's attitude was "If my idea turns out not to align with the organization's needs, then I'm not going to let it happen. I will allow a personal failure," which, by the way, we do not hold against anyone.

We realize that, for IBM iFundIT to be sustainable, we have to embrace a certain degree of failure and still celebrate participation.

Muller's last points about objective-driven funding and dealing with rejection are often-debated topics. Intuitively, the people we talk to about these sorts of internal crowdfunding efforts want to open up the barn door and let everything out to avoid constraining innovation. What we have found is that this is a surefire recipe for failure. Unless you set parameters around what the organization needs, it's impossible to constructively turn away proposals or provide feedback to submitters. It's also extremely difficult to develop any sort of business model or expectation for financial return on projects.

Just as with consumer crowdfunding, internal crowdfunding, as IBM found, requires engagement; proposers have to actively campaign to make people aware of what they're proposing, gather fans, and ideally, spread the word beyond their own efforts. Simply posting a "great idea" and expecting people to run with it didn't work. According to Muller:

> Active campaigning is important both for the project proposer and for the people who are running the trial or running the campaign. We did weekly newsletters for the Watson trial and we could see very, very clearly a bump in participation every Monday when the newsletter came out.
>
> At Almaden, they held a site-wide meeting and gave everybody 120 seconds to promote their project. In the CIO's group, because they were not co-located, they promoted it in a more decentralized way and online. I think the clear lesson is that internal crowdfunding requires heavy promotion. In some cases, people who had funded a project that they really liked also engaged in promotion.
>
> The other very amusing and successful promotion technique at Almaden was to borrow a social robot that could be operated by a person at a remote site. The social robot ran up and down the halls at Almaden promoting the social robot project and of course it was funded. Promotion by project proposers is important and promotion of the entire campaign by the owner or executive is also important to guide people.

In the end, it's not just the idea being proposed but whether the crowd believes in it enough to not only contribute funding—which is the foundational level of participation—but to help spread the word, making the project their own.

THE MANUFACTURING HACK

Suman Mulumudi had some time to take a break between middle school and high school. If you have kids, nephews, nieces, or grandkids you know how awkward that transition can be. It's a period when everything is changing; adolescent bodies and brains seem to go hyperdrive as both start to grow at rates greater than their owners can easily acclimate to.

Most teens wander somewhat aimlessly through those years—at best on autopilot, with their activities distracting them enough to stay out of trouble. But not Suman. His restlessness found a different outlet. When he was in sixth grade, a few parents pooled money to buy his school a *MakerBot Thing-O-Matic*. Cofounded by Bre Pettis, a one-time Seattle public school teacher, MakerBot has been selling home-based 3D printers since 2009 and is one of the best-known brands in the consumer 3D printer market.

Fairly straightforward machines, 3D printers use plastic resin to print objects in three dimensions by printing in successive layers. More than a curiosity, these printed objects can take forms limited only by the imagination of the user, from simple toys to wearable jewelry to intricate objects with working gears to, lately, even food and internal organs. (While MakerBot only provides 3D printers for home and light industrial use, 3D printers are becoming pervasive in many commercial settings from the automotive industry to medicine.) To help Mulumudi pass the summer productively, his parents decided to get him his own MakerBot Replicator 2 Desktop 3D Printer.

While most of his fellow makers were adorning their iPhone cases with their favorite action heroes or steam punk design, Mulumudi took another route. Because his father is a cardiologist, he was accustomed to hearing about the nuances of the heart during conversations at home. He was intrigued by his father's descriptions of how subtle, low-frequency sounds were difficult to identify using acoustic stethoscopes, and he was fascinated by the fact that doctors weren't able to hear and record the data from heart sounds, especially in an era when so much is being digitized.

It was interesting because, to me, it seemed rather outrageous that heart sounds were not recorded regularly. It's shocking to realize that in the twenty-first century, where so many things can be analyzed in such detail with digital technologies, the stethoscope, which is a staple instrument in the world of medicine, doesn't do that. One fundamental problem I had identified is the fact that it's nondigital and the fact that when you're listening for heart sounds, doing an auscultation [listening to sounds inside the body through the use of a stethoscope], you're looking for third heart sounds and murmurs.

People have tried to put a microphone over the chest, but that doesn't work. Interestingly enough, that's how the first stethoscope was invented.

Before 1816, Mulumudi explained, doctors used to put their ears to patients' chests. Then a young woman went to see the French physician René Laennec. He rolled up a piece of paper like a megaphone and put the narrow end to his ear. Mulumudi says:

So basically, murmurs and third heart sounds are both low frequency and quiet, and their location, their amplitude, and their length can be indications of various heart conditions. They're very difficult to hear, so general practitioners can have quite a bit of difficulty confidently identifying them. These patients end up going for echocardiograms, which can be somewhat expensive and you can get a lot of false positives as well as a lot of missed false negatives from the fact that doctors just don't have the same level of training and experience in identifying them. When a doctor identifies an abnormal heart sound, the patient is often sent to get an echocardiogram. Though it is an end all doubt test, it is logistically and economically impractical to perform it on all patients. With increased auscultation accuracy, false positives could be reduced, reducing the number of unnecessary echocardiograms. Additionally, this increased accuracy can also reduce the number of false negatives.

At the same time, there's something called the phonocardiograph; it's an old technology that would literally record the heart's sounds and give you a printout graph of the waveform. It's a ten- to twenty-year-old technology. The problem with it, at the time, was that it was expensive and they were big machines. The technology never really caught on, so it ran out of favor in comparison to the analog stethoscope. However, it became very clear that being able to see these heart sounds as waveform output has the possibility of increasing the accuracy of diagnostics.

So the problem in front of me was two-fold: first, I had to consider the fact that there is currently no good way of digitally recording and storing heart sounds; second, that there's still no good phonocardiograph out there, something that is truly practical and useful at the same level as a regular stethoscope. So with those two things in mind, I moved forward.

Let's stop for a moment and point out the obvious. This is a fifteen-year-old talking about his experiences between middle school and high school. If you find yourself impressed by Mulumudi's maturity and his ability to articulate his thoughts, you may also be thinking, "Well, this is just an exceptionally bright kid who is very advanced for his age." There is no doubt that Mulumudi is bright. While we often have to go back and ask interview subjects to rephrase what they've said in order to make it useful in the context of the book, that was not the case with Mulumudi. What you see here is what he shared with us.

Should we discount Suman Mulumudi as an outlier and high achiever who is not representative of a typical Gen Zer? In our opinion, we would do so at our own peril. Mulumudi is the voice of a generation. His views are remarkably spot on for the ethic of Gen Zers, whatever their age.

We chose to feature Mulumudi's story precisely because of his ability to capture the essence of the creative and disruptive energy that Gen Z possesses in a way that causes you to lose track of his age.

If we had not told you that Mulumudi was fifteen, would you have guessed it? Of course not. We had to keep reminding ourselves during the interview. Yet he is also not as much of an outlier as you may think. In researching this book we had the chance to speak with many kids born into Gen Z, or close to it, and we were consistently impressed. These are kids driven by a sense of purpose and self-assuredness that can easily be interpreted as arrogance or even cockiness. But, as we said in chapter I, the magnitude of the challenges they are taking on is such that we had better be grateful for their belief in their abilities and potential.

In San Diego we spoke with a young woman who, although not Gen Z by birth, expresses many of the attitudes of Gen Z. She had just dropped out of Harvard—where she felt there was little they could teach her—to create global awareness for the prevalence of the underground sex trade of young girls.

For Gen Z, transparency creates a call to action that is not just difficult to ignore but which also drives a deep conviction that they can make a difference. That may not sound much different than the drive behind many of history's great achievers, but the difference with Gen Z is that they all have the tools with which to act on this drive in a practical way.

That's what Suman Mulumudi so vividly illustrates. Curiosity and creativity are not new. It is the ease with which that creativity can be enabled through disruptive technologies, such as 3D printing, that radically changes the Gen Z experience. The MakerBot gave Mulumudi the ability to take a bright idea from concept to reality. With a bit of ingenuity and much experimentation, he built a new type of stethoscope that allowed patients to be far more proactive in identifying specific heart abnormalities in collaboration with their health-care partners.

Using his MakerBot and basic off-the-shelf components, Mulumudi built an acoustic diaphragm into his iPhone case that tuned in to low-frequency sound waves that were then transmitted through a built-in tube in the case to the iPhone's microphone.

Mulumudi had created the first iPhone-based stethoscope, which he named the *Steth IO*. Soon thereafter, the then-fifteen-year-old launched a company, *StratoScientific*, in partnership with his father. Another 3D device followed quickly—the LesionSizer is intended to identify arterial stenosis, allowing optimal placement of stents in arteries. He has applied for patents on both.

For Mulumudi, the ability to turn ideas into actual devices in nearly real time was crucial in removing barriers to moving forward:

The idea that you can fabricate any object removes some level of restriction from your ability to imagine things. Our thought process tends to be contained within a box. We have the idea of this predefined reality, which is what we can build, what we feel as though we could feasibly and realistically accomplish. Expanding that area of what you feel comfortable building also expands your level of comfort with imagining. It frees your creativity in that fashion, makes it much more flexible, much more versatile.

Just as insightful are some of his views on how Gen Z thinks about solving problems. We asked him to talk about the degree to which Gen Z has a greater ability to think outside the box:

> I think it's a combination of two things. One, I think that the box is definitely changing, it's expanding. Simultaneously, I think that people are getting access to technology much younger, which means that they've had less experience, but more technologies to do things with.
>
> Experience obviously gives you an advantage; an intuitive feel about how to go about creating things or how you think through challenges. At the same time, experience, if you become too dependent on it, can be limiting. It's not that experience is bad, but you may treat it like a crutch.
>
> For example, I had access to 3D printing at a young age. I developed experience, and absolutely, the more experience, the better. It is not that lesser experience is better, but while I've leveraged my experience, I was also willing to think in ways that are not necessarily in line with my experience, meaning that I am not limited by just what I have seen. **The box really is your experience, and to think outside of the box you first need to accept the fact that the box—your experience—is not the only pathway.** I think that becomes easier to do when you are provided with technologies to create at a younger age.

We probed deeper to find out what Mulumudi thought about differences in the way older generations looked at the role of failure in innovation.

> It's difficult for me to speak on how the view of mistakes in my generation compares to older generations just because I'm not a member of the older generation. I really don't know how they would look at it, but speaking from my perspective, the perspective of a ninth grader, I think there's definitely at least some change in looking at mistakes and failure as a path to success.

I truly believe if you have not failed, then you have not succeeded, because if you have not failed, you have not tried anything uncertain, you have not thought outside of the box.

There are two things that I think bring people fear of failure. The first one is public embarrassment, the idea that somehow by failing, you're ultimately judged. I fail to understand why someone would see public embarrassment as a reason for not trying something new; I think that's more of an insecurity. It's learning to become secure with yourself, secure with the fact that what you are doing, what you are striving to do, and those things that you want to do in life, are something that you yourself defined and the judgment of others is only the judgment of others. Ultimately, it's you who has the choice to accept their judgment or accept your own.

If you're not willing to fail, if you're not willing to take the risk, then you're not going to go any farther. For me at least—and this is may be more of a personal choice and I think many people would disagree—I **would rather fail, lose something, fall down, and have the opportunity to step up rather than just staying at the same level.** If I really only have one shot and one life to live, I'm prepared to throw out the easy way and strive to be the most I can. My personal view is I've got nothing to lose in the end, so I might as well do as much as I possibly can in-between. That's at least my personal view on risk taking.

We see Mulumudi's view expressed by many who adopt the Gen Z frame of mind. However, there is more going on than just a shift in attitude. The catalyst is clearly the MakerBot's ability to translate ideas into physical objects.

It's far too easy to dismiss 3D printing as a novelty, a gadget, or a toy. But that ignores its incredible power in bridging the costly and time-consuming translational gap that has stood between ideas and products in the manufacturing space, where even simple prototypes can be prohibitively expensive, which is why new products often come from established manufacturers. The result is incremental innovation.

This is why we see 3D printing as such a significant disruptor: it increases the rate of experimentation, creates cost-effective personalization of manufacturing, and provides a real-time bridge between ideas and objects. In many ways, it is consistent with the ongoing Gen Z theme of increasing transparency, because it allows new ideas to surface according to their actual merit. Mulumudi says:

> Kurt Cobain has an interesting quote about the duty of the youth, and I've formed an adaptation over the past few years: "Each generation's job is to question the last." I think sometimes it seems like, from the perspective of older generations, that questioning and rebellion and mistrust are the same thing. In my mind they are very different.
>
> The idea to put trust into someone, for someone in an older generation to say that your wisdom and your knowledge and your experience is valuable does not necessarily mean you don't ask a question about it. It does not mean you don't question it, because at the end of the day, we're all subject, if you will, to the same laws of nature.
>
> It's absolutely important that someone in the younger generation questions what someone in the older generation says, not out of mistrust, not out of disrespect, but out of the quest, if you will, for knowledge, the quest for truth, the quest for "the best right way." I think that having the freedom to question is important. Sometimes that questioning is misunderstood not as a curiosity, but as disrespect. It's my opinion that asking questions is so amazingly essential to being able to ask for the justification and to be able to build the right kind of mind-set that will ask for justifications, and if none exists, then challenge the status quo because the justification does not exist.

Finally, we asked Mulumudi his thoughts on multigenerational work environments:

> I think the multigenerational workforce holds a great promise because it means that it's not just one perspective running the world. You have different types of people, from different backgrounds, different generations, different ages who can contribute another way of looking at ideas. It promotes a change in the status quo; it promotes a versatile, flexible, and creative thought process. At the same time, I think there is work to be done in reducing the generational friction that exists. I don't think

that we as a society are always accepting of or consider different perspectives. We sometimes can be too quick to dismiss different age groups and I think that can sometimes be counterproductive to moving in the direction of globalization as we become more aware of different perspectives, which I believe holds great promise for the future.

As 3D printing becomes a more widely used technology, the sort of experience that Mulumudi describes will become the norm. 3D printing will be as commonplace to Gen Z as electronic publishing is to Gen X. Both are ways to convey ideas, but the impact will be much greater because of the opportunity to translate ideas into the physical world of real and useable objects.

Of all the ways in which the world will change, the effect of 3D printing may well be one of most difficult to project. 3D printers such as the MakerBot are platforms for innovation; they ignite latent potential and bring ideas to life. Crowdfunding can then help to scale those ideas.

However, accelerating cycles of innovation and increasing access to capital create a final problem that has been nipping at the heels of previous generations and has finally caught up with Gen Z. It's the issue of protecting intellectual property.

THE INTELLECTUAL PROPERTY HACK

In 2000 we wrote a white paper for Delphi with the title *Web Magna Carta*. It was intended to be a wake-up call to builders and buyers of software, alerting them that dramatic changes were taking place in the way software was sold over the web and in the cloud. One of the boldest claims we made was that "Software shall be free."

At the time this was an extremely difficult idea to fathom—and it was not particularly popular. In fact, two attendees at one of our seminars from Microsoft lambasted us for even thinking that such a thing was remotely possible in an enterprise setting. They called the thinking naïve, adding that no business would trust free software, nor would "real" developers ever work for free. During the previous year, Microsoft cofounder Bill Gates had referred to

Linux, one of the earliest open source operating systems, as software for the "student and hobbyist market."[8]

In fact the general consensus among most people in the software industry was that there clearly had to be a profitable business model in order for companies to develop and provide software solutions. At that time, the software industry was also becoming increasingly protective of its intellectual property (as we'll discuss in a bit).

However, a countertrend known as "open source" software was emerging. Open source had its origins in numerous initiatives but is most commonly associated with work done by Finnish American software engineer Linus Torvalds in 1991; Torvalds's work was in turn based on work done by Richard Stallman at MIT in the 1970s and '80s.

Open source software is used under what are known as copyleft terms—as opposed to copyright. According to the website of the GNU Operating System, sponsored by the Free Software Foundation: "Copyleft says that anyone who redistributes the software, with or without changes, must pass along the freedom to further copy and change it. Copyleft guarantees that every user has freedom."[9]

During the past decade, open source software such as Linux has found its way into large enterprise software systems in organizations as varied as the U.S. government, the FAA, DreamWorks, Bank of America, and the New York Stock Exchange.

Coincidentally, last year Microsoft was one of the top twenty contributors to Linux. Although we'd love to say, "I told you so," the reality is that open source does not always mean free. In fact, one of the largest enterprise software companies today is Red Hat, an early adopter, promoter, and developer of open source and Linux. Red Hat's software is far from free;[10] Red Hat generates over $1 billion in annual sales, mostly through paid support and customized solutions. Making money off of open source is pretty straightforward. Think of it this way; if lumber and all of the hardware needed to build a house were free, even if the basic house was built for free, you'd still need to pay for utilities, maintenance, and care, and upgrades. However, Red Hat is also one of a handful of companies that is trying to renegotiate the terms for software patents. It's not an easy thing to do or rationalize as a for-profit company, as is evident in the patent policy posted on its website: "Red Hat has consistently taken the position that software patents generally impede innovation in software development and that software patents are inconsistent with open source/free software."[11]

If you're wondering how it is that Red Hat protects itself and its customers from patent litigation from companies that are much more attached to the notion of patent protection, here is Red Hat's response, also from its published patent policy:

> At the same time, we are forced to live in the world as it is, and that world currently permits software patents. A relatively small number of very large companies have amassed large numbers of software patents. We believe such massive software patent portfolios are ripe for misuse because of the questionable nature of many software patents generally and because of the high cost of patent litigation.
>
> One defense against such misuse is to develop a corresponding portfolio of software patents for defensive purposes. Many software companies, both open source and proprietary, pursue this strategy. In the interests of our company and in an attempt to protect and promote the open source community, Red Hat has elected to adopt this same stance. We do so reluctantly because of the perceived inconsistency with our stance against software patents; however, prudence dictates this position.

Clearly, the conflicting messages in the Red Hat policy point to the fact that patents are at a crossroads. But it's not just patents that are under attack; the concept of intellectual property in general is under intense scrutiny by Gen Zers. The fundamental issue comes back to whether the systems we have in place for protecting intellectual property support the objectives of a society that is transparent and open, and in which knowledge is accessible to all.

One of the best examples of the changing attitudes toward intellectual property is Google's long battle with publishers and authors over its scanning of more than twenty million books, the majority of which are protected under copyright. In 2012, Google reached an undisclosed settlement with publishers. However, the Authors Guild sued Google separately. In a decision that dismissed the case and gave Google the right to index, search, and display portions of copyrighted works, U.S. Circuit Judge Denny Chin, said:

> In my view, Google Books provides significant public benefits. It advances the progress of the arts and sciences, while maintaining respectful consideration for the rights of authors and other creative individuals, and without adversely impacting the rights of copyright holders. It has become an invaluable research tool that permits students, teachers, librarians, and others to more efficiently identify and locate books. It has given scholars the ability, for the first time, to conduct full-text searches of tens of millions of books. It preserves books, in particular out-of-print and old books that have been forgotten in the bowels of libraries, and it gives them new life. It facilitates access to books for print-disabled and remote or underserved populations. It generates new audiences and creates new sources of income for authors and publishers. Indeed, all society benefits.

This trend toward openness is not limited to profit-motivated organizations such as Red Hat and Google. One of the largest examples is the not-for-profit Wikipedia—the online, crowdsourced encyclopedia built entirely by volunteers who give freely of their time and knowledge.

Wikipedia has created a collection of 4.5 million articles and has been credited with the demise of printed encyclopedias such as the *Encyclopedia Britannica*. Wikipedia has no advertising budget; it is written, edited, and policed by its members. Yet it has become extraordinarily influential—many would claim more so than any other reference source—and is the seventh-most-visited website in the world (behind Facebook, Google, YouTube, Yahoo, Live.com, and VK.com—the Russian equivalent to Facebook).[12]

A large part of Wikipedia's success is not just the volume of information it contains but the trust people associate with it, because of its strict guidelines about the form and substance of submissions as well as a policy of disallowing paid submissions (that is, those commissioned by someone who would benefit from the article).

Right now we are clearly in the midst of a significant transition in attitudes towards the role and value of patents, as well as the impediments to innovation that they create. In the graduate classes we teach there is a fifty–fifty split among students on the topic of abolishing patent protection. Yet, in undergraduate classes an overwhelming 80 percent feel that patent protection is an absurd holdover from an era when innovation moved much more slowly. They believe that the vast majority of patents are nothing more than a license for large corporations to stall innovation so that they can maximize the value of outdated technology investments.

We've heard many people dismiss this attitude as a sign that these students just need to "grow up," but that is not our interpretation. While there may be an element of idealism in this perspective, there are also the seeds of change, planted by young people who have the ability to reexamine behaviors and attitudes that have outlived their utility.

Surprisingly, one of America's most prominent early inventors, Benjamin Franklin, felt strongly that new inventions should not be patented and instead should be available for the benefit of all.

You can chalk up Franklin's views to those of an idealist who was rather well off to begin with. But what about Elon Musk, founder of Tesla, and one of the most admired contemporary innovators, who recently open-sourced all of Tesla's patents? In our own research we found that 74 percent of individuals, across all ages, believe that the Patent and Trademark Office is outdated and in need of a significant overhaul, while 20 percent believe it will eventually serve no useful purpose.

Although changes in attitudes have always accompanied generational shifts—each generation challenging the wisdom of their parents—the lines dividing the behaviors were more than lines in the sand, they were fortresses of pride built over decades. The reason we have not dismantled the patent and trademark system is that it feeds the means by which those who built it capitalize on it, both its efficiency and its inefficiency. For example, one of the fastest-growing areas of patent litigation concerns patent trolls. These are legal practices or entire firms dedicated to acquiring unused patents from their owners in order to enforce the patents against small and medium-sized businesses that have products that might infringe on the patent. Note the emphasis on the word "might." Because, in fact, the issue is not whether the patent is

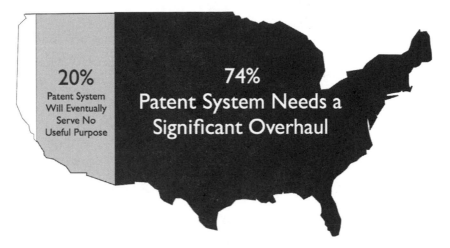

Figure 7-2: State of U.S. Patent System by Percentage of Survey Respondents (Source: Delphi Group)

being infringed but whether the troll can make the case that the legal costs of defending against the claim outweigh the costs of a licensing fee. The result is a legal sinkhole that serves no purpose other than enriching the trolls and stifling innovation. In fact, in one of the most perverse twists in the patent wars, Google was once an investor in what has become the world's largest invention marketplace, Intellectual Ventures (IV). IV, founded by former Microsoft CTO Nathan Myhrvold, was started in the wake of the dot-com bubble to buy the patents of distressed and defunct dot-com companies. Originally, the idea was to create a "defense fund" that would prevent infringement upon the patents for the benefit of the original owners. Yet as IV grew, so did its ability to feed off of the patent system in place.

The absurdity of some of the higher-profile cases boggles the mind. In one instance, an attempt was made by a company called Innovatio IP Ventures to sue every hotel, coffee shop, and other establishment using Wi-Fi, claiming that the use of Wi-Fi infringed on its patents. Even residential end users of Wi-Fi could have been sued. Ultimately, the case was settled, but Innovatio still walked away with nearly $3 million.

In another case, American Express patented CID/CVV codes, those three or four little numbers on your credit card's face or back that are used to verify a transaction. In an effort to make the security process available to all, American Express actually donated the patent to a nonprofit so that anyone could use it. However IV, through one of its companies, purchased the patent from the nonprofit and proceeded to enforce it against American Express competitors.

Perverse? Yes. But that's the way the system works. Does it make sense? If you are playing by the rules, it makes perfect sense. This is what patents are supposed to do, protect those who own them, enrich the inventor, and create a marketplace for their use in which value flows from the beneficiary of the patent to the creator.

But stop for a minute. **When you consider the instantaneously collaborative behavior of Millennials and Gen Z, who feel a moral obligation to share every thought they have as well a deep conviction that a sharing economy is far superior to an artificially protected one, it's not hard to envision the way attitudes about patents and intellectual property rights will play out over time as Gen Z enters the workforce.**

We'll be more than a bit surprised if we do not see radical global reform of the patent and trademark system within the next ten to twenty years, along with an accompanying rise of the copyleft and open source movement across not just the technology industry but in many other sectors, including such sacred industries as manufacturing and even pharmaceuticals.

We know that sounds sacrilegious, but when the average number of drugs[13] being approved yearly in the pharmaceutical industry hasn't changed since 1975, while research and development has increased tenfold during the same period,[14] something is clearly wrong with the way we are currently collaborating and innovating. Under these circumstances, hacking the system is not an interesting sidebar but a necessity.

PULLING THE ANDON CORD

Lifehacking is no less revolutionary than the Magna Carta was in setting forth a new form of governance in which people have a greater say in the forces that rule their lives. The difference, of course, is that the Magna Carta was yet another attempt to appease and pacify an angry population for whom the only outlet was overt civil unrest and disobedience. The agreement was meant to instill in the people a hope that those few noblemen who had power and influence could bring about change.

Gen Z, however, is more like a factory assembly line. One of the staples of the Toyota production system is what's called an "andon" line. This is a cord that runs the length of the assembly line and can be pulled by anyone working on the line when a defect or anomaly is spotted. Once the andon cord is pulled a supervisor comes over to see what the problem is and, if it cannot be rectified in the time required for the task at that station to be completed, the assembly line is stopped. **On a normal day in Toyota's Kentucky manufacturing plant, the andon cord is pulled an incredible five thousand times.**

Like workers on the Toyota production line, Gen Z is not waiting for someone else to pull the andon cord. Everyone has a voice and everyone can stop the process.

It is that extraordinary capability, and, in many cases, the obligation, that Gen Z has to use whatever technological means available to hack the systems that have for so long defined how organizations operate, which is most impressive and profound. Gen Z understands that the tasks ahead, from environmental sustainability to universal education, are ones that will require entirely new ways of doing business. And that is exactly where we'd like to bring the ideas that form the foundation for Gen Z to a conclusion in our next and final segment.

Put It Into Action:
Chapter 7 #lifehacking #GenZ

Learn from Gen Z Leaders

- Catherine Bracy, director of community organizing at Code for America
- Justine Ezarik, instant celebrity via her iJustine persona
- Lorde, singer–songwriter
- Michael Muller, PhD, head of the invention development team for the collaborative user experience group at IBM
- Suman Mulumudi, inventor of *Steth IO*

Are you ready for Gen Z?

- Which of the three hacks (funding, manufacturing, and intellectual property) have you been involved in—or at least contemplated?
- Do you see the value of each of these hacks, or are you sensing a resistance to one or more of them? Why?
- As a consumer, are you funding projects via crowdfunding platforms?
- If you are an inventor or start-up, have you looked into crowdfunding as an alternative to traditional means of raising capital?
- Is your organization considering internal crowdfunding platforms as a way to accelerate innovation by finding the best projects and experiments to fund?
- Have you experimented with 3D printing technology casually or with a specific commercial application in mind?
- How are you using goods, products, or services that are based on copyleft rather than copyright?
- Has your company considered using a copyright alternative, such as a Creative Commons license, for otherwise copyrightable material?

Find out whether you're ready for The Gen Z Effect by taking the full assessment at TheGenZEffect.com.

CONCLUSION

Welcome to Gen Z

If you want to build a ship, don't drum up people to collect wood and don't assign them tasks and work, but rather teach them to long for the endless immensity of the sea.

—ANTOINE DE SAINT-EXUPÉRY

In the course of the last five thousand years, we've traveled across innumerable generations, each one marking its unique place in history and time. Some transformed the world, while others were simply part of an indistinguishable continuum from one generation to the next.

Yet we have no doubt that many felt their point in history was an apex for humankind—a place from which great change and grave decisions would shape the future—perhaps even end it. Some were right, such as those who lived through the great enlightenment of ancient Greece in 500 BC and the birth of democratic principles; the fall of the Roman Empire in AD 476; the scientific revolution of the late 1600s; the Industrial Revolution of the 1800s; World War II; and the space race.

The immense burden of responsibility for the world is now at our doorstep. The challenges we laid out at the beginning of this book—escalating terrorism; climate change; income disparity; global unemployment among youth; global debt at 313 percent of global GDP[1]; climbing energy costs; an imperative to move toward renewable sources of energy; the contrast of a world awash in billionaires while nearly 1 billion humans lack access to clean water and 2.5 billion lack basic sanitation—seem nearly insurmountable.

But we did not set out to write a book about generational prejudice or despair. *The Gen Z Effect* is a book about hope, the hope that connecting humanity—all of us—will give us the ability to take on these problems, evolve our civilization, and transform our world.

So, what have we learned about Gen Z?

1. **Gen Z** is simple. By the time this book is published there will be more mobile devices in service than there are human beings alive. Our cars, homes, toothbrushes, and medicines will be talking to one another. We've struggled through decades of technology that required us to understand "how it worked," and now it just does. Technology—once among the greatest forces separating generations—will unite us across all ages. Technology is becoming the great equalizer; it's foundational to the Gen Z Effect because it creates common ground.

2. **Gen Z** is hyperconnected. We are finally almost totally connected—constantly, simply and intuitively—across every boundary and border, including the most powerful and unyielding borders of all, age and geography.

3. **Gen Z** is educated. Universal education has been an elusive goal. For the most of history and for many of the world's inhabitants, a secondary and post-secondary education have been unattainable, precluded by the necessity to survive and eke out a meager living. But as we've seen, access to education is opening at an amazing rate. Gen Z will be the first generation to realize the ambition of universal access to affordable education.

4. **Gen Z** is unified. As one of our study respondents put it, "The ability to share experiences and knowledge across generations has been a real positive influence for us. Different generations learn from each other. It's breathed new life into our organization and has helped us realize our potential."

For us, the ultimate promise of the Gen Z Effect, and the driver of our passion in writing this book, is that every human being across every

demographic will have the opportunity to be equally involved in creating the future.

Chip and Dan Heath, in their 2007 book *Made to Stick*, cited a phenomenon called "the curse of knowledge" where, once you know something, it's hard to remember what it was like to not know it. That's our hope for you after having read this book: that you will never again look at generational divides and accept them as a law of nature, and, through that lens of understanding you will decide to become part of Gen Z, the last generation of the information age and the first generation of the age of hyperconnectivity; a simple shift that we believe will change the world more profoundly than any revolution ever has.

IT REALLY IS *YOUR* CHOICE

Whatever may drive each of us—from our culture and our beliefs to our values and opinions—we are all also driven by the most fundamental need of every human being, to absorb knowledge and connect with others with whom we share interests.

Gen Z is not just another waypoint on that journey. It is, in our humble opinion, the destination of many millennia, a mile marker for humankind. **We have arrived at a singular moment in history when we will observe the final connection of every last human to one global community.**

With that, the potential for a new world, unencumbered by the legacy of generational divisiveness—something we have taken for granted as a law of nature—may finally be realized.

But there is work to be done for all of us, as individuals, organizations, and nations. We've outlined much of that work in the course of this book but we do not want our description of what could be to take the place of what still needs to be in order for change to happen.

Throughout this book we've offered examples and suggestions that we believe are essential in helping you and your organization prepare for and benefit from the Gen Z Effect. They do not represent *everything* that needs to be done, but they are the *core* of a new set of behaviors and attitudes.

Our objective has been to start a conversation, controversial as it may be, that will continue for some time to come. At the core of that conversation is the most basic and yet most difficult change in the way we've been trained to think about society and business as a collection of distinct generations. The obstacle of generational divisiveness is something we no longer need to hold onto. It has outlived its usefulness.

TOSS THE GENERATIONAL FICTION

We know how brazen our premise for this book is. We have asked you to let go of something you've likely never questioned, the label of generations. One of the hardest things for any of us to do is leave behind truths that we believe to be self-evident. We have grown up with these beliefs and they are embedded so deeply in the way we look at the world that any threat to their validity is a direct assault on our sensibilities.

In the case of generations, we adopt an even deeper attachment to their existence because we identify ourselves with a generation. It is who we are and why we behave the way we do—or at least it is the way we *used to* identify ourselves. Yet beliefs—of any sort—are only valuable when they produce useful outcomes. Otherwise, they are simply dogmas that control our behaviors, robbing us of free will and preventing us from moving forward.

As we've seen throughout the book, the idea of belonging to a generation no longer serves to drive us forward. Instead, it shackles us to the past, prevents us from collaborating effectively, and drives a wedge between groups of people who share more in common than age-based barriers would suggest. The defining characteristics of a generation—distinct technologies, modes of working, and an inability to adapt to new ideas and experiences—no longer apply. The tools we use to live, work, and play are nearly identical now.

Will some of us still choose to detach from society and run off to our own island, like Herman Melville's "insular Tahiti," far from others? Of course, but many more of us—the vast majority—will live, work, and play together on a common technological and social platform. The better we are at doing that, the more likely we are to take on the increasing complexity of our world and the enormity of our common challenges.

196

In your own life—and in your organization—the questions you should be asking are:

- Do I attach myself so closely to a specific generation that I limit my ability to challenge outdated beliefs and behaviors?
- Do I quickly label others as belonging to a generation, biasing my opinions of their beliefs and behaviors?
- Am I holding onto old technologies that I've become accustomed to—while others slingshot past me—only because they are the technologies I've come to know?

YOU HAVE ARRIVED

Actually, we have all arrived, and we are all—if we care to be—builders of the future.

It may appear a daunting task—to take on the building of the future as an individual—but we do all play a role, slight though it may be for most of us. We'll all be hyperconnected as an indomitable global force, but we are still individuals; connections enhance us, they do not eliminate us. If anything, the six forces we've described in this book amplify the voice, influence, and impact of the individual.

But how does an individual change the world? In a February 1972 interview, Buckminster Fuller said it much better than we ever could:

Think of the *Queen Mary*—the whole ship goes by and then comes the rudder. And there's a tiny thing at the edge of the rudder called a trim tab.

It's a miniature rudder. Just moving the little trim tab builds a low pressure that pulls the rudder around. Takes almost no effort at all. So I said that the little individual can be a trim tab. Society thinks it's going right by you, that it's left you altogether. But if you're doing dynamic things mentally, the fact is that you can just put your foot out like that and the whole big ship of state is going to go.

So I said, call me Trim Tab.[2]

Gen Z left the dock long ago. Whether you bought a ticket, ended up stuck on board when the ship pulled away, or are hanging from the railings, you are a passenger on a magnificent journey that will pass by vistas never before seen or imagined. You can watch and be amazed or you can stay in the comfort of your stateroom, hoping to wake when it's over. It's your choice.

Just know that there are no more safe harbors on this voyage, only open sea. Welcome to Gen Z.

APPENDIX

A Short Guide to Reverse Mentoring

Because reverse mentoring is new for 86 percent of organizations, we've put together a short guide that you can use to build awareness and interest in your own reverse mentoring program.

What is reverse mentoring? Reverse mentoring is a learning relationship between a mentor who is young and exceptionally literate in a new aspect of technology or social behavior and a protégé who has more life experience but is not as familiar with a new technology or social behavior.

Who uses reverse mentoring? While only 14 percent of companies have a reverse mentoring program in place, there are some fairly prominent players among them, including GE, The Hartford, Ogilvy & Mather, HP, and Cisco.

Why reverse mentoring? Mentoring relationships can be among the most valuable and meaningful professional and life relationships. The premise is simple: allow experienced mentors to pass on their know-how, successes, failures, and confidence to less experienced individuals. This is precisely the premise behind reverse mentoring, except that the reverse mentor is a younger individual who has less life experience but more direct experience with new technologies and behaviors. The reverse mentor is skilled in both cutting-edge technologies and, more importantly, the social behaviors and attitudes that these technologies create.

Appendix

Why is reverse mentoring valuable? While it is simple to describe and understand, reverse mentoring is rare. If you ask most people to identify a reverse mentor they are likely to come up with a child or grandchild, niece or nephew. Few of us have had reverse mentors on the job.

One of the greatest intangible values of a reverse mentoring relationship is the confidence it often conveys to both individuals. The protégé benefits from the cutting-edge perspective of the mentor and the mentor benefits from the exposure and recognition gained in working with a more senior individual.

Although reverse mentoring may be intended primarily to expose senior employees to new technologies, behaviors, and ideas, it also provides younger employees with the reassurance that they have valuable insights and points of view that are worth sharing.

What can a reverse mentor expect to contribute in terms of time and energy? This will vary based on the needs of the situation. Typically, a mentor should expect to spend regular one- to two-hour sessions with the protégé in order to allow a relationship to develop. This may mean monthly or twice-monthly sessions initially. What is essential is a negotiation of the mentor's availability and the protégé's needs at the outset and on an ongoing basis.

How long will a reverse-mentoring relationship last? Although traditional mentoring relationships can last for decades—sometimes even a lifetime— the ideal reverse mentoring relationship is usually more focused on a shorter period of intense learning. Reverse mentoring focuses on a specific set of experiences rather than the transfer of lifelong learning. However, there are cases where reverse mentoring relationships continue for long periods of time. It's up to the individuals involved and depends upon the specifics of their organization's commitment to and support of the time investment involved.

How do mentors and mentees find each other? Traditional mentoring is often an organic process in which mentor and protégé connect through a mutual contact or affiliation. However, reverse mentoring relationships start when a protégé reaches out to a mentor for some initial advice or guidance. Given that this is most often done in an organizational context, support has to be available for the mentor to dedicate the time required to build a worthwhile relationship. Often, companies put in place formal reverse mentoring programs, such as the one pioneered by GE's former CEO Jack Welch in 1999, which directs protégés to reach out to mentors.

Why is reverse mentoring not more widely used? Mentoring is used in 56 percent of the six hundred organizations polled by Delphi Group. However, reverse mentoring has been amazingly absent from the business landscape—used by only 14 percent of these same 600 organizations. It's not clear why more attention is not paid to reverse mentoring. We speculate that some of it is due to the intense pressure on most professionals to focus their energy on tasks that have a clear return on the investment of their time, or because we substitute peer-to-peer relationships for mentoring. Whatever the case, most people have simply never thought to reach out and ask someone to reverse mentor them.

Who makes the best reverse mentor? While there are many subtleties that have to do with the chemistry between mentor and protégé, there are some fundamentals that qualify good mentors. Among these are:

➤ A willingness to contribute time and energy for the satisfaction of seeing somebody else's growth and success
➤ Deep experience in success and failure with new technologies and attitudes that they are willing to share in an unembellished way with the protégé—the good, the bad, and the ugly!
➤ A sincere interest in developing connected communities that cross age groups and the sharing of knowledge among the community, regardless of members' age
➤ An ability, interest, and organizational support to take time out of their schedule to invest in mentoring
➤ A positive experience of having been mentored (traditionally or reverse) and thereby understanding its value

This short reverse mentoring guide is just the beginning. In order to effectively use reverse mentoring you need to undertake it as a core discipline of your organization, which is supported by leadership and culture. If you have a mentoring program in place then you're already halfway there. If you do not use mentoring then consider the critical importance of putting in place a formal mechanism through which your organization can share knowledge across generational boundaries in both directions.

A SPECIAL DEDICATION

Just before we began our collaboration for *The Gen Z Effect,* we lost a dear friend and long-time colleague, Carl Frappaolo.

Carl was one of Delphi Group's founders and a pioneer in the field of knowledge management. He possessed a great and restless mind, a frighteningly sharp wit, and the uncanny ability to step onto any stage or into any situation, no matter how challenging, and put people at ease. Carl could walk into a lion's den and walk out not only smiling and unscathed but with the lions left behind writhing from laughter.

Over the course of twenty-five years, we worked together with Carl to not only build two remarkable businesses but also to build an even more remarkable friendship in which we shared countless ideas and opinions about the way technology was changing the world.

Carl's endless sense of humor and tireless joy of life drove us both to reach deeper into, and achieve a greater understanding of, our own sense of purpose. It was a dialog that not only contributed enormous intellectual energy but, more importantly, imparted an enthusiasm that made our work truly enjoyable.

It is cliché to say that one loves his work, that it is meaningful and satisfying to work hard without it hardly feeling like work, but that was the reality of working with Carl. His enthusiasm was a chronic incurable condition that often amazed us and always provided an antidote for boredom.

Losing such an ally in our journey has been a sad reminder for both of us that in life and in work joy is not optional, passion is not a byproduct, and friendship is not an afterthought—not if what you are trying to achieve is greater than what you can achieve yourself.

We believe Carl would have been very comfortable in the company of Gen Z, if not for all of its new behaviors and technologies, then for its message of hope, purpose, and promise—a philosophy he embraced and lived.

NOTES

INTRODUCTION

1. Sudeep Reddy, "Number of the Week: Total World Debt Load at 313% of GDP," *Real Time Economics, The Wall Street Journal,* May 11, 2013, http://blogs.wsj.com/economics/2013/05/11/number-of-the-week-total-world-debt-load-at-313-of-gdp/.

2. Work-life expectancy is defined as the ages during which an individual can be gainfully employed in either a part-time or full-time capacity.

3. For those who are well versed in physics it should be noted that we have not included in our description of gravity's effect on falling objects other variables such as air resistance, the altitude from which the object is being dropped, or terminal velocity into our simplistic example.

4. If you're doing the math, 13 x 5 = 65, which is one more than the sixty-four years of age in our four-year age groupings. The reason for the discrepancy is that we actually start the first band not with age one but rather birth (age zero), so that the bands are delineated as; zero to four, five to nine, ten to fourteen, etc.

CHAPTER 1

1. DJ Saul, "3 Million Teens Leave Facebook in 3 Years: The 2014 Facebook Demographic Report," *iStrategyLabs,* January 15, 2014, http://istrategylabs.com/2014/01/3-million-teens-leave-facebook-in-3-years-the-2014-facebook-demographic-report/.

2. "Zero to Eight: Children's Media Use in America 2013," Common Sense Media, Fall 2013, https://www.commonsensemedia.org/sites/default/files/research/zero-to-eight-2013.pdf.

3. Demographers often refer to what we are calling micro-generations as "cohorts." Cohorts share a particular point in time or an event, for example, those of us alive

when the first man stepped foot on the moon could be seen as cohorts by virtue of having shared that experience. We've simply chosen to use the term micro-generation to make the point that generations are being compressed to very small intervals of time.

4. Philip Elmer-DeWitt, "Jan. 1984: How Critics Reviewed the Mac," *Apple 2.0, Fortune.com*, January 12, 2009, http://fortune.com/2009/01/12/jan-1984-how-critics-reviewed-the-mac/.

5. Jeff P comment on "The Future of Reader Store in the US & Canada Sony," accessed May 12, 2014, https://blog.sony.com/2014/02/the-future-of-reader-store/comment page 1/.

6. "Mobile Messaging Futures 2013-2017," *Portio Research*, accessed April 26, 2014, http://www.portioresearch.com/media/4532/Mobile%20Messaging%20Futures%202013-2017%20SAMPLE%20PAGES.pdf.

7. Joel Penney, "The Sip: Marco Rubio's Viral Moment and the Triumph of Political Style," *Viral Politics*, February 19, 2013, http://viralpoliticsblog.wordpress.com/2013/02/19/the-sip-marco-rubios-viral-moment-and-the-triumph-of-political-style/.

8. Bryan Wood, "Twitter / Bryanwx: A Woman Attempting To Take…," February 13, 2014, https://twitter.com/bryanwx/status/434106544263675904.

CHAPTER 2

1. "World Population to 2300," United Nations, 2004, accessed April 24, 2014, http://www.un.org/esa/population/publications/longrange2/WorldPop2300final.pdf.

2. Mary Kruhm, "Mead, The Polymath," in *Margaret Mead: A Biography*. (Westport, CT: Greenwood Press, 2003).

3. Tony Bradley, "Study: The Traditional Office Will Soon Be Extinct," *PC World*, June 17, 2014, http://www.pcworld.com/article/2364272/study-the-traditional-office-will-soon-be-extinct.html.

4. GSA Office of Governmentwide Policy, *Workspace Utilization and Allocation Benchmark*, July, 2012, http://www.gsa.gov/graphics/ogp/Workspace_Utilization_Banchmark_July_2012.pdf.

CHAPTER 3

1. The number of years it takes a technology to mature is one of the most hotly debated topics, as the length of time depends on when you start the clock. If you begin at the invention of the technology, fifty years is a conservative number. For example, radio took anywhere from thirty-eight to fifty-eight years to mature, depending on whether you start with Heinrich Hertz from radio waves in 1887 or Guglielmo

Marconi, the telegraph, in 1907. However, if you start with commercial deployment, that time has been shrinking because of the increasing availability of a technology infrastructure. For example, TV piggybacked on much of the work already done with radio transmission and therefore took from thirteen to thirty-nine years, again depending on when we mark the starting point.

2. Gisle Hannemyr, "The Internet As Hyperbole," accessed March 26, 2014, http://hannemyr.com/en/diff.php.

3. Total number of connections is calculated with the formula Number of Nodes(n) $n(n-1)/2$.

4. Number of devices based on authors' compilation of sources from each industry and Delphi Group research on sensors and device proliferation.

5. Phaedrus.

6. Bill Moyer, "Segment: Sherry Turkle on Being Alone Together," October 18, 2013, http://billmoyers.com/segment/sherry-turkle-on-being-alone-together/.

7. *Alexander Graham Bell's Telephone Patent Drawing and Oath, 03/07/1876*, n.d., http://research.archives.gov/description/302052.

8. Wikimedia Commons, "Osborne 1 open," accessed April 26 2014 wikimedia.org/wiki/File:Osborne_1_open.jpg.

9. Diane Mapes, "We're Married, Sleeping Separately," *CNN.com*, September 12, 2008, http://www.cnn.com/2008/LIVING/personal/09/12/lw.sleep.alone.when.married/.

10. Andrea Peterson, "The Six Types of Conversations on Twitter," *The Washington Post*, February 20, 2014, http://www.washingtonpost.com/blogs/the-switch/wp/2014/02/20/the-six-types-of-conversations-on-twitter/.

CHAPTER 4

1. Wikimedia Commons, "Internet Users per 100 Inhabitants," accessed April 26, 2014, http://en.wikipedia.org/wiki/File:Internet_users_per_100_inhabitants_ITU.svg.

2. http://data.worldbank.org/.

3. Based on reports from Apple's Quarterly Financial Reports starting in 2010.

4. Gartner, Inc., "Gartner Says Worldwide Tablet Sales Grew 68 Percent in 2013, With Android Capturing 62 Percent of the Market," March 3, 2014, http://www.gartner.com/newsroom/id/2674215.

5. Erickson Living, "Seniors Shed Common Myths as They Adopt Social Media," December 9, 2013, http://www.ericksonliving.com/blog/technology-for-seniors/seniors-shed-common-myths-as-they-adopt-social-media.asp.

Notes

6. Paul Sloan, "49 Percent of Online Seniors Use Facebook," *CNET*, June 8, 2012, http://www.cnet.com/news/49-percent-of-online-seniors-use-facebook/.

7. Aaron Smith, "Older Adults and Technology Use," *Pew Research Center's Internet & American Life Project*, April 3, 2014, http://www.pewinternet.org/2014/04/03/older-adults-and-technology-use/.

8. "GWI Social January 2014 GlobalWebIndex Report Series," accessed April 26, 2014, http://insight.globalwebindex.net/gwi-social-january-2014.

9. Fred D. Davis, "User Acceptance of Information Technology: System Characteristics, User Perceptions and Behavioral Impacts." *International Journal of Human-computer Studies / International Journal of Man-machine Studies* 38, no. 3 (1993): 475-487, accessed April 26, 2014, doi:10.1006/imms.1993.1022.

10. Andrew Maier, "A Chat with Bill Gribbons," March 21, 2013, http://networkedblogs.com/Jxwoj.

11. Nathan Clevenger. "How the iPad Conquered the Enterprise," *Datamation*, July 29, 2011, http://www.datamation.com/mobile-wireless/the-ipad-and-enterprise-it.html.

12. Richard Padilla, "Apple Q1 2014 Numbers: $158.8 Billion in Cash, 65 Billion Apps Downloaded, and 420 Total Retail Stores," *Mac Rumors*, January 27, 2014, http://www.macrumors.com/2014/01/27/apple-q1-2014-sales-numbers/.

13. As of March 26, 2014 from http://www.apple.com/about/job-creation/ - there were 291,250 iOS app economy jobs in the U.S., and 275,000 registered iOS developers in the U.S. alone.

14. Mihaly Csikszentmihalyi, *Flow: The Psychology of Optimal Experience*, (New York: Harper & Row, 1990).

15. "Social Support and Lasting Weight Loss," Weight Watchers, last modified, December 17, 2011, https://www.weightwatchers.com/util/art/index_art.aspx?tabnum=1&art_id=20911&sc=804.

16. "CES Press Release—2015 International CES, January 6-9," *Consumer Electronics Association*, December 2, 2013, http://www.cesweb.org/News/Press-Releases/CES-Press-Release.aspx?NodeID=31f2b670-9a21-418a-b5d9-23dde67a758c.

17. Susannah Fox and Maeve Duggan, "Tracking for Health," *Pew Research Internet Project*, January 28, 2013, http://www.pewinternet.org/2013/01/28/tracking-for-health/.

18. Jan Soults Walker, "Benefits Of Steam Washing Machines," *houselogic*, November 24, 2010, http://www.houselogic.com/home-advice/appliances/steam-washers-dream-come-true-jetsons-style/.

19. "A history of Microsoft Windows," Microsoft, accessed April 26, 2014, http://windows.microsoft.com/en-us/windows/history#T1=era0.

CHAPTER 5

1. Robert B. Cialdini, *Influence: Science and Practice*, 5th ed. (Boston: Pearson Education, 2009).

2. "RetailNext Hits New Heights in Retail Big Data," *RetailNext,* April 3, 2014, accessed April 26, 2014, http://retailnext.net/press-release/retailnext-hits-new -heights-in-retail-big-data/.

3. "Gross Domestic Product 2012," *World Bank,* accessed April 26, 2014, http://data bank.worldbank.org/data/download/GDP.pdf.

4. Patti M. Valkenburg and Moniek Buijzen, "Identifying Determinants of Young Children's Brand Awareness: Television, Parents, and Peers," *Journal of Applied Developmental Psychology* (2005): doi:10.1016/j.appdev.2005.04.004.

5. "Interbrand Best Global Brands," *Interbrand,* accessed April 24, 2014, http://www .interbrand.com/en/best-global-brands/2013/Best-Global-Brands-2013.aspx

6. Clearly, both Google and Facebook monetize their social media through paid advertising. However, the point is that, while the business model requires the support of paid advertisers, the content is open to everyone. That is a far cry from the media empires of the past, which were staffed with legions of gatekeepers who filtered and approved editorial content.

7. "The Top 10 Industries that Contributed Most to Google Earnings," *WordStream Inc.,* Accessed April 26, 2014, http://www.wordstream.com/articles/google -earnings.

8. "Upworthy.com Traffic and Demographic Statistics," *Quantcast,* accessed April 26, 2014, https://www.quantcast.com/upworthy.com.

9. Mark Michell, "Google's 8 Simple Rules for Being a Better Manager," *Government Executive,* January 15, 2013, http://www.govexec.com/excellence/promising-practices/ 2013/01/googles-8-simple-rules-being-better-manager/60882/.

10. Gary Burnison, "What Thomas L. Friedman Didn't Report About Getting Hired by Google," April 13, 2014, https://www.linkedin.com/today/post/article/ 20140313201538-281874400-what-thomas-l-friedman-didn-t-report-about -getting-hired-by-google.

CHAPTER 6

1. "120 Years of American Education: A Statistical Portrait, 1993," *National Center for Education Statistics,* January, 1993, http://nces.ed.gov/pubs93/93442.pdf.

2. "School Enrollment, Primary (% net)," *World Bank,* accessed April 26, 2014, http:// data.worldbank.org/indicator/SE.PRM.NENR/countries/1W?display=graph.

3. "YouTube U: The Power Of Stanford's Free Online Education," *Co.Exist*, November 11, 2011, http://www.fastcoexist.com/1678792/youtube-u-the-power-of-stanfords -free-online-education.

4. "MOOCs in 2013: Breaking Down the Numbers," *EdSurge*, December 22, 2013, https://www.edsurge.com/n/2013-12-22-moocs-in-2013-breaking-down-the-numbers.

5. A course visit is a single instance of a student viewing a module, or part of a module, of a MOOC course. Of course, the actual number of course visits for each student will depend on the length of the course, the number and length of the course modules, and the proficiency of the student. In our experience delivering MOOCS for our own courses, we have found that the average number of course views per student is typically ten. This includes those students who do not complete the course as well as those who view modules multiple times.

6. "Stories," Khan Academy, accessed April 26, 2014, https://www.khanacademy.org/ stories.

7. "Employee-to-employee (E2E) Learning: Google's g2g Program," *Udemy*, accessed April 26, 2014, https://www.udemy.com/organizations/employee-to-employee-e2e -learning-bring-googles-g2g-program-to-your-team/.

8. An independent US nationwide in-home placement study, *Research Strategy Group Inc,* March 2013.

CHAPTER 7

1. "Frequently Asked Questions About Small Business," *Small Business Administration Office of Advocacy,* March 2014, http://www.sba.gov/sites/default/files/FAQ _March_2014_0.pdf

2. Anthony Breitzman, PhD and Diana Hicks, PhD, "An Analysis of Small Business Patents by Industry and Firm Size," *Small Business Administration*, November 2008, http://archive.sba.gov/advo/research/rs335tot.pdf.

3. " US Angel Group Update: 2013 Year in Review," *CB Insights,* accessed April 24, 2014, http://www.svb.com/uploadedFiles/Content/Blogs/Halo_Report/halo-report -2013.pdf.

4. "MoneyTree Report—Q4 2013/ Full-year 2013," *PwC*, accessed April 26, 2014, http://www.pwc.com/en_US/us/technology/assets/pwc-moneytree-q4-and-full -year-2013-summary-report.pdf.

5. "Kauffman Index of Entrepreneurial Activity," *Ewing Marion Kauffman Foundation,* accessed April 26, 2014, http://www.kauffman.org/what-we-do/research/kauffman- index-of-entrepreneurial-activity.

6. "One Billion Dollars," accessed April 26, 2014, https://www.kickstarter.com/1billion.

7. Justine Ezarik, "iPhone Bill,", accessed April 26, 2014, https://www.youtube.com/watch?v=UdULhkh6yeA.

8. Roger Parloff, "How Linux Conquered the Fortune 500," *Fortune,* May 6, 2013, http://money.cnn.com/2013/05/06/technology/linux-500.pr.fortune/.

9. "What is Copyleft?," *GNU Project Free Software Foundation,* accessed April 26, 2014. https://www.gnu.org/copyleft/.

10. Red Hat does provide some software for free, such as Fedora.

11. "Patent Policy," accessed April 26, 2014, http://www.redhat.com/legal/patent_policy.html

12. "Wikipedia.org Traffic Statistics," *SimilarWeb,* accessed April 26, 2014, http://www.similarweb.com/website/wikipedia.org.

13. The term *drug* is used here to represent what the pharmaceutical industry and the FDA term NME, or new molecular entities. These are new drugs that contain a molecule not already approved by the FDA.

14. "Pathway to Global Product Safety and Quality," *U S Food and Drug Administration,* accessed April 26, 2014, http://www.fda.gov/downloads/aboutfda/centersoffices/oc/globalproductpathway/ucm259845.pdf.

CONCLUSION

1. Sudeep Reddy, "Number of the Week: Total World Debt Load at 313% of GDP," *The Wall Street Journal,* May 11, 2013, http://blogs.wsj.com/economics/2013/05/11/number-of-the-week-total-world-debt-load-at-313-of-gdp/.

2. "A Candid Conversation with the Visionary Architect/Inventor/Philosopher, R. Buckminster Fuller," *Playboy,* February, 1972.

REFERENCES

Bell, Alexander Graham. "Telephone Patent Drawing and Oath, 03/07/1876." http:// research.archives.gov/description/302052.

Bradley, Tony. "Study: The Traditional Office Will Soon Be Extinct." *PCWorld*, June 17, 2014. http://www.pcworld.com/article/2364272/study-the-traditional-office-will -soon-be-extinct.html.

Breitzman, Anthony, and Diana Hicks. "An Analysis of Small Business Patents by Industry and Firm Size." *Small Business Administration*, November 2008. http://archive. sba.gov/advo/research/rs335tot.pdf.

Burnison, Gary. "What Thomas L. Friedman Didn't Report About Getting Hired by Google." *LinkedIn*, April 13, 2014. http://www.linkedin.com/today/post/article/ 20140313201538-281874400-what-thomas-l-friedman-didn-t-report-about-getting -hired-by-google.

"A Candid Conversation with the Visionary Architect/Inventor/Philosopher, R. Buckminster Fuller." *Playboy* magazine, February 1972. http://bfi.org/sites/default/files/attachments/ pages/CandidConversation-Playboy.pdf.

CB Insights. "US Angel Group Update: 2013 Year in Review." Accessed April 24, 2014. http://www.svb.com/uploadedFiles/Content/Blogs/Halo_Report/halo-report -2013.pdf.

Cialdini, Robert B. *Influence: Science and Practice*, 5th ed. Boston: Pearson Education, 2009.

Clevenger, Nathan. "How the iPad Conquered the Enterprise." *Datamation*, July 29, 2011. http://www.datamation.com/mobile-wireless/the-ipad-and-enterprise-it.html.

Common Sense Media. "Zero to Eight: Children's Media Use in America 2013." Fall 2013. http://www.commonsensemedia.org/sites/default/files/research/zero-to-eight-2013 .pdf.

References

Consumer Electronics Association. "CES Press Release—2015 International CES, January 6–9." December 2, 2013. http://www.cesweb.org/News/Press-Releases/CES-Press-Release.aspx?NodeID=31f2b670-9a21-418a-b5d9-23dde67a758c.

Csikszentmihalyi, Mihaly. *Flow: The Psychology of Optimal Experience*. New York: Harper & Row, 1990.

Davis, Fred D. "User Acceptance of Information Technology: System Characteristics, User Perceptions and Behavioral Impacts." *International Journal of Man–Machine Studies* 38, no. 3: 475–487.

EdSurge. "MOOCs in 2013: Breaking Down the Numbers." December 22, 2013. http://www.edsurge.com/n/2013-12-22-moocs-in-2013-breaking-down-the-numbers.

Elmer-DeWitt, Philip. "Jan. 1984: How Critics Reviewed the Mac." *Fortune.com*, January 12, 2009. http://fortune.com/2009/01/12/jan-1984-how-critics-reviewed-the-mac/.

Erickson Living. "Seniors Shed Common Myths as They Adopt Social Media." December 9, 2013. http://www.ericksonliving.com/blog/technology-for-seniors/seniors-shed-common-myths-as-they-adopt-social-media.asp.

Ewing Marion Kauffman Foundation. "Kauffman Index of Entrepreneurial Activity." Accessed April 26, 2014. http://www.kauffman.org/what-we-do/research/kauffman-index-of-entrepreneurial-activity.

Ezarik, Justine. "iPhone Bill." Accessed April 26, 2014. http://www.youtube.com/watch?v=UdULhkh6yeA.

Fast Company. "YouTube U: The Power Of Stanford's Free Online Education." November 11, 2011. http://www.fastcoexist.com/1678792/youtube-u-the-power-of-stanfords-free-online-education.

Fox, Susannah, and Maeve Duggan. "Tracking for Health." *Pew Research Internet Project*, January 28, 2013. http://www.pewinternet.org/2013/01/28/tracking-for-health/.

Free Software Foundation. "What is Copyleft?" Accessed April 26, 2014. http://www.gnu.org/copyleft/.

Gartner, Inc. "Gartner Says Worldwide Tablet Sales Grew 68 Percent in 2013, With Android Capturing 62 Percent of the Market." March 3, 2014. http://www.gartner.com/newsroom/id/2674215.

General Services Administration. "Workspace Utilization and Allocation Benchmark." July 2012. http://www.gsa.gov/graphics/ogp/Workspace_Utilization_Benchmark_July_2012.pdf.

Global Web Index. "GWI Social January 2014 GlobalWebIndex Report Series." Accessed April 26, 2014. http://insight.globalwebindex.net/gwi-social-january-2014.

References

Hannemyr, Gisle. "The Internet As Hyperbole." Accessed March 26, 2014. http://hannemyr.com/en/diff.php.

Interbrand. "Interbrand Best Global Brands." Accessed April 24, 2014. http://www.interbrand.com/en/best-global-brands/2013/Best-Global-Brands-2013.aspx.

"Internet Users Per 100 Inhabitants," Wikimedia Commons. Accessed April 26, 2014. http://en.wikipedia.org/wiki/File:Internet_users_per_100_inhabitants_ITU.svg.

Khan Academy. "Stories." Accessed April 26, 2014. http://www.khanacademy.org/stories.

Kickstarter. "One Billion Dollars." Accessed April 26, 2014. http://www.kickstarter.com/1billion.

Kruhm, Mary. "Mead, The Polymath." in *Margaret Mead: a Biography.* Westport, CT: Greenwood Press, 2003.

Maier, Andrew. "A Chat with Bill Gribbons." March 21, 2013. http://networkedblogs.com/Jxwoj.

Mapes, Diane. "We're Married, Sleeping Separately." *CNN.com*, September 12, 2008. http://www.cnn.com/2008/LIVING/personal/09/12/lw.sleep.alone.when.married/.

Michell, Mark. "Google's 8 Simple Rules for Being a Better Manager." Government Executive, January 15, 2013. http://www.govexec.com/excellence/promising-practices/2013/01/googles-8-simple-rules-being-better-manager/60882/.

Microsoft. "A History of Microsoft Windows." Accessed April 26, 2014. http://windows.microsoft.com/en-us/windows/history#T1=era0.

Moyer, Bill. "Segment: Sherry Turkle on Being Alone Together." October 18, 2013. http://billmoyers.com/segment/sherry-turkle-on-being-alone-together/.

National Center for Education Statistics. "120 Years of American Education: A Statistical Portrait, 1993." January, 1993. http://nces.ed.gov/pubs93/93442.pdf.

Neff, Jack. "Procter & Gamble Spends 35% Of Marketing Dollars On Digital." *Advertising Age*, August 20, 2013. http://adage.com/article/digital/procter-gamble-spends-35-marketing-dollars-digital/243718/.

OECD. "Education at a Glance 2012: OECD Indicators." Accessed April 24, 2014.

"Osborne 1." *Wikimedia Commons.* Accessed April 26, 2014. http://en.wikipedia.org/wiki/File:Osborne_1_open.jpg.

Padilla, Richard. "Apple Q1 2014 Numbers: $158.8 Billion in Cash, 65 Billion Apps Downloaded, and 420 Total Retail Stores." *Mac Rumors*, January 27, 2014. http://www.macrumors.com/2014/01/27/apple-q1-2014-sales-numbers/.

References

Parloff, Roger. "How Linux Conquered the Fortune 500." *Fortune*, May 6, 2013. http://money.cnn.com/2013/05/06/technology/linux-500.pr.fortune/.

Penney, Joel. "The Sip: Marco Rubio's Viral Moment and the Triumph of Political Style." *Viral Politics*, February 19, 2013. http://viralpoliticsblog.wordpress.com/2013/02/19/the-sip-marco-rubios-viral-moment-and-the-triumph-of-political-style/.

Peterson, Andrea. "The six types of conversations on Twitter." *The Washington Post*, February 20, 2014. http://www.washingtonpost.com/blogs/the-switch/wp/2014/02/20/the-six-types-of-conversations-on-twitter/.

Portio Research. "Mobile Messaging Futures 2013-2017." Accessed April 26, 2014. http://www.portioresearch.com/media/4532/Mobile%20Messaging%20Futures%202013-2017%20SAMPLE%20PAGES.pdf.

PwC. "MoneyTree Report - Q4 2013/ Full-year 2013." Accessed April 26, 2014. http://www.pwc.com/en_US/us/technology/assets/pwc-moneytree-q4-and-full-year-2013-summary-report.pdf.

Quantcast. "Upworthy.com Traffic and Demographic Statistics." Accessed April 26, 2014. http://www.quantcast.com/upworthy.com.

Reddy, Sudeep. "Number of the Week: Total World Debt Load at 313% of GDP." *The Wall Street Journal*, May 11, 2013. http://blogs.wsj.com/economics/2013/05/11/number-of-the-week-total-world-debt-load-at-313-of-gdp/.

Redhat. "Redhat Patent Policy." Accessed April 26, 2014. http://www.redhat.com/legal/patent_policy.html.

Research Strategy Group Inc. "An independent US nationwide in-home placement study." March 2013.

RetailNext. "RetailNext Hits New Heights in Retail Big Data." April 3, 2014. Accessed April 26, 2014. http://retailnext.net/press-release/retailnext-hits-new-heights-in-retail-big-data/.

Saul, DJ. "3 Million Teens Leave Facebook in 3 Years: The 2014 Facebook Demographic Report." *iStrategyLabs*, January 15, 2014. http://istrategylabs.com/2014/01/3-million-teens-leave-facebook-in-3-years-the-2014-facebook-demographic-report/.

Sloan, Paul. "49 Percent of Online Seniors use Facebook." *CNET*, June 8, 2012. http://www.cnet.com/news/49-percent-of-online-seniors-use-facebook/.

Small Business Administration. "Frequently Asked Questions about Small Business." March 2014. http://www.sba.gov/sites/default/files/FAQ_March_2014_0.pdf.

Smith, Aaron. "Older Adults and Technology Use." *Pew Research Center's Internet & American Life Project*, April 3, 2014. http://www.pewinternet.org/2014/04/03/older-adults-and-technology-use/.

References

Soults Walker, Jan. "Benefits Of Steam Washing Machines." *Houselogic/The National Association of Realtors,* November 24, 2010. http://www.houselogic.com/home-advice/appliances/steam-washers-dream-come-true-jetsons-style/.

Udemy. "Employee-to-employee (E2E) Learning: Google's g2g Program." Accessed April 26, 2014. http://www.udemy.com/organizations/employee-to-employee-e2e-learning-bring-googles-g2g-program-to-your-team/.

United Nations. "World Population to 2300." Accessed April 24, 2014. http://www.un.org/esa/population/publications/longrange2/WorldPop2300final.pdf.

US Food and Drug Administration. "Pathway to Global Product Safety and Quality." Accessed April 26, 2014. http://www.fda.gov/downloads/aboutfda/centersoffices/oc/globalproductpathway/ucm259845.pdf.

Valkenburg, Patti M., and Moniek Buijzen. "Identifying Determinants of Young Children's Brand Awareness: Television, Parents, and Peers." *Journal of Applied Developmental Psychology* (2005): doi:10.1016/j.appdev.2005.04.004.

Weight Watchers. "Social Support and Lasting Weight Loss." Last modified December 17, 2011. http://www.weightwatchers.com/util/art/index_art.aspx?tabnum=1&art_id=20911&sc=804.

"Wikipedia.org Traffic Statistics." *SimilarWeb.* Accessed April 26, 2014. http://www.similarweb.com/website/wikipedia.org.

Wood, Bryan. "Twitter post, February 13, 2014. http://twitter.com/bryanwx/status/434106544263675904.

WordStream Inc. "The Top 10 Industries that Contributed Most to Google Earnings." Accessed April 26, 2014. http://www.wordstream.com/articles/google-earnings.

World Bank. "Gross Domestic Product 2012." Accessed April 26, 2014. http://databank.worldbank.org/data/download/GDP.pdf.

World Bank. "School Enrollment, Primary (% net)." Accessed April 26, 2014. http://data.worldbank.org/indicator/SE.PRM.NENR/countries/1W?display=graph.

INDEX

Index

Index

Index

Index

Index

ABOUT THE AUTHORS

Thomas Koulopoulos is the founder of the Delphi Group, which for twenty-five years has been providing thought leadership to global organizations on the intersection of business and technology. He is the author of nine previous books, including *Cloud Surfing*. Said the late Peter Drucker, father of modern-day management theory, "Tom's writing makes you question not only the way you run your business but the way you run yourself." For the past two decades, his books have foreseen major shifts in business and technology, from the rise of internet search engines, to the advent of social media, to the impact of the cloud on businesses and consumers. *The Gen Z Effect* follows that trajectory, providing a prescient view of how tectonic shifts in generational behavior, demographics, and technology will forever change the way we live, work and play. Visit him at www.TKSpeaks.com.

Dan Keldsen has over twenty years of experience working as a consultant, analyst, and technology strategist, with organizations from the Fortune 50 to State and Federal government agencies and non-profits. Dan co-led groundbreaking research on attitudinal differences and alignment between Boomers and Millennials in one of the earliest Enterprise 2.0 research projects (2007-2008), and was noted as one of the Most Influential Enterprise 2.0 Writers of 2009 by SeekOmega. He has contributed to *Business Model Generations* by Alex Osterwalder and Yves Pigneur, *The New Small* by Phil Simon, and been featured in *The Laws of Subtraction* by award-winning author Matthew E. May, and *Innovation: How Innovators Think, Act and Change Our World* by Kim Chandler McDonald. He is a frequent speaker and has been quoted in the *Wall Street Journal*, the *Economist*, *InformationWeek*, *CMSWire*, and *FierceContentManagement*, among other publications. Visit him at www.DanKeldsen.com